AMERICA'S ECONOMIC WAR – YOUR FREEDOM, MONEY AND LIFE

A Citizen's Handbook for Understanding the War between
American Capitalism and Socialism

Gerard Francis Lameiro, Ph.D.
Founder and CEO, Lameiro Economics LLC
"America's Citizen-Philosopher"

Published by Lameiro Economics LLC.
For more information, please visit: http://www.LameiroEconomicsLLC.com .

ISBN: 1-4392-5515-6
EAN: 9781439255155

First Print Edition

Printed by BookSurge
http://www.booksurge.com .

To order additional copies, please visit: http://www.amazon.com
or http://www.booksurge.com .

Booksellers may purchase copies in any quantity by contacting the BookSurge Customer Service Department at 866-308-6235 option 6 or by email to customerservice@booksurge.com .

For more information or to contact Dr. Lameiro, please visit:
http://www.LameiroBooks.com .

Cover and book design by MDW Graphics and Type,
http://www.mdwgraphics.com .

God

Contents

Global Socialism and the United Nations
- Global Socialism and the U.N.'s Lack of a Superior Moral Legitimacy
- Global Socialism, Norming, and Back-Door Socialism

Part II – The Combatants

The Christian Foundations of American Capitalism
- Individualism
- Equality under the Law
- Freedom
- Private Property
- Free Enterprise and Capitalism
- Charitable Giving and Compassion
- Universities
- Science and Technology

The Architecture of American Capitalism
- Key Laws
- Key Freedoms
- Key Requirements
- Key Institutions
- Key Infrastructure

The Characteristics of American Capitalism
- Faith (and Morality)
- Freedom (and Peace)
- Free Markets (and Prosperity)
- Family (and Trust)
- Spiritual and Material Human Growth

American Capitalism – A Summary

The Seduction of Socialism – Part 1
- The Seduction of Christian Socialism
- The Seduction of Democratic Socialism

The Characteristics of Socialism
- Atheism (and Immorality)
- Control (and Violence)
- Economic Inefficiency (and Poverty)
- Groups of "Victims" (and Distrust)
- Moral Decay and Social Disintegration

Socialism – A Summary

The Seduction of Socialism – Part 2
- The Seduction of Hampered Capitalism
- The Seduction of Welfare State Socialism
- The Seduction of Progressive Socialism

Four Degrees of Freedom, Peace, and Prosperity

Three Reasons Why There are No Sustainable, Hybrid "Third Way" Systems
- Reason #1 – "Third Way" Systems Lead to Bankruptcy Directly or into Socialism (and then Bankruptcy)
- Reason #2 – "Third Way" Systems Lead to Capital Exhaustion
- Reason #3 – "Third Way" Systems Lead to Political Strife and Upheaval

Hampered Capitalism and Welfare State Socialism – A Summary

The American Political Landscape – A New Way to View It

Part III – The Strategies and Battles

The War Room – A Quick Listing of All 47 Major Battles and 3 Special Battles
- 9 Major Battles against the Christian Church and Religious Freedom
- 6 Major Battles against the Family and Religious Freedom
- 13 Major Battles against the Constitution and Religious Freedom, Political Freedom, and Economic Freedom

- Constitution, Religious Freedom, Political Freedom, and Economic Freedom
- Free Market, Free Enterprise, and Economic Freedom

If American Capitalism Loses the War ...
- Christian Church, Family, and Religious Freedom
- Constitution, Religious Freedom, Political Freedom, and Economic Freedom
- Free Market, Free Enterprise, and Economic Freedom

It's No Longer ...
- It's No Longer Republicans vs. Democrats – It's American Capitalists vs. Socialists
- It's No Longer Red States vs. Blue States – Red is the Color of Socialism, Blue is the Color of Freedom
- It's No Longer Negative Campaigns that Win Elections – It's Positive Campaigns that Win Mandates

The American Economy – A Quick Turn-Around, a Bad Recession, or a Ten-Year Depression?

Seven Free Market Principles that Can Generate Economic Prosperity Soon

When Will the War End?

Who Will Win the War?

Part V – The Appendices

ix

Why You Should Read This Book

You might not realize it right now because you are busy with work or school or family concerns, but, you and your family's freedom, money and life are all at risk today. The purpose of this book is to help you understand what is going on within America today and why it is vitally important to you and your family. America's Economic War is raging and changing the nature of American Culture, American Government, and the American Economy. Each and every one of us is dramatically impacted. Yet, few of us recognize that America's Economic War is taking place at all. Indeed, fewer still understand the causes of the war, or its impact and potential dangers.

This book explains America's Economic War in enough detail to gain a true understanding of the extent, scope and impact of this war. It focuses on the real dangers you face. It shows you who the combatants in the war are and it explains their philosophy, rationale and logic. It details the 47 major battles and the three special battles taking place now. It also looks at some of the consequences of the war and predicts the likely winner.

Answers to Questions about America's Economic War and the American Economy

You should read this book if you want answers to these practical questions and more:

- What is America's Economic War?
- Why is my economic freedom, political freedom, and religious freedom at risk?
- Why is my prosperity at risk?
- Why is my life at risk?
- What's really going on in the American Economy today?
- Will our economy turn-around quickly, or get bogged down in a bad recession, or worse, collapse into a ten-year depression?
- Why do we confront a constant stream of bad economic reports and financial crises?
- Why do we face increasing inflation with mounting food and energy prices?
- What really causes inflation?
- Why is inflation actually an insidious tax?
- Why do we have a health care system that is often complex, bureaucratic and costly?

- Why do our political leaders engage in fierce political battles with one another?
- Why do our political campaigns get so nasty, negative and destructive?
- Why does our culture and morality continue to decline?
- How can we restore a positive culture?
- How can we have positive political campaigns?
- How can we achieve economic prosperity soon?
- How can we build a great American Civilization looking forward to a brighter future?
- When will America's Economic War end?
- Who will win America's Economic War?

Answers to Questions about Economic Systems and Economics

You should also read this book if you want to learn about economics and how economic systems really work. This book provides answers to these questions and more:

- What is American Capitalism?
- What are the Christian foundations of American Capitalism?
- What is the Architecture of American Capitalism?
- What are the characteristics of American Capitalism?
- What are the characteristics of a Free Market?
- Why is American Capitalism a moral economic system?
- What is Lameiro's First Law of Economics?
- Why does American Capitalism promote peace and prosperity?
- Why does socialism promote violence and poverty?
- What is socialism?
- What are the characteristics of socialism?
- What is Socialism's Chain of Control?
- How do some socialists use deceit, deception, and fear as weapons against American Capitalism?
- Why are so many smart people seduced into believing socialism is a good economic system?
- Why is socialism an immoral economic system?

America's Economic War is a test of America's moral strength and courage, a test of its Constitutional principles, and a test of its great engine of economic freedom and prosperity.

You should read this book to get a solid understanding of America's Economic War and how American Capitalism can help all of us to achieve a brighter future for ourselves, our children and our grandchildren.

Part I

The Dangers

Chapter 1

Your Freedom, Your Prosperity, and Even Your Life are in Danger

"And you shall know the truth, and the truth shall make you free."
John 8:32

Are you struggling to understand what's really going on in the American Economy today? Do you want to know if our economy will turn-around quickly, or get bogged down in a bad recession, or worse, collapse into a ten-year depression? Do you want to understand why we confront a constant stream of bad economic reports and financial crises? Why we face increasing inflation with mounting food and energy prices? Why our leaders engage in fierce political battles with one another? Why our political campaigns are so nasty, negative and destructive? Do you want to understand why American Culture and our morality are in steep decline? Do you want to put all this into context and really understand what's going on in America today?

This book answers all these questions and many more by describing America's Economic War. This war impacts the American Economy, American Government, and American Culture. These impacts are deeply profound and indeed, both life-changing and life-threatening. This war directly affects you and your family, your finances and your security, your health and your safety, and even your life itself. It's vitally important that you understand this war and the dangers posed to you and your family.

America it's time to wake up to the war that is being fought right before your eyes! While you are working, taking care of your family, and even spending a little time enjoying life, something dangerous is happening. Some people are tearing down America. These people are trying to destroy our economic freedom, political freedom, and our religious freedom. Inch-by-inch, they are attacking the institutions of America and American Capitalism. The Christian Church, the Family, the Constitution, our Freedom, our Free Market, and Free Enterprise, all are under relentless assault. Today, America is engaged in an economic war, actually a civil war, which touches every American. Your freedom, your prosperity, and even your life are in danger.

The good news is that American Capitalism can win America's Economic War. This book will arm you with the knowledge to understand this war.

America's Economic War – American Capitalism vs. Socialism

If you look in your heart, you will know that men and women, by their God-given nature, seek to be free. They thrive under freedom too. In sharp contrast, elite rulers over the ages (be they kings, emperors, dictators, ruling parties, fascists, communists, or other socialists) have sought to stifle liberties and impose control over their pitiful subjects.

American Capitalism is that wonderful economic system created under God and based on human freedom. Socialism is the name given by this author to all other economic systems that are based on the tyranny of a ruling elite and their control over economic resources. While American Capitalism harnesses the power of freedom to produce human growth and economic affluence, socialism relies on coercion, compulsion and violence to control people and their lives. Socialism is based on power and inevitably leads to moral bankruptcy and abject poverty.

Today, America faces an economic war in which the advocates of socialism are attacking American Capitalism and its underlying institutions. Its objective is to destroy American Capitalism and America as we know it. Its • objective is to replace American Capitalism with American socialism. With some socialists, their objective is to create a larger system of global socialism under a United Nations (U.N.) controlled world government.

If socialists win this economic war, either American socialism or global socialism will bring with it the destruction of much or all of our economic, political, and religious freedom. It will also usher in an age of increasing violence, illness, and destitution. It would be a human tragedy.

What's going on in America Today?
... In Our Economy

Have you been shaken to see our economy hit by one financial crisis after another? Have you been shocked to learn your 401(k) or IRA accounts have dramatically declined in a period of just a few months? Have you been bewildered to see our government spending hundreds of billions of dollars, possibly trillions of dollars, to bail out one failing company or organization after another? Are you surprised that even universities are seeking bailouts? Believe it or not, these economic explosions are a direct result of socialist thinking and socialist policies made by our government. They are all part of America's Economic War as we will see later in this book.

Indeed, socialism has a history of attempting to use so-called "crises" to take economic freedom away from individuals and to increase the power of a handful of elite rulers. It's not surprising then, with government bailouts, come stringent new government regulations and sometimes even outright government ownership stakes in the "rescued" companies. It's also not surprising, with government bailouts, that the government increases its power and control over individuals and that government gains a greater and greater share of the nation's wealth. With socialism, power becomes concentrated in the hands of a few elite rulers. Under complete socialism, the elite rulers (be they kings, emperors, dictators, ruling parties, fascists, communists, or other socialists) ultimately control all of the nation's resources and wealth.

It's ironic in one sense, but it's true nevertheless. Socialists create "crises" in order to "fix" them later because so-called "crises" give socialists the opportunity to limit individual freedom and to gain additional power over others.

Most of today's economic "crises" could have been avoided had the Free Market been allowed to function freely. For example, a stable and sensible monetary policy is a key to a prosperous economy. Stable monetary policy simply means that the dollar's value is stable and changes very little over time. Without monetary stability, the value of a dollar changes so much (and/or so often) that the Free Market's pricing mechanism is confused and poor investment, business and personal decisions are made. This leads to bad utilization of economic resources and a lower standard of living for all of us. Sometimes, bad monetary policy can lead to inflation, hyperinflation, or even in extreme cases, financial chaos. We cover more on monetary policy and inflation in Chapter 5.

To take another example of how the government hampered the Free Market resulting in our recent economic "crises," consider the recent mortgage housing bubble. Relying on faulty socialist thinking, our government chose to pursue socialist housing policies. These policies were a primary driving force in the housing bubble and the subsequent painful housing bust.

To illustrate, does it make sense for the government to force banks to make sub-prime (risky) mortgage loans to individuals who are unable to afford a given home? It doesn't take much thought to realize that there were bound to be many foreclosures down the road. In the Free Market, banks make their own business decisions based on the likelihood that their decisions will make the bank profitable or not. The government should not force banks to make stupid and foolish business decisions.

Or, does it make sense to allow people to buy homes with no down payments, to have no equity stakes in their homes? Obviously, with no equity invested, they can walk away from their homes with no losses. Once again, such *no-down payment mortgages* were economically reckless.

We can assign blame for most of today's economic "crises" to our government's socialist thinking, socialist policies, and direct interference with the Free Market. Moving forward, why should you pay higher taxes to make up for the government's socialist policy mistakes?

As we will see throughout this book, the impact of America's Economic War on your finances is profound. Whether the American economy will turn-around quickly, or get bogged down in a bad recession, or worse, collapse into a ten-year depression is a subject of Chapter 8.

... In Our Politics
Have you been upset with elections over the past several years? Are you tired of nasty, negative, and destructive campaigns? Are you sick of bitter, court-contested, recounts of close elections? Do you wonder why election campaigns are focused on scandals and bizarre accusations and sleazy innuendos? Like so many Americans, are you relieved and grateful to get the elections over with?

Socialists have a long tradition of avoiding debate and discussion and instead, of assailing and damaging their opponents with *ad hominem* personal attacks. The reason for this tactic is simple. Socialism is a failed philosophy, both theoretically and in practice. Socialist experiments always eventually fail. Socialism always leads to moral and economic bankruptcy. Socialists can't win debates. So, they are left with attacking their opponents.

Negative campaigns are one more manifestation of America's Economic War as we will see in Chapter 7.

... In Our Culture

Have you looked around lately and seen some troubling signs that our culture is declining? Have you heard some disturbing news reports about violent crimes? Have you flipped to some cable TV program and been blown away by sexual depravity? Have your children come home from school and shocked you with what they have been learning? Do you feel like you are losing control of your children? Believe it or not, there is a simple explanation.

American Culture, and for that matter culture in general, is a by-product of a nation's spiritual and moral thinking. It is part of the civilization or moralization of a people. American Capitalism, as we will see later in this book, was built on Christianity and its spiritual and moral thinking. To atheists and agnostics who don't believe in faith (but only believe in reason), this thought might be hard to buy. However, without the Christian Church's faith in reason itself (and its striving for truth), reason (as we know it) would not exist and capitalism would never have been created. But, more on that in Chapter 3.

Today, American Culture is being polluted by the influence of socialism. Socialism is an economic system that is <u>not</u> built on a spiritual or moral order. Instead, socialism is founded on the notion of materialism.

Materialism is the idea that there is no spiritual reality; rather, life consists of nature – the physical world, what we can see and hear and touch. To the early proponents of socialism, there was no spiritual world, only a tangible, physical world. To them, there were no eternal moral truths. In fact, morality (or what passed for socialist morality) was a fluid idea that changed with the times.

As you might think, radical environmentalism is a spin-off of socialism and materialism. In some ways, environmentalism often takes on the character of a religion whose god is nature. Take global warming, for example. Many environmentalists take the dire predictions of global warming on faith, since they don't have enough solid scientific evidence to back up their outlandish claims.

Humanism, secular humanism, and atheism are all closely associated with materialism. All focus on a physical world and either downplay or deny a spiritual world. Atheism, or the denial of God's existence, is usually associated with socialism.

In America today, our moral culture is eroding and declining. Immorality is becoming more acceptable and more commonplace. This is due to the increasing influence of socialist thinking and the barrage of socialist attacks on America's institutions and American Capitalism. In recent years, the battles over cultural issues have even been called a "cultural war." This so-called "cultural war," however, is really just one series of battles in the much larger war, America's Economic War between American Capitalism and socialism.

Later in this book, we will see why and how socialism leads to cultural decline and social disintegration. For now, let's turn our attention to the dollars and cents of America's Economic War.

American Capitalism – The Greatest Economic System Ever Created

American Capitalism, the greatest engine of human economic growth and prosperity ever known in the history of the world, is being attacked, damaged and weakened as these words are being written. If socialists have their way, it will be destroyed completely and it will be replaced by a socialist or interventionist system consisting of government-dictated centralized planning, control, coercion, compulsion and violence. Your freedom will disappear, your prosperity will evaporate, and even your life will be in jeopardy from a backward and inefficient, socialized health care system that will require extensive rationing of services.

America's standard of living is the envy of the world. According to the U. S. Census Bureau, the median American family income (in 2006 inflation-adjusted dollars) was over $58,500.[1] Even our "poor" today live better than kings and princes in pre-capitalist ages past. Just think. If a leader of a third world country comes down with a serious illness, he generally flies to the U. S. to take advantage of our health care system. He typically doesn't book a hospital room in a socialist country.

Consider too, our technological innovation; it is unsurpassed in the world.

There is a long list of new American technologies that have spawned vast new global industries. Google, the ubiquitous Internet search engine company, started when two Stanford graduate students Larry Page and Sergey Brin (with maxed-out credit cards) showed their new software technology to Sun Microsystems' Co-Founder Andy Bechtolsheim in 1998. Andy's confidence in their invention and his check for $100,000 helped launch another American success story.[2] Google (at the time of this writing) has a market capitalization of approximately $210B.[3]

Indeed, America's patent database is rich with inventions that were inspired by the incentives of Free Enterprise. Our management techniques provide stunning models for the efficient utilization of resources and the treatment of employees. Our educational system has been instrumental in creating new knowledge and educating young people to lead productive and fulfilling lives.

But, unfortunately, with socialism creeping into our schools and coming onto our campuses, professors and teachers have frequently introduced indoctrination instead of education and political correctness instead of academic freedom and free speech. It is truly tragic to see today's universities invite an anti-American dictator to speak and yet, deny a high-ranking U. S. government official from speaking in that same venue. It is also troubling to watch today's schools invite a proponent of free sex and drugs to a school assembly to use that forum to encourage impressionable young high school students to "experiment."

Under American Capitalism, American productivity is astounding. Americans make up roughly 5% of the world's population. Yet, those same Americans have generated a Gross Domestic Product (GDP) equal to about 20% of the entire GDP of the world. America also produces approximately 23% of the electricity in the world, 18% of natural gas, and nine percent of oil production.[4] The U. S. is third in oil production, only following Saudi Arabia and Russia.[5] In fact, if environmental regulations did not impede American oil production, no doubt we would produce more oil and we would cut or eliminate any dependency we now have on foreign oil.

Even Karl Marx and Frederick Engels, the revolutionary proponents of socialism, acknowledged in 1848 how capitalism had succeeded in improving production:

The bourgeoisie, by the rapid improvement of all instruments of production, by the immensely facilitated means of communication, draws all, even the most barbarian, nations into civilisation. ... The bourgeoisie, during its rule of scarce 100 years, has created more massive and more colossal productive forces than have all preceding generations together.[6]

"Bourgeoisie" is their term for capitalists. It is true that socialists know that capitalism is superior to socialism in the realm of economic matters. Yet, they persist in their blind faith to the morally and economically inferior system of socialism.

The fact that American Capitalism is a far better economic system than socialism is unquestionable. American Capitalism creates more growth. American Capitalism creates more productive jobs. American Capitalism creates more technological innovation and inventions. American Capitalism creates more management innovations. American Capitalism creates better working conditions and more innovative programs and benefits for workers. American Capitalism creates more manufacturing and process innovations. American Capitalism creates faster, better and cheaper products. American Capitalism creates new medications and innovative health care technologies. American Capitalism raises worker productivity which increases real wage rates. American Capitalism continually raises the American standard of living.

Despite all the economic data, all the economic studies, all the economic theories, all the economic analysis, all the economic realities, there are those who still are waging war against American Capitalism. Why don't they use reason? Are they caught up blindly in a misleading faith – the religion of socialism?

If we lose America's Economic War, the greatest economic engine the world has ever known will be destroyed. The poverty of socialism will engulf America and the world.

Compare our wealth-producing American Capitalism to all those "socialist utopias" with their depressed economies and destitute people. Is it any wonder why so many people want to come to America? Is it any wonder why Americans don't risk their lives to swim to Cuba?

Socialism –
A Fancy Name for Moral and Economic Bankruptcy

In some ways, the word "socialism" has a nice ring to it. It sounds like a party; everyone is getting along and having a good time. Too bad that socialism is just the opposite.

Socialism starts off with a very weak foundation. We mentioned that foundation earlier – materialism. Socialism doesn't believe in a spiritual or moral order. There is no God to pray to when you need help. Of course, you can pray to a tree. A tree after all is a material thing and socialism believes in material things. But, trees can never answer prayers.

For those socialists who do believe that morality is needed, there is an additional problem. Socialists usually believe that moral values evolve and change with the times and economic circumstances. So, how does a socialist know what moral values to use this year? Or, this month? Or, today? If you follow socialism to its logical conclusion, all moral and economic decisions ultimately devolve into questions of power. Why, you ask?

With socialism, there are no eternal moral standards to judge different potential human actions. Should we build one fuel efficient car or should we build ten bicycles? (Remember in socialism there is no Free Market to help make economic decisions.) Should we define marriage as a special lifelong, loving relationship between a man and a woman to raise and nurture children, or should we define marriage as an arbitrary relationship, existing for a period of time, between any two adults of different genders or the same gender? (Remember in socialism there is no spiritual thinking to guide moral decisions.)

With socialism and no enduring moral standards, there will likely be many people with their own versions of the "best" moral standards and "best" type of socialism. Conflicts (and sometimes violence) usually ensue. The winners will always be the people with power, the ruling elite (be they kings, emperors, dictators, ruling parties, fascists, communists, or other socialists). Socialism always boils down to power. Socialism always results in moral bankruptcy.

In economic terms, socialism manifests itself in government-dictated centralized planning, control, coercion, compulsion and violence. Socialist governments use the powers of government (physical coercion, prison and even death) to enforce its economic plans and decisions.

Government is the only institution in society that is given the legal power of physical coercion, compulsion and violence. Police power used to protect citizens from criminal behavior (such as robbing you at gunpoint) and military power used to protect citizens from external attack (such as an invading army or a terrorist plot) are legitimate uses of government power. But, broadening government power to include rigidly controlling the nation's economy is another matter. Such power wielded by socialist governments leads inevitably to economic bankruptcy. Let's look at some examples of socialist economies.

Zimbabwe is a case in point. According to the 2009 Index of Economic Freedom, a joint project of the Heritage Foundation and *The Wall Street Journal*, Zimbabwe is the second least free (that is, second most controlled) nation in the world (ranking just above North Korea).[7] Zimbabwe, once a leading producer of food in Africa, was changed under socialism into a poverty-stricken country with a starving population. Price controls are common. Private property rights are virtually non-existent. Tax rates are very high. Corruption is widespread. Inflation is about 10,453%. Unemployment is 80%. Per capita GDP was a meager $2,065.[8] As you can see, Zimbabwe is a real "socialist utopia."

Another "socialist utopia" is Syria. Syria is governed under the repressive Ba'athist Party, a secular socialist party. Like other socialist countries, bribery and corruption is widespread and private property rights are not well protected. Syria has no stock market and capital markets are virtually non-existent, making new wealth creation nearly impossible. Syria's inflation is relatively high and regulatory overhead is stifling. Syria's per capita GDP was only a meager $3,610.[9]

But, what about other countries that have adopted an initially less stringent form of socialism known as welfare state socialism? They are widely regulated and controlled, but not to the extent of socialist dictatorships like Zimbabwe and Syria. Will welfare states also go bankrupt?

To the extent that freedom is restricted and socialism is adopted by a country, economic growth is weakened and economic decline sets in. To illustrate this slower track to economic bankruptcy, let's take a quick look at Europe.

Europeans clearly do not enjoy the extent of labor freedom that exists in the United States. Government regulations in European nations are extensive and pervasive. They run the gamut from wage and hour controls, to workplace rules and collective bargaining requirements, to even mandating the language that can be spoken. That's why European per capita GDP is usually much lower than in America, while their unemployment levels tend to be much higher.

The fundamental problem with Europe's version of socialism is that it is unsustainable in the long run. It is not pure socialism as envisioned by the early philosophers of socialism and it is certainly not pure capitalism. It is a form of socialism that focuses on inefficient social programs. As will be seen in Chapter 5, welfare state socialism ultimately leads to economic bankruptcy. It just takes longer than complete socialism. The more a government hampers capitalism, the quicker total socialism and economic bankruptcy ensue. When socialism is fully implemented, extreme poverty always results.

The financial drain of European socialism with its high tax, high regulation and high unemployment as well as its welfare state practices will likely bankrupt Europe the same way as it has bankrupted other socialist countries in the past.

Despite socialism's nice-sounding name, the moral and economic bankruptcy of socialism is a dismal recipe for a nation. It's also a terrible prescription for you and your family.

The Danger to You and Your Family

American Capitalism must win America's Economic War we face today. If not, an era of American socialism or global socialism will destroy our moral culture and devastate our economy. Religious freedom, political freedom and economic freedom will be lost and the suffering to average people and families will be enormous. No institution will avoid the damaging impacts of socialism. The Christian Church, the Family, the Constitution, our Free Market, and Free Enterprise will be irreparably harmed. No one will be able to avoid the onslaught of a truly dark, dark age. America as we know it will not exist.

American Culture and Morality are at Risk

If American Capitalism loses America's Economic War, American Culture and our traditional Christian-based morality will be destroyed. An immoral socialist culture will engulf America.

In terms of dating, relationships, marriage and family matters, you can expect some tectonic changes. Traditional marriage and families as we know them will no longer exist. They will be replaced with meaningless sexual hook-ups, single lonely parents, and government-financed child support. These trends are already settling into our culture. In traditional American Culture, it takes a family to raise a child. With socialism, it takes the entire village (that is, the government).

In a socialist culture, you can expect to lose control of your children to the government. The government will dictate the rules for raising children. Parents will have little power over school curriculum and important personal matters. Parental notification and permission for abortions will be non-existent. Free condoms and free birth control pills will be available for pre-teens as well as teens, again without parental notification and parental permission. Parents might not even be allowed to accompany their children to the doctor's office for a physical exam.

Sexuality will be dramatically changed as well under socialism. Sexuality will revert to the pagan customs of the ancient, pre-Christian, Greeks and Romans. Homosexuality will be widespread and accepted. Promiscuity, pedophilia, prostitution, group sex and even bestiality will be commonplace along with adultery. In an amoral socialist culture, all will be considered "normal" sexual outlets. Those holding on to the "old, outdated Christian morality" will be criticized, shunned, and sent to sensitivity programs (so they can "fit in" better).

In a 21st century version of socialism, we might even see sex and marriage between robots (that mimic human appearance, behavior and functionality) and people according to David Levy of the University of Maastricht in the Netherlands.[10] The dehumanization of men and women will always go hand-in-hand with socialism.

Sexual abuse and the objectification of people will be rampant and widespread. The pleasure principle will prevail. The emotional and psychological damage to both children and adults will be profound. If you look around today, you can see how the growing influence of socialism is making inroads into creating a sexually-perverted and sexually-soaked culture.

In the arena of entertainment, the impact of socialism is also becoming evident. Sexual depravity will populate and permeate programming and media of all types. TV, movies, art and literature will all trumpet sexual deviation. The adult entertainment industry, on and off the Internet, will no longer be limited to viewing by adults. Children will become widespread consumers of this content as well, with or without their parent's permission. The amoral socialist sexual culture will be celebrated and promoted in all entertainment channels.

In addition to unhealthy sexual content, the entertainment industry will also portray brutality and violence on an unprecedented scale. This is a natural reflection of socialism's low regard for the value of an individual human life. Socialism sees political and economic groups as power sources and power centers. Individuals, with the exception of a few ruling elite, have no meaning or significance or value to the government and socialist society. Under socialism, the "culture of death" will triumph over the "culture of life."

If American Capitalism loses America's Economic War, you and your family will have to live in the sexually-depraved culture of death. The ramifications of this new immoral socialist culture will be widespread, touching all parts of our spiritual, political and economic lives. All of our lives will be negatively and adversely impacted. Our world and America will be a miserable place in which to live.

Our American freedoms, bought by the sweat and blood and lives of thousands of brave army, navy, marine, and air force men and women, will be another victim of socialism. Let's look more closely at how socialism will destroy your religious, political and economic freedom.

Freedom vs. Socialism's Chain of Control

American Capitalism is built on the solid foundation of Christian spiritual and moral thinking. Indeed, it is no accident that our Founding Fathers referred to God in their writings. A first principle of American democracy is that our freedoms come from God. They specifically do not come from any king or government leader; they do not come from any state or government; and they do not even come from any of our founding documents. God is the author of freedom.

Thomas Jefferson's words inscribed at the Jefferson Memorial capture his insight, wisdom and support for this first principle:

God who gave us life gave us liberty. Can the liberties of a nation be secure when we have removed a conviction that these liberties are the gift of God?[11]

Jefferson's words even seem to anticipate today's attempt to remove God from the American public square by proponents of socialism and atheism. As you probably know, socialists are working hard to remove the phrase "under God" from our Pledge of Allegiance and to remove "In God We Trust" from our currency.

Socialism is the antithesis of freedom. Indeed, socialism is government-dictated centralized planning, control, coercion, compulsion and violence. How does this control come about?

First, in order to create a "socialist utopia," socialism must control the economy. To do this, it must eliminate our economic freedom.

Second, in order to eliminate our economic freedom, socialism must control the government. To do this, it must eliminate our political freedom.

Third, in order to eliminate our political freedom, socialism must control the culture and morality. To do this, it must eliminate our religious freedom.

The accompanying diagram sums up Socialism's Chain of Control.

Socialism's Chain of Control is also closely related to Lameiro's First Law of Economics.

Lameiro's First Law of Economics
While most people think of economics as a somewhat separate field of study, Lameiro's First Law of Economics shows the importance and interrelationship of religion/culture, politics, and economics:

All economic systems consist of an economy, embedded within a political system that in turn is embedded within a religious/cultural system.[12]

As this law implies:

It is impossible to study an economy completely, isolated from the political system in which it lives and from the underlying religious/cultural system of a given human civilization. An economy does not exist in a vacuum.[13]

To understand America's Economic War then, it's vital to recognize both Lameiro's First Law of Economics and Socialism's Chain of Control. It is also critical to realize that America's Economic War is raging in a parallel series of battles within the American Economy, within American Government, and within American Culture.

To implement Socialism's Chain of Control, socialism must eliminate religious freedom, political freedom and economic freedom. To obtain this level of control, socialism must attack and destroy (or, at the very least, make ineffective) the other institutions of American Capitalism: the Christian Church, the Family, the Constitution, our Free Market, and Free Enterprise.

Socialism's Chain of Control

To Create a "Socialist Utopia"
Socialism Must Control the Economy

To Control the Economy
Socialism Must Eliminate Economic Freedom

To Eliminate Economic Freedom
Socialism Must Control the Government

To Control the Government
Socialism Must Eliminate Political Freedom

To Eliminate Political Freedom
Socialism Must Control the Culture

To Control the Culture
Socialism Must Eliminate Religious Freedom

Your Religious Freedom is at Risk

If socialism is successful in its attacks on American Capitalism, the ramifications will be staggering. Without true religious freedom, you and your family can expect that the free exercise of your religion will be strictly curtailed. For example, if you are Christian, you might not be allowed to wear a cross to school or work. It might offend someone (such as an atheist or someone from another religion). You might not be able to bring a Bible to school or work and read it on your lunch hour. Again, it might be offensive for someone else to even see a Bible on your desk. Similarly, talking about your religion in public might be seen as imposing your views on someone else in your group. Or, someone might overhear your conversation and feel uncomfortable with moral discussions.

To illustrate how socialist thinking can impact religious freedom, consider one of the Lewis-Palmer High School's 2006 graduating valedictorians in Colorado. Erica Corder apparently broke the rules by mentioning Jesus during her graduation speech. According to a news report, Erica was told that she would not receive her diploma unless she apologized for her commencement speech.[14] Would Erica have been forced to apologize if she quoted a socialist or atheist leader or even the leader of a non-Christian religion?

In contrast to the treatment of Christians and to the lack of tolerance for Christian beliefs, consider the California school where teachers forced seventh grade students to pretend to be Muslims for several weeks. This exercise included memorizing verses from the Qur'an and playing *jihad* games.[15] Jihad is an Arabic word for a holy war against heretics and infidels. Will this school also require students to memorize an equivalent number of verses from the Bible and perform a "Sermon on the Mount" play?

With socialism, a priest or minister might be accused of deceiving his congregation "with false tales and superstitions" of an all-powerful God in order to "dupe" his Church attendees into making donations to the Church. Furthermore, preachers might be restricted by the government against "hate speech" for professing their belief that homosexuality is a sin or that theft of private property is wrong. In both cases, ministers might face criminal proceedings and/or civil litigation.

Besides banning the Christian cross, the Bible, and religious speech in public as well as prohibiting sermons that touch on political and cultural issues, you and your family will probably see many other restrictions on your religious freedom. Christmas trees and nativity scenes on your lawn might be outlawed; while Winter Holiday trees and lights will be government-regulated and government-approved. If your Aunt dies, you might not be allowed to place a Christian cross or Scripture verse on her cemetery monument (assuming, of course, that you are permitted to bury your relative at all). Along with socialism's devaluation of the individual and environmentalism's ethic of protecting the earth, under socialism the pagan ritual of cremation will be preferred to the traditional Christian burial.

On top of all these affronts to religious freedom, you will suffer living in a culture hostile to religion, in general, and Christianity, in particular. While Christianity will be scoffed at and downplayed, the "religion of socialism" will be celebrated. You and your family will be subjected to the immorality of socialism and its culture of death. The drumbeat of political correctness and social indoctrination will be pervasive and constant. Widespread, and often subtle, discrimination of Christians will be commonplace as well. You and your family might join other families in hiding your Christian values and beliefs from the rest of the world to avoid being ostracized and ridiculed.

In addition to eliminating your religious freedom, socialism will also eliminate most of your political freedom. Just as religious free speech will be curtailed, so too will all other forms of free speech. Let's survey the landscape of political free speech.

Your Political Freedom is at Risk

On college and university campuses (long a hallmark of academic freedom and free speech), you can already see the impact of political correctness, political indoctrination, and the ruthless oppression of free speech, under the growing influence of socialism. Examples abound of professors and instructors browbeating their students over political free speech, free inquiry and the exploration of non-politically correct ideas. To illustrate, a Georgia Tech student was threatened on her first day of a public policy class with getting an "F" in the class if she attended a Conservative Political Action Conference.[16] So much for freedom of inquiry, encouraging open-minded political debate, and real education.

Another means for limiting your free speech popular among its socialist proponents is labeling some speech as "hate speech." Under the guise of not offending certain socially-identified and socially-protected groups, your free speech is already being curtailed. While it is true that someone can offend another person with their speech, there are many, many problems with regulating speech (not the least of which is the First Amendment of our Constitution). With socialism, you and your family can expect all manner of comments (both verbal and written) covering all sorts of religious, moral, cultural, political, and economic topics to be strictly controlled by the government. Under socialism, you can expect to have the government scan all your emails for "hate speech" or other politically incorrect speech.

A major issue with "hate speech" is that the government can declare virtually anything "hate speech" and then, prosecute you or your family for engaging in it. For example, what if your ten year old child calls another schoolmate "fat?" Will fat people be designated as a special group under socialism? Is calling someone fat a reason to discipline your son? Or, what if your husband owns a dry cleaning business and tells a customer that his competitor's work is shoddy? Is criticizing a competitor "hate speech?" What if you get into a discussion with your friends at the health club and tell them you really prefer the Free Market and competition to socialism? Will you be violating the government-controlled limits on speech? Many socialists think American Capitalism is a terrible system and promoting it is wrong. In all of these cases, you or your family might be accused of "hate speech" and punished.

With the advent of "hate speech," there are also more specific "hate crimes." "Hate crimes" are ordinary crimes that have a specific "hateful component" to them, based on a "hateful attitude" toward the victim or a social group that the victim is associated with. Presumably, socialists believe that a "hate crime" is a worse crime than the ordinary crime without the "hateful component."

With some "hate speech" and many "hates crimes," the "thought police" will likely need to check on the books and magazines you and your family buy and read, the websites you visit, the organizations you belong to, as well as the events you attend, to determine if some of your speech (or activities) might be "hateful" and therefore, illegal. You and your family can expect to be forced to attend sensitivity training for actual (or even potential) "hate speech" violations. Persistent "hate speech" offenders can expect imprisonment as can those guilty of "hate crimes."

Closely tied to "hate speech" are "speech codes" on campus. According to socialists, the justification for speech codes is the elimination of potential "hostile environments" or "sexual harassment" situations by restricting speech. Just like other socialist arguments for "socialist utopias," speech codes are sold with socialism's "good intentions." However, socialism always eliminates your freedom. Plus, the results of their social engineering efforts never achieve their lofty-sounding goals anyway.

Take the University of Maryland's sexual harassment policy, for example. It bans:

... idle chatter of a sexual nature, sexual innuendoes, comments about a person's clothing, body, and/or sexual activities, comments of a sexual nature about weight, body shape, size, or figure, and comments or questions about the sensuality of a person.[17]

This means that in addition to banning ostensibly rough and crude comments, the speech code also restricts someone from saying: "Beth, your new dress looks great." Why should the government regulate your family's everyday conversations?

You and your family can expect just this type of regulation under socialism. Indeed, your freedom of speech will be severely limited. In addition, other people's freedom of speech also will be limited under socialism and this too will impact you adversely. Indeed, under the influence of socialist thinking, political free speech has already been substantially restricted in America. You can expect that these onerous regulations will likely be enhanced if socialism wins America's Economic War. How does political free speech get restricted and how does it impact your family? Let's look at some examples.

Suppose your neighbor down the block decides he or she wants to run for Congress. Maybe, the incumbent seems to be out of touch with his constituents and your neighbor believes they can do a much better job of lowering taxes, eliminating government waste, and restoring our freedoms. As your neighbor will quickly learn, to run an effective political campaign and to compete with an entrenched incumbent requires money. The potential new candidate can't get their message out for free. TV, radio and newspaper ads cost money. So do bumper stickers and lawn signs. Thus, one of the very first tasks of your neighbor is to raise money for the campaign (assuming that they are not already very wealthy and can afford to finance a campaign solely out of their own personal funds).

Your neighbor will immediately run into the maze of government regulations known as the Federal Campaign Finance Law overseen by the Federal Election Commission. This regulatory agency has jurisdiction over all U.S. House, U.S. Senate, Presidential and Vice Presidential campaign finances. Without going into all the issues here, the Federal Campaign Finance Law (including the Bipartisan Campaign Reform Act of 2002 also known as McCain-Feingold) makes it more difficult to raise money by placing a variety of restrictions on campaign financing.[18]

By making it tougher to raise money and support potential new candidates for office, the government has already limited political free speech by restricting the ability of some individuals to seek federal office. Your political freedom is also directly impacted. You have fewer candidates to listen to, fewer ideas to mull over, and fewer candidates to vote for. Is it any wonder why so many citizens don't bother to vote? Their opinions and voices are stifled, while incumbents are given a built-in edge.

Let's look at another example of limiting political free speech. The "Fairness Doctrine" is a case in point. While ostensibly promoting diversity of opinion, this positive-sounding socialist policy would stifle political free speech on the radio. Today, talk radio is largely dominated by conservative talk show hosts. Why? Because radio audiences find conservative talk shows of interest and value. These shows are generally quite successful. In stark contrast, liberal talk shows don't seem to draw comparably-sized audiences. The "Fairness Doctrine," in a nutshell, will force conservatives off the air. It will do this by forcing radio station owners who carry conservative talk radio to also carry equal amounts of unpopular liberal talk radio programs. The impact will simply be to eliminate the voice of conservative talk radio hosts such as Rush Limbaugh. The "Fairness Doctrine" is another tool of socialists to limit political free speech.

A related, emerging debate is raging over various socialist proposals to regulate the Internet. Network Neutrality or Net Neutrality (also known as the "Web Fairness Doctrine"[19]) is another one of those nice-sounding, freedom-killing, socialist ideas designed to take away your freedom. Net Neutrality attempts to force Internet Service Providers (ISPs) to provide any content, from any source, to any destination, requiring any amount of Internet resources, without additional costs to anyone (except, of course, the

ISP businesses that foot the bill). Socialists have even been able to confuse some groups into thinking that Net Neutrality would protect their free speech, when in the long run it would have the opposite effect.

The long term impacts of Net Neutrality to you include: the further restriction of political free speech by forcing some other content (not demanded by free market forces) to be carried at below traffic cost, the drain of resources that could be used for potential investment in new and better Internet infrastructure and technology, and increased costs passed on to the consumer. Net Neutrality is just another socialist scheme to eliminate your political freedom.

Besides eliminating you and your family's religious freedom and political freedom, socialism will also eliminate your economic freedom. Let's look at a few ways in which socialism wants to restrict your economic freedom.

Your Economic Freedom is at Risk – The So-Called Health Care "Crisis"

A good place to start is in the field of health care. America's health care system is broken; costs (including insurance premiums) continue to increase significantly, while quality is often marginal. Why?

Under socialist thinking, America's health care system is increasingly over-regulated. Unfortunately, there is no longer a free market in health care in America. The American health care system is a hampered market, throttled back from reaching its full potential. You and your family are paying more for insurance, assuming you even have insurance. Plus, your choices of doctors and medical procedures are restricted by government interference in the market. Quality is down; costs are up. Government controls and regulations are the economic villain. Your economic freedom is limited in this important area of your family's life.

Two Cato Institute researchers sum up the situation succinctly:

... in America's health care sector, a dense thicket of laws and regulations disables the competitive process ... Government discourages patients from shopping for value and encourages them to disregard costs. It pays doctors and hospitals according to volume with no regard to quality. It restricts the choices available to patients and blocks competition among providers of medical goods and services. Through tax policy, subsidies, and regulation,

government reduces patients' freedom to choose, reduces competition, and obstructs the market processes that deliver higher quality at lower prices.[20]

In stark contrast to those parts of the health care market that are government-regulated, consider two market segments that experience less government control: laser eye surgery and cosmetic surgery. Both of these health care market segments have experienced declining costs.[21] When consumers have the economic freedom to pick their own health care providers and their own medical procedures with the help of their freely-chosen doctors, quality goes up and prices go down. Competition provides choice and efficiency, as well as innovation.

Today, socialists are calling for more laws and more regulations to "fix" our health care system. It's truly ironic that socialism wants to repair the system that it has broken using the failed approaches that created all the problems in the first place. Indeed, this is a classic pattern of welfare state socialism: (1) hamper the market with regulations, (2) the market reacts by becoming less effective at meeting people's needs, (3) criticize the market for not meeting everyone's needs, (4) claim the market is failing, and (5) use the complaints to call for more government intervention and regulations. The cycle continues. Each time through the cycle, the market becomes weaker and less efficient. Eventually, shortages and rationing occur. Eventually, poverty in that area of the economy results. The accompanying figure illustrates Socialism's Cycle of Increasing Regulations and Control.

Socialism's Cycle of Increasing Regulations and Control

Regulate
the Market

Call for
More
Regulations

Market is
Less
Effective

Claim
Market is
Failing

Criticize the
Market

But, as bad as America's health care system is today under a hampered market, things will get worse if American Capitalism loses America's Economic War. For a taste of complete socialized health care, Britain and Canada gives us some awful food for thought. Rush Limbaugh cites the case in Britain of Elizabeth Jones that was twice turned away from a hospital on the date of birth of her baby. The hospital was full and was not able to accommodate Elizabeth. Elizabeth finally delivered at home without help from the local British National Health Service maternity ward.[22]

Other horrifying stories and statistics abound. Under socialism, British patients with dental problems sometimes can't find a dentist. Some patients even resort to pulling out their own teeth. In Canada, wait times for medical care can be staggering. Wait times for emergency heart surgeries range from five to six weeks, while wait times for emergency neurosurgeries are 10.7 weeks.[23] Emergencies can't wait. Lives are at risk. Patients are stuck under socialism. Yet, socialists in the United States look to Britain and Canada as models for America's health care system.

Under socialism, your economic freedom will be severely restricted or eliminated if the government takes over the health care system. Even your life and the lives of your family members are in jeopardy under a socialist health care system. Let's look next at another example of how socialism will try to restrict your economic freedom.

Your Economic Freedom is at Risk –
The So-Called Global Warming "Crisis"

The apocalyptic myth of an impending global warming "crisis" is another tool of socialism. Its purpose is to wrest economic power from your hands and give it to socialists who will run your life for you. The so-called global warming "crisis" is about controlling the economy, controlling you, and eliminating your economic freedom. It accomplishes this by convincing you to alter your lifestyle or risk the survival of the planet.

So far, it seems to be working. Scientific facts are being ignored (even by some scientists who should know better). Socialists have declared a "scientific consensus" that doesn't exist in reality. Opponents are criticized, ridiculed, threatened or ignored. Debate is stifled. Discussion is termed unnecessary. School children are frightened. People are changing their lifestyles. The economy is taking a hit, while socialists are grabbing power and control.

Socialists thrive on crises. Before global warming, do you remember the global cooling "crisis" that occurred some years ago? Or, how about the pollution crisis? Or, how about the energy crisis? Or, the population explosion crisis? Or, for that matter, any of the other socialist crises? Crises are socialist weapons in America's Economic War.

Looking more deeply at global warming, a large body of scientific evidence clearly shows that the so-called global warming "crisis" is a *convenient untruth* of socialism. It's a *convenient* excuse to seize more control of the economy and restrict you economic freedom. Plus, it's an *untruth*. It's simply a manufactured crisis. What do we really know?[24]

First, there is no "scientific consensus" on a global warming "crisis." If allowed to speak, many scientists do not buy into the so-called global warming "crisis."

Second, there is scientific evidence that as carbon dioxide levels increase, global temperatures can increase or decrease. It is not a given that carbon dioxide levels cause global warming. Instead, there is scientific evidence that the sun's cosmic rays are correlated very well to global temperatures. Other factors might be involved as well. Global warming and cooling seem to be a natural process that has occurred on the earth for thousands of years.

Third, there is no scientific evidence to link global warming to devastating, major hurricanes. There is some indication hurricanes are more related to the ocean's currents and salinity variations.

Fourth, the claims that global warming is responsible for melting ice caps and glaciers, rising sea levels, droughts, fires, floods, tornadoes, extinctions of species, disease, and even deaths are simply "claims." There is scientific evidence to refute all of those claims. More research might prove enlightening. There is scientific evidence that the development of corn-based ethanol as an alternative fuel will hurt groundwater depletion and soil erosion, and will help to create oxygen-free "dead-zones," such as one large dead-zone already found in the Gulf of Mexico. So, socialist tampering with the Free Market by subsidizing ethanol might actually hurt the environment.

Finally, it is a fact that people only account for about 3% of carbon dioxide levels, while approximately 97% of carbon dioxide levels are naturally occurring on this planet. People's carbon footprints (and their corresponding lifestyles) are probably not a significant factor in increasing carbon dioxide levels in the atmosphere. But, even if people's lifestyles were a factor, levels of carbon dioxide do not necessarily make a difference in the earth's long-term global warming and cooling process.

The accompanying table summarizes some of the claims socialists make with regard to the so-called global warming "crisis" and some of the information that refute these claims. The table also includes reference notes for the above material.

Socialist Claims about the So-Called Global Warming "Crisis" and the Information to Rebut Those Claims	
Socialist Claims	Reality
There is no need for further debate or discussion on the global warming "crisis" because there is "scientific consensus"	1. "Scientific consensus" is a political term and is not a scientific term. Science and the scientific method constantly seek new knowledge and new understanding. Hypotheses are critically tested against experimental data. Bad theories are discarded. 2. The socialist proponents of the so-called global warming "crisis" want to stifle debate and eliminate discussion. They have closed their minds to experimental data that contradicts their theories. 3. The U.N. Intergovernmental Panel on Climate Change's *Summary for Policymakers* was not a scientific consensus, but a political consensus. Of the 2500 panel members, most were not scientists and only a small group of members actually wrote the *Summary for Policymakers.*[25] 4. The "Oregon Petition" had more than 17,000 signers (most of whom were scientists) that declared: "There is no convincing scientific evidence that human release of carbon dioxide, methane, or other greenhouse gasses is causing or will, in the foreseeable future, cause catastrophic heating of the Earth's atmosphere and disruption of the Earth's climate.[26] 5. The American Meteorological Society's (AMS) "consensus" statement was voted on by only a few governing members of the society. Estimates indicate that many, if not most, AMS members are skeptical of this consensus statement.[27]

Socialist Claims about the So-Called Global Warming "Crisis" and the Information to Rebut Those Claims

Socialist Claims	Reality
Global warming is caused by increased carbon dioxide in the atmosphere	1. There has been some global warming during the past 30 years. But, the correlation with carbon dioxide levels is uncertain.[28] 2. For much of the 20th century, at the same time carbon dioxide levels were increasing, temperatures were actually decreasing.[29] 3. One study, covering a 3,000 year period, found an incredibly high correlation between the sun's cosmic rays and the earth's temperature. This indicates that global warming and cooling might be a very long-term phenomenon caused by the sun, not carbon dioxide.[30]
Global warming is responsible for recent devastating hurricanes	1. From 1925-1965, there were 39 major hurricanes that hit the United States.[31] 2. From 1966-2006, the number declined by 56% to only 22 major hurricanes hitting the United States.[32] 3. This decline happened even though the global mean temperature rose an estimated 0.4 degrees Celsius and carbon dioxide climbed 20%.[33] 4. Atlantic Ocean currents as described by the Thermohaline Circulation (THC) and naturally occurring variations in ocean salinity seem to correlate with hurricane activity. This indicates that ocean salinity variations might be responsible for changes in hurricane activity, not global warming.[34]
Global warming is responsible for many other global calamities including: melting ice caps and glaciers, rising sea levels, droughts, fires, floods, tornadoes, extinctions of species, disease, and death	1. Scientific evidence does not support these broad claims.[35] 2. Global warming might actually have many positive effects by helping agriculture and forestry.[36] 3. Some attempts to mitigate global warming might actually be harming the earth's environment. A World Resources Institute study indicates that the development of corn-based ethanol as an alternative fuel will hurt groundwater depletion and soil erosion, and will help create oxygen-free dead-zones, such as one large dead-zone already found in the Gulf of Mexico.[37]

Socialist Claims	Reality
People's lifestyles are to blame for the global warming "crisis"	1. There is no global warming "crisis." Therefore, people's lifestyles are not an issue at all. 2. The "Oregon Petition" had more than 17,000 signers (most of whom were scientists) that declared: "There is no convincing scientific evidence that human release of carbon dioxide, methane, or other greenhouse gasses is causing or will, in the foreseeable future, cause catastrophic heating of the Earth's atmosphere and disruption of the Earth's climate.[38]
People must change their lifestyles and reduce their carbon footprints to save the planet from the global warming "crisis"	1. There is no global warming "crisis." Therefore, people's lifestyles are not an issue at all. 2. About 97% of carbon dioxide is not man-made. It occurs naturally.[39] 3. Reducing people's carbon footprint will probably not impact the environment appreciably, but it will have serious economic consequences.
The poor will be hurt the most by the global warming "crisis"	1. Most of us will be poorer if socialism uses the so-called global warming "crisis" to control the economy and restrict our economic freedom.

Let's focus now on how this phony "crisis" is putting your economic freedom at risk. How does the so-called global warming "crisis" impact you and your family?

The mythical global warming "crisis" is all about controlling energy and controlling the American Economy. Energy is the lifeblood of the American Economy and American Capitalism. American Capitalism literally runs on energy. Without energy, nothing works. If socialists gain control of our energy, they also gain control of our economy. That's why socialists are so eager to promote the global warming "crisis" and are so hesitant to allow any debate on the topic. If socialists have their way, you and your family's lifestyle will be dramatically altered, your personal finances will be hit hard, and your economic freedom will be severely restricted.

How is the so-called global warming "crisis" linked to the American Economy? It's pretty simple as the accompanying diagram shows. First, socialists claim that the planet will not survive global warming. It's a life and death crisis of global proportions. Second, socialists allege that carbon dioxide must be controlled in order to save the earth from destruction. Third, socialists propose government or U.N. controlled carbon dioxide emissions "cap and trade" programs (more on these later). Finally, with these programs in place, socialists would control our energy supply and usage, impacting virtually everyone and everything in the economy.

Cap and trade programs are straight-forward too. They are an insidious way to create and enforce a system of energy rationing. With these programs, the government (or possibly the U.N.) regulates how much carbon dioxide emissions each person and each company (and possibly each country) will be permitted. Sometimes other emissions besides carbon dioxide will be regulated as well.

By limiting emissions, your energy usage is fixed. This is the "cap" portion of cap and trade. It sets a cap or top limit on your energy usage. The "trade" portion refers to a part of the system that allows you to purchase part of someone else's cap that might not be needed. An alternative idea is to buy additional energy rations, that is, trade dollars for permission to use more energy. The dollars might be used to plant new trees in a third world country or finance other government boondoggles.

Using the So-Called Global Warming "Crisis" to Control America's Economy

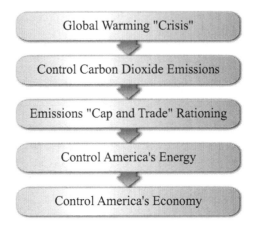

    AMERICA'S ECONOMIC WAR – YOUR FREEDOM, MONEY AND LIFE

Now, let's bring this back to your family. Here's how it might work in your home. The amount of gasoline you can use in all your cars will be restricted. If you want to take a two-week summer vacation and drive across the country, you might have to purchase some trees in Africa to obtain the necessary emission rations. Notice how you will be paying not only for the gasoline, but also for the right to purchase the gasoline. Some system!

If you want to buy a new SUV, you will find it too expensive relative to your gasoline "cap." If you live in a warm climate, your electricity "cap" might not permit you to air condition more than one hour per day. Plus, you might have to cut back on using all those appliances at home. One TV per household might be all you can expect too. Two TV's will probably be an "energy luxury." The restrictions go on and on. Your economic freedom will disappear.

If this were the only impact, it would be bad enough. But, it's not all. There will be inequities in determining what people and what companies (and possibly what countries) get what caps. Socialist countries generally experience widespread corruption. You can expect the cap and trade programs will experience corruption too. There will be calls for new regulators to regulate the existing cap and trade regulators who have allowed the corruption. That's how socialism operates.

Another major impact on you and your family will be financial. Your expenses will go up and up. Energy costs will skyrocket. Costs always skyrocket when there are shortages caused by government. One attempt by socialists to mitigate global warming is already costing your family money. The government's ethanol biofuel policy has raised corn prices dramatically (by 70% in one six month period alone). This, in turn, triggers significant price increases in food items such as meats, eggs, and soft drinks because corn is used for animal feed and for corn syrup.[40]

In addition to the costs associated with cap and trade programs and other government regulations and programs, socialists have also proposed various new carbon taxes to restrict your freedom and take away more of your money. Socialists will add these taxes to the already existing high taxes you pay on gasoline and other sources of energy. For example, California drivers pay about 62.8 cents per gallon of gasoline for Federal and State taxes.[41] In effect, this represents a 26.5% sales tax on gasoline costing $3.00 per gallon.[42] If socialists have their way, a carbon tax of 20% or more might be added per gallon of gasoline.

You and your family can expect other forms of carbon taxes as well. According to a news report, Boulder, Colorado is the first city in the U.S. to institute a carbon tax on electricity.[43] Carbon taxes on natural gas and coal are likely too. Another possible hit to your wallet is the gradual phase-out of the home mortgage interest deduction based on the square-footage of your home. In other words, socialists want to force you to live in a smaller home in order to curtail the carbon emissions associated with heating your home. They want you to downsize your lifestyle and your checking account.

Not only will you have to pay for carbon taxes and for higher energy costs, but you will also have to pay (by trading) for more emission rations to make your life more bearable. Without extra energy rations, you might find your life very uncomfortable. Moreover, you can expect the prices of all other products and services that involve energy to go up in price (since prices for goods and services include the energy costs associated with manufacturing and transportation).

To sum up, the so-called global warming "crisis" is an attempt to control the economy by controlling energy. You and your family's economic freedom will be severely restricted, your lifestyle will be dramatically altered, and your personal finances will be hit very hard.

Your Prosperity is at Risk

By now, the picture is probably coming into sharper focus for you. America's Economic War is all about your freedom, your money and your life. American Capitalism offers you religious, political and economic freedom. It permits you to freely earn a living, or become an entrepreneur and create new products and services along with new wealth. It permits you to live the lifestyle you have honestly earned and you truly desire. American Capitalism does not guarantee you the life you want, but it does guarantee you the freedom to pursue your life's dreams.

The Declaration of Independence eloquently sums up American Capitalism with these still profound words:

We hold these truths to be self-evident, that all men are created equal, that they are endowed by their Creator with certain unalienable Rights, that among these are Life, Liberty and the pursuit of Happiness. – That to secure these rights, Governments are instituted among Men, deriving their just powers from the consent of the governed ...

The pursuit of happiness translates into our ability to work, to earn, to play, and to spend money as we think best. In short, it is to live in freedom. It is not to have a government control our actions.

With socialism, your freedoms are taken away. With welfare state socialism (the precursor of complete socialism), your freedoms are taken away incrementally, until that day in which you and your family are no longer free at all.

While American Capitalism creates economic wealth, socialism destroys economic wealth. Under American Capitalism, resources are directed toward the greatest fulfillment of human needs and wants through the operation of an unimpeded, free market. Under socialism, resources are depleted in a highly ineffective, highly inefficient, highly wasteful, government bureaucracy controlled by a powerful elite.

With American Capitalism, you are in control. With socialism, the government is in control.

With American Capitalism, the individual votes every day for precisely those goods and services of highest priority to them. You and your family vote every day too. You do it with your buying decisions and money. Even the slightest change in consumer demand for goods and services is immediately factored into production and investment decisions that are rapidly trans-mitted throughout the Free Market. There are no delays in communicating human needs and wants with the Free Market.

In sharp contrast, with socialism the government has no effective process for allocating scarce resources and directing them to meet human needs and wants. Even if a socialist government has some concern for its people, without the Free Market it does not have the mechanism to understand and meet their needs. Without the Free Market, there is no free (and instantaneous) flow of economic decision-making information. Also, many socialist governments don't even pretend to care about their citizens. Many socialist governments just focus on the needs of their powerful elite.

American Capitalism is highly effective in satisfying consumer needs.

Socialism is an abysmal failure in satisfying consumer needs.

If socialism wins America's Economic War, your prosperity will be eliminated. Under the crushing twin burdens of excessive taxation and excessive regulation, economic growth will stagnate, wages and salaries will dissipate, and financial opportunities will evaporate.

On a personal level, if socialism wins America's Economic War, you can expect much higher taxes than you already pay, much lower real salary and wage growth (or no growth at all), fewer jobs to choose from (if you have a choice at all), higher prices in the supermarket, higher prices for cars, higher costs for gasoline, higher costs to heat your home, higher costs for water and other utilities, higher costs for travel, higher costs for cell phones, shortages of key goods and services, no luxury goods and services, few investment choices (assuming you have any investment choices at all), limited financial services, and higher government fees for any government services (such as automobile license plates).

In summary, with socialism you can expect much higher costs, lower income, shortages, rationing, and a much lower standard of living. You can expect to go from the #1 economy in the world to a standard of living associated with a second or third world country. Remember socialism always leads to moral and economic bankruptcy.

America's Economic War poses a very great danger to you and your family's prosperity. It also puts you and your family's lives at risk in many different ways. Let's see why.

Your Life is at Risk

Remember the socialist health care system in Canada. Earlier in this chapter, we cited statistics on how long the wait times were for emergency surgeries. Wait times for emergency surgeries were measured in weeks, not hours or minutes! With socialism and a socialist health care system, you can expect health care rationing with long lines for both critical care and routine care, placing your health and your life at risk.

Under a socialist health care system, without the incentives of Free Enterprise, you can also expect few entrepreneurs to step up and start new drug companies and new health-related companies. New drugs and new innovations in health care that might have become available under American

Capitalism will never be created. People who might have been saved with new medications, new therapies, and new procedures will never get those chances. The government-controlled economy will stifle such efforts.

In America today, socialists even condemn drug companies as evil because they are trying to make a profit, as if profit were immoral. But, it is that very profit incentive that spurs on the innovation that creates new products and services that meet the needs of patients with diseases and illnesses. If your daughter comes down with a serious illness, would you prefer to give her a drug that cures the illness (and give a drug company some profit at the same time)? Or, would you prefer to give your daughter nothing and let her die (in order to prevent the drug company from making a profit)? That's probably a pretty easy decision for any loving parent to make. Socialists just don't seem to understand the profit motive and the Free Market.

Under socialism, misguided government regulations can also cause your life to be at risk. The asbestos scare provides another example to consider.

Asbestos is a strong flame-retarding substance that was once used to insulate steel and to prevent the melting of building materials in the event of a fire. It was often utilized in the construction of schools and large office buildings. In order to make it easier to apply asbestos to building materials, Herbert Levine, an inventor and entrepreneur, created a technique for spraying wet asbestos onto the frames of large buildings to help prevent and restrain fires. The company he formed was named Asbestospray.[44]

Back in the 1970's, some government officials were concerned about the fact that workers exposed to high levels of asbestos fibers were reportedly more likely to become ill. The ultimate result was a ban on using asbestos in new buildings and later, the removal of asbestos from existing buildings.[45]

In 1971, New York City specifically banned asbestos. When the World Trade Center was constructed, wet asbestos spraying was only used up to the 64th floor. Herbert Levine was quoted prophetically as saying: "if a fire breaks out above the 64th floor, that building will fall down." The two airlines that brought down the World Trade Center towers crashed into floors 96 – 103 (One World Trade Center) and floors 87 – 93 (Two World Trade Center) respectively, confirming Herbert Levine's prediction.[46]

Additional research on asbestos indicates that it is probably not as risky as once thought. The Heartland Institute reports that:

Research has confirmed that asbestos workers who do not use protective breathing apparatus suffer increased health risks. For the remaining 99+ percent of the U.S. population, however, asbestos health risks are virtually nil.[47]

It has even been reported that no adverse health effects have ever been associated with the wet asbestos spraying process used in skyscraper construction prior to the ban.[48]

How many lives would have been saved in the 9/11 tragedy if the government had not banned asbestos? How many lives are at risk today? How many government regulations have caused more harm than good?

Today's so-called global warming "crisis" (based on junk science) is reminiscent of the asbestos "crisis" which was also built on inadequate scientific investigation. **Socialists rush to scientific judgments and create "crisis" after "crisis" to support their attempts to win America's Economic War**. Unfortunately, with the increasing influence of socialist thinking, you and your family's lives are at increasing risk. If socialists win America's Economic War, you can expect things to get worse.

Consider one final example where you and your family's lives are at risk as a result of onerous government regulations. In an attempt to lessen America's dependence on foreign oil and to cut air pollution, Congress created the Corporate Average Fuel Economy (CAFÉ) program, the so-called CAFÉ standards. CAFÉ standards mandate that manufacturers sell cars that get better gas mileage. To meet these standards, regulatory formulas are somewhat complex and convoluted.[49]

It turns out that CAFÉ standards, not only did not achieve the goals proponents sold them on, but they also created some very negative, unintended consequences. One study estimates that an additional 46,000 people died as a result of driving lighter weight vehicles that were manufactured as a response to the CAFÉ program. CAFÉ standards also probably result in many additional injuries that are not fatal.[50]

In a pronouncement of judicial activism, the 9th U.S. Circuit Court of Appeals has ordered the National Highway Traffic Safety Administration (NHTSA) to increase the unsuccessful CAFÉ standards even higher, apparently in an attempt to mitigate the so-called global warming "crisis."[51] Will we get still more regulations, more deaths and more injuries with socialist thinking?

A much better approach is to permit the Free Market to develop solutions to America's challenges. Certainly, reducing carbon dioxide emissions (to diminish the so-called global warming "crisis") at the cost of tens of thousands of American lives is not a good trade-off. The Free Market offers far better solutions than government regulations.

With socialism, you can expect your life, your prosperity, and your liberties, all to be at risk. Socialism will destroy your religious freedom, your political freedom, and your economic freedom. It will devastate your prosperity. Ultimately, it will imperil your health and life. Socialism is a dismal failure everywhere it is tried. If left unchecked, socialism always results in moral and economic bankruptcy. Fortunately, America can still stop socialism and its terrible effects. America will not naively ignore the threat.

America is at War
If America's institutions continue to be assaulted by socialists, America, as we know it, will disappear and moral and economic bankruptcy will take its place. Today, many Americans are fighting the assault on the Christian Church, the Family, the Constitution, our Freedom, our Free Market, and Free Enterprise. Some religious Americans, who are not Christian, are even fighting for the Christian Church. For, if Americans lose the right to exercise Christianity, then surely all other religions will lose their religious freedom soon thereafter.

America is a predominantly Christian nation, formed on Christian principles, yet allowing and empowering complete freedom of religion for its citizens. It has never dictated to its citizens what spiritual beliefs they must hold. It has never established a government-run religion all must participate in. It has shown its Christian heritage in its motto "In God We Trust," in its Pledge of Allegiance "under God," and in its courtrooms that display the "Ten Commandments." Atheistic socialists have no right to obliterate America's Christian heritage or the religious, political, and economic freedoms that rest upon that Christian heritage.

Atheistic socialism is a tyranny of a very small minority, a tyranny of an elite. It is a hoax. It is immoral. Its arguments are based on false premises, faulty logic, and perverted language. Yet, many people, including some of America's finest minds, have succumbed to its seductive allure. Socialism sounds good; but, socialism is bad.

For many in America, it's fashionable to criticize American Capitalism and to attack America's institutions. For many in America, they think our wonderful economy, our liberties, and our lifestyle will continue without the Christian Church, without morality, without Family, without the Constitution, without Freedom, without the Free Market, without Free Enterprise, and without American Capitalism. They are fooling themselves.

Remember that American Capitalism is that wonderful economic system created under God and based on human freedom. Socialism is the name given to all other economic systems that are based on the tyranny of the ruling elite. While American Capitalism harnesses the power of freedom to produce human growth and economic affluence, socialism relies on coercion, compulsion and violence to control people and their lives. Socialism is based on power and inevitably leads to moral bankruptcy and abject poverty.

America is at war. You and your family's religious freedom, political freedom, and economic freedom are at risk. You and your family's prosperity are at risk. You and your family's lives are at risk.

This book will arm you with the knowledge to understand America's Economic War. Let's take a quick tour of the rest of this book.

A Quick Tour of This Book
With an introduction to America's Economic War between American Capitalism and socialism, as well as an understanding of the dangers that socialism poses to you and your family already covered in Chapter 1, Chapter 2 warns you about some of the insidious weapons that some socialists deploy against American Capitalism. These weapons include distorting the meaning of common words, stifling debate and discussion, camouflaging socialist plans, and using fear to control you and your family. Chapter 2 also covers the looming threat of global socialism. Understanding these weapons and additional threats are vital to understanding America's Economic War.

In Chapter 3, we see why **American Capitalism is God-Inspired Freedom and Individualism**. Chapter 3 traces the important Christian foundations of American Capitalism, and discusses the powerful Architecture of American Capitalism. It shows why the characteristics of American Capitalism are:

- Faith (and Morality)
- Freedom (and Peace)
- Free Markets (and Prosperity)
- Family (and Trust)
- Spiritual and Material Human Growth

With this basic understanding of American Capitalism, it is possible to explain why American Capitalism is indeed moral and why American Capitalism is the best economic system ever created in the history of the world.

In contrast, Chapter 4 shows us why **Socialism is Power-Based Control and Elitism**. It discusses why socialism is characterized by:

- Atheism (and Immorality)
- Control (and Violence)
- Economic Inefficiency (and Poverty)
- Groups of "Victims" (and Distrust)
- Moral Decay and Social Disintegration

Chapter 4 also explains the allure and seduction of socialism to some people. It shows why Christian socialism is a theological mistake and why democratic socialism is a political and economic mistake.

Taken together, Chapters 3 and 4 show why American Capitalism works and why socialism fails. Plus, these chapters show why we need American Capitalism to be free and prosperous.

In Chapter 5, we deal with the attempts made by some people to combine American Capitalism and socialism into an alternative, potential "third way" or third economic system. Chapter 5 reveals why hampered capitalism (highly taxed and tightly regulated capitalism) as well as welfare state socialism (the nanny state), both attempts at a "third way," can't work effectively and are not viable in the long run. It also discusses "progressives" and their mistaken efforts to "progress" toward welfare state socialism. Chapter 5 clearly debunks the seductive arguments for hampered capitalism, welfare state socialism, and progressive socialism.

Chapters 3, 4 and 5 taken together provide subtle insights into understanding the confusing arguments we hear on TV and we read in the news every day. They will help you separate truth from fiction. They will help you understand what policies will help the nation to grow economically and what policies will move us toward economic stagnation or even economic bankruptcy. They will also help you understand why various people think the way they do.

Chapter 6 presents socialism's war strategy for attacking and destroying the institutions of American Capitalism. It lists the 47 major battles and three special battles against the Christian Church, the Family, the Constitution, Freedom, the Free Market, and Free Enterprise. It also details many of the battles raging to destroy our religious freedom, political freedom, and economic freedom.

For readers who choose to delve into more detail about any or all of the battles listed in Chapter 6, Appendix A (at the end of the book) provides more detailed battle summaries. These summaries contain more information on each battle, battlefront examples, and over 365 reference notes for further study or research.

Chapter 6 also highlights and discusses the three most critical battles in America's Economic War:

- The Battle against Faith in God,
- The Battle against the Constitution as Originally Written, and
- The Battle against Private Property.

Plus, it covers some important debates such as the important argument dealing with freedom of speech and the freedom to offend. It also describes why "hate speech" and offensive speech limits are clearly unconstitutional. Finally, Chapter 6 explains the seduction of environmental socialism and the seduction of universal health care socialism.

In Chapter 7, we learn about another socialist war strategy. This chapter covers socialism's strategy to control you and your family in these ways:

- Control the Message (What You Can Hear),
- Control the Conversation (What You Can Say),
- Control the Agenda (What You Can Think),
- Control the Mood (What You Can Feel),
- Control the Economy and Your Life (What You Can Do), and
- Control the Election Process (What Type of Leaders You Can Elect).

Chapter 8 focuses on life in America when America's Economic War is over. Chapter 8 summarizes two distinct visions for America. One vision assumes American Capitalism wins America's Economic War; it's upbeat, positive, and optimistic. The other vision is pessimistic. It describes what America might be like if American Capitalism loses to socialism. Appendix B and Appendix C present these visions in an organized format for study or reference.

Chapter 8 also discusses some major political and economic consequences of America's Economic War, including the potential morphing of the political parties, the possible changes to electoral maps, and the potential changes to election campaigns.

In addition, Chapter 8 answers the important question: Will the American economy turn-around quickly, or get bogged down in a bad recession, or worse, collapse into a ten-year depression? It also provides seven Free Market principles that can generate economic prosperity soon. Finally, Chapter 8 predicts when America's Economic War will probably end and which side will likely win.

With that brief overview of this book, let's move on to Chapter 2 and get an understanding of some of the weapons socialists use against American Capitalism.

Chapter 2

Caution: Some Socialists Use Deceit, Deception and Fear as Weapons

"When words lose their meaning people will lose their liberty."
Confucius[52]

Truth is the friend of Freedom and American Capitalism, while truth is the enemy of coercion and socialism. At the core of socialism's strategy, tactics, and efforts to win America's Economic War are deceit, deception and fear. Without these weapons, socialism has little chance of success. But, with truth and courage, these weapons will fail. American Capitalism will win America's Economic War with truth and courage.

Socialism's assault on the truth is perhaps its greatest act of immorality. In attacking American Capitalism by attacking truth itself, socialism undermines all moral thinking. This is because all moral thinking (all morality and reason) depend upon understanding the meaning of truth, acknowledging its existence, and permitting its free pursuit.[53] Respect for the truth is the foundation of intellectual freedom. Respect for the truth is also a fundamental requirement for civilization.

In order to win its war against American Capitalism, socialism ignores truth and resorts to deceit and deception by changing the use and meaning of words. This is done to paint socialism's awful thinking in a more favorable light and to confuse debate and discussion. Let's look at some important words that socialists use and let's understand the true meaning of these words.

It's Not Conservatives vs. Liberals – It's American Capitalists vs. Socialists

The first word socialists misuse is "liberal." This has been going on for a long time.[54] If you think about it, the word liberal is derived from the word "liberty." The word "liberal" really means a person who stands for liberty and freedom. Socialists don't stand for either liberty or freedom. Socialism is the exact opposite. Socialism seeks government control of our lives.

If you trace its origins, liberalism goes back to England in the eighteenth century. Some might trace its origins even further back in history. Then, liberalism stood for such principles as majority rule, equality under the rule of law, freedom of speech, freedom of press, tolerance of all opinions, etc.[55] Certainly, these principles are in conflict with the practices of socialism. For example, consider the socialist demonstrators that shout down an opponent on a college campus. Is that tolerance for all opinions? Or, think about how a scientific skeptic of the so-called global warming "crisis" is treated by socialists. There are no open-minded scientific differences permitted within socialism. Socialists are not liberal by any means.

How about the word "conservative?" It might or might not surprise you to realize that conservatism refers to maintaining the status quo. Conservatives want to keep things more or less the same way they existed in the past. That's why conservatives are associated with American Capitalism. American Capitalism represents the status quo from 1776 to current day America (with, of course, the increasing impact of socialist thinking creeping into America).

Conservatives traditionally do not promote radical new approaches to new challenges. Rather, they seek to solve new problems with proven methods (things that worked in the past). This has inadvertently helped socialism to be accepted by those seeking a better nation and world. Socialists always try to exploit the good intentions of those naïve enough to believe that government control and coercion will solve problems. The young, especially those uneducated by failing schools and universities, are easy targets for socialism's phony moral allure.

Using the words "conservative" and "liberal" is actually causing much of the confusion in American politics today. While conservatives typically support the institutions of American Capitalism, not all conservatives are really capitalists. For example, they frequently do not pursue free market solutions to problems, and they sometimes permit the erosion of freedom in the name of compromise. Often, they act like socialists who are on a slow track in implementing socialist programs.

Adding to the confusion, there are some true "liberals" who seek positive change and growth, who mistakenly advocate socialist policies (something detrimental to their own liberal philosophy).

Finally, another group of socialists call themselves "progressive." They believe that moving America toward a "socialist utopia" is progressive, as if working toward moral and economic bankruptcy is ever progressive. Progressives over the years have come to promote different specific socialist policies and programs. Progressives, for example, often promote a government take-over of the health care system and the stringent regulation of the Free Market. But, the true meaning of the word "progressive" (when socialists use it) is *regressive economic growth.*

So to summarize, we have these groups today (and other groups as well):

- Conservatives who are true capitalists, and who support Freedom and the Free Market
- Conservatives who are not true capitalists, but act more like slow-track socialists
- Liberals who are true liberals, but act like socialists
- Socialists who are true socialists, but call themselves liberals
- Socialists who are true socialists, but call themselves progressives

Isn't life fun?

Is it any wonder there is confusion among voters? Is it any wonder that many people don't vote? Is it any wonder that many voters are disappointed by what politicians actually do when they get in office? That's why some conservatives have felt betrayed in the past. They work to elect a conservative, only to find that conservative supports socialist programs when in office.

Chapter 5 looks at a new way to segment the American Political Landscape into meaningful groups based on their visions for America's present and future. It outlines an accurate and practical framework with 17 different belief segments to untangle this political spaghetti for you and your family. This approach will further enhance our understanding of the war between American Capitalism and socialism.

It's not conservatives vs. liberals. That's the language of the past. It's American Capitalists vs. socialists. If you keep that distinction clearly in mind, the entire American Political Landscape will become easier to understand and navigate. Issues will come into sharp focus. You will be better able to understand America's Economic War.

Clearly, socialists distort the use of the words "liberal" and "progressive." What other words do they distort?

Some Socialists Distort the Meaning of Words

The word "social" is a key word in the language of socialism. It appears in the terms "social justice" and "social equality" and in dozens of other terms and concepts related to socialism. Its meaning has been abused and distorted. In all cases, its usage is the basis of considerable confusion and deception.[56] Even the word "socialism" itself is the root cause of much misunderstanding. Let's see how socialists misuse these words and what the words really mean.

As we mentioned in Chapter 1, "socialism" has a nice ring to it. It sounds like a party; everyone is getting along and having a good time. Socialists are trying to promote socialism with the use of the word "socialism." It gives the impression of a "Great Society."

It's interesting to note, too, that socialists also were trying to build themselves up when they decided to call themselves "liberals," appropriating the word from classical liberalism that stood for liberty and freedom. In a very ironic twist, socialists were also trying to denigrate the system of Freedom and Free Markets when they named that system "capitalism" (a name we obviously continue to use today) in place of its original name "liberalism."

But, socialism is not a synonym for a "Great Society" or a "Party Nation." It's a moral and economic system based on atheistic materialism and government-dictated centralized planning, control, coercion, compulsion and violence. It's far from social. When implemented completely, it is distinctly anti-social[57] and better named "Anti-Socialism."

Socialism is about power, and power in the hands of the government or state. If socialists were to have called their thinking "totalitarian" or "dictatorial" not many people would have signed on to support it. Those terms are much closer to the truth, however. So, socialism is a nice way to sell an immoral economic system.

Instead of the word "social," a more appropriate word to use is "state." In place of the word "socialism," a more precise word is "statism" since socialism is a system based on state or government control. But, people probably will continue to use the words "social" and "socialism" because they have become so ingrained in our vocabulary. Also, "socialists" will likely continue to identify themselves as "liberals" and "progressives" as these words sound more positive and obscure their true agenda.

What about the terms "social justice" and "social equality?" How are they used by socialists and what do they really mean?

"Social justice" and "social equality" sound so very good and so morally appealing.[58] Again, socialists use the friendly-sounding word "social" with the uplifting words "justice" and "equality" to deceive you. Both justice and equality are moral virtues within American Capitalism. They apply to human actions and grade those actions in a moral sense. Is stealing property "just?" Are all employees treated "equally?" They have specific meanings that most people intuitively understand. However, when the word "social" is added to them, wow! The meanings change dramatically.

To socialists, "social justice" and "social equality" are rallying cries against American Capitalism. In their misguided perception, American Capitalism is evil because it rewards some with larger economic gains and it punishes others who fail to produce as much value for consumers. Socialists believe that everyone regardless of intelligence, knowledge, natural capabilities and skills, as well as personal efforts should be rewarded equally. This means that the heart surgeon should be paid the same as the supermarket cashier. The baseball player should be compensated the same as the electrician. The TV star should be rewarded the same as the high school teacher. It also means that the hard worker should be paid the same as the lazy worker or the worker who always shows up late for the job. All should be compensated equally. Is this justice?

With socialists, social justice implies equality of outcome for everyone. This concept is fraught with problems. First, is it just to pay everyone the same amount of money for different work? Clearly, some professions and jobs are more important to society than others. Inventing a new drug might be much more valuable than cooking a good hamburger (even though before dinner the hamburger might seem like a very high priority). Second, if everyone gets the same share of the economic pie regardless of effort, what is the incentive for anyone to help produce the economic pie?[59] With welfare state socialism, unemployment rates are high and the welfare rolls are high for a reason. Why work for a living if the government will guarantee you a comfortable living with little or no effort? Under complete socialism, all are poor except for the elite. There is no comfortable standard of living for the average citizen under complete socialism.

A third issue with the concept of social justice is also very pragmatic. Who is in charge of social justice and social equality? Who will get more? Who will get less? What groups will be favored and at whose expense? Presumably, the only organization that can accomplish this utopian goal is the government. Government-dictated centralized planning, control, coercion, compulsion and violence run by a socialist elite will be required. After all, some people might object to taking away their hard-earned money and property, and giving it away. The threat of fines, imprisonment and even death will be necessary to enforce the illusion and the nightmare of social justice.

If socialism destroys the Free Market and its system to reward innovation, production, and hard work, there is a fourth problem. Who will work in what jobs? Who will do the heavy-lifting? Who will get the soft, easy jobs? Again, the task of assigning and enforcing jobs will ultimately fall to the government, run by a socialist elite, aided by their social experts, social engineers, and social workers. How very "social" all of their social planning sounds, doesn't it?

One quick note on all this socialism. With power concentrated in the hands of just a few, it is very easy to see why corruption is rampant under socialism. There are few, if any, checks on the power of the socialist elite. In addition, their power is so absolute, that it can pay richly to bribe the elite. It is also sometimes the only way to get something done in a socialist bureaucracy. Lord Acton put it so eloquently when he said: "Power tends to corrupt, and absolute power corrupts absolutely."[60] Corruption is certainly another element of socialist immorality.

Let's think about one last word that socialism redefines to fit its own purposes. That word is "democracy." If a socialist uses the word "democracy" or its close cousin, the phrase "social democracy," it does not mean the same thing as we traditionally mean in America by the word democracy. If a socialist states that they seek democracy now, they really mean they want a group of socialist elite to create a socialist government that will rule on behalf of the people. What the socialist elite "think is best for the people" must actually be "what is best for the people" in their minds. No further deliberation, debate or discussion is needed.

Under socialism, "democracy" is the control of the government by a small group of socialist leaders. It does not matter if they came to power by election or revolution. Once in power, by socialist definition, they are a democracy and have "what is best for the people" in mind.

In sharp contrast, under American Capitalism, democracy starts off with the strong belief in the Principle of the Sovereignty of the People.[61] This means power belongs to the people. This means the individual is sovereign, not an elite group running the government. With American Capitalism, the people cede this power through free and open elections to representatives who hold office for a limited period of time. This is majority rule.

Note that with American Capitalism power is in the hands of the individual. With socialism, power is in the hands of an elite group of socialists who think they know what is best for everyone <u>or</u> who pretend to know what's best for everyone to get elected <u>or</u> who don't care and are outright dictators.

As you can see from the many examples above, socialists distort the meaning of words to deceive you and your family. Socialists hope you will give up your power and sovereignty. Socialists want to eliminate your religious freedom, political freedom, and economic freedom. Socialists want to control the economy. Socialists want to control you and your family's lives and lifestyles. Socialists want you to fit into their "socialist utopia."

Besides words, you need to be very cautious about socialist plans. Let's see why.

Some Socialists Camouflage Their Plans
Of necessity, most socialist plans require one or more of the following:
- the seizure of additional power (away from the people);
- new taxes;
- increases in existing taxes;
- new fees;
- increases in existing fees;
- new licenses;
- increases in license requirements for existing licenses;

- new regulations, mandates and directives;
- more control or coercion exerted through existing regulations, mandates and directives;
- less religious freedom;
- less political freedom;
- less economic freedom;
- less prosperity;
- shortages and rationing;
- lower standard of living;
- poorer health; and
- shorter life expectancy.

As a result, socialists often prefer to camouflage their plans with nice-sounding platitudes, vague generalities, and expressions of their good intentions. Presenting their true plans to voters will risk detailed economic analysis and certain criticism. Plans that will result in a loss of freedom and diminished prosperity will always be rejected by informed voters. That's one reason why some socialists must consistently hide their true plans from you and your family.

Another major reason some socialists camouflage their plans is that when compared to free market alternatives they seem utterly inferior. Held up to close scrutiny, socialists plans for controlling you and your family's lives and lifestyle are morally, politically, and economically bad. No matter how hard socialists try to make their plans sound good, socialist plans simply do not work.

In America's Economic War, you need to be on the lookout for socialists that promise you big government solutions, to national problems or personal problems, at little or no cost to you, but at a cost to others. You and your family also need to look for signs that your freedoms will be limited for the promised benefits.

Another sign of a socialist-camouflaged plan is that there are "bad guys" and "victims." The "bad guys" are usually certain socialist-designated groups in society like businesses or CEOs. The "victims" are other socialist-designated groups like workers or teachers or the elderly. Socialism sees "bad guys" oppressing "victims." They are all too happy to save the "victims," assuming you are willing to hand over your freedom, your money, and in some cases, your life.

Socialists continually employ the tactic of "divide and conquer." Divide the nation into "good guys" (another name for "victims") and "bad guys" (usually those who promote, protect, and support American Capitalism). Two quick examples come to mind. Socialists who wish to take-over the health care system consider consumers the "victims" of the greatest health care system in the world, America's health care system. Health insurance companies and drug companies are the "bad guys," despite the fact that they provide enormous value to patients, doctors, and hospitals.

Take the military as another example. In the mixed-up world of socialism, socialists consider the American military the "bad guys" today even though they are dying for our protection and freedom, as well as the protection and freedom of unknown millions of people in the Middle East. How can some socialists call our military men and women murderers, rapists, and torturers? They are our heroes! In contrast, why do some socialists seek to protect the rights of terrorists, the "good guys" in the eyes of some socialists?

Socialists need to camouflage their plans from the American people. They need to hide their plans from you and your family. Otherwise, you will reject their plans, programs and policies outright.

Besides deceit, deception, and camouflage, what other weapons do socialists use in America's Economic War?

Some Socialists Use Fear to Control You

Fear is a powerful emotional weapon in the arsenal of socialism. Fear has that special quality of shutting down clear thinking and reasoning. Fear grips a person. It can cause panic. It can cause people to make very poor decisions.

Some socialists play on this unique quality of fear and use it to control you and your family. Examples abound. Chapter 1 discusses the so-called global warming "crisis." Some socialists use fear of destroying the planet to control you and your family's lives and lifestyles. They want you to curtail and even ration your use of energy. They are content if your children go to bed in fear of floods and animal extinctions. They are happy if you are afraid of driving your SUV, or turning on your air conditioner. They relish negative thinking, gloom, and pessimism in the interests of controlling you and the American Economy.

Chapter 1 also mentions other examples of socialists trying to use fear to control you and your family including the global cooling "crisis," the pollution "crisis," the energy "crisis," the population explosion "crisis," and the asbestos scare. For example, before global warming was touted as a "crisis," socialists were lamenting the fact that the planet was cooling too rapidly. Average global temperatures were declining, droughts were taking place, growing seasons were shortening, and famines were happening.[62] When thermometers started to rise, socialists started to revise their story. The fear of global cooling was out. But, then, the fear of global warming took its place.

With the pollution "crisis," socialists instilled fear into parents and children that air and water pollution were killing our planet. Children should use water paints instead of oil paints to save the planet.[63] With the population explosion, socialists claimed that people were over-populating the earth and that this population growth would cause great famines.[64] Of course, socialists typically neglect the facts and the impacts of new technology and food production techniques.

As an aside, with regard to the serious and tragic problem of food shortages and starvation in certain areas of the world, Freedom and Free Markets are the answer. In the words of Julian L. Simon,

Any country that gives to farmers a free market in food and labor, secure property rights in the land, and a political system that ensures these freedoms in the future will soon be flush with food, with an ever-diminishing proportion of its work force required to produce the food.[65]

In addition to the population explosion "crisis," there are many other examples of socialist fears, scares, and "crises." Some fears surround potential health hazards. You might recall the fear that electromagnetic radiation from power lines and appliances could cause cancer. Some parents were concerned for their children's safety when schools were located near power lines. Others worried about even using an electric blanket at night.[66] Another fear was that cells phone could cause cancer.[67]

Today, there are still more fears about your health. Some socialists claim you and your family eat too well, or you are too fat (as if that is their business), or you eat trans-fats. Have you wondered if the trans-fat scare is really valid? Have you wondered how long the trans-fat scare will last? Will it last as long as the cranberry scare[68] or the alar apple scare?[69]

The list of socialist fears, scares, and so-called "crises" goes on and on. But, from all these fears and "crises," a pattern emerges. Some socialists use fear to control you and your family, and ultimately, to control the American Economy. It's all about power and control, not your health and safety. It's all part of America's Economic War. Fear is just another socialist weapon in this war.

Let's look at one more socialist weapon in America's Economic War.

Global Socialism and the United Nations

The threat of socialism winning America's Economic War is real. The threat of global socialism controlling the world's economy is also real. Global socialism is one more weapon aimed at American Capitalism. What is global socialism? Why is it a threat to American Capitalism and America's sovereignty? Plus, what is the deception behind the threat?

To begin with, global socialism is nothing more than socialism on a global scale. It has all the same elements. It is based on atheistic materialism. It is immoral. It is elitist. It strives for power and control over people's lives. It disdains freedom and liberty. Global socialists want to control the world economy and the world, just as socialists in America want to control the American Economy and America. But, global socialism poses a special danger to America.

Global socialism is a two-pronged threat to both American Capitalism and America's sovereignty. First, global socialists seek to impose socialism on the entire world community of nations including America (circumventing the will of the American people and by-passing our Constitution). This is an affront to America's sovereignty as a free and independent nation. Second, global socialism is a weapon of American socialists who can't pass certain legislation in Congress and attempt to use the United Nations and other Non-Governmental Organizations (NGOs) to accomplish in a world forum what can't be accomplished politically at home. To understand the nature of these two threats to America, let's start by looking at the United Nations.[70]

Global Socialism and the U.N.'s Lack of a Superior Moral Legitimacy

The United Nations was created on October 24, 1945 as the result of the efforts of about 50 nations that came together[71] to create an international organization devoted to peace, human rights, justice, and social progress.[72] Today, the U.N. consists of about 192 member nations.[73] Given the U.N.'s positive charter and goals, as well as the fact that it contains nearly 200 member nations, many global socialists claim the U.N. has an international moral legitimacy and standing that give it the right to make pronouncements on the entire world. Some have even gone as far as saying that the U.N. Secretary General is the rough, secular equivalent of the Pope.[74] This is particularly note-worthy since some people see socialism as a quasi-religion with nature or the material world as their false god.

To some global socialists, it is proper for the U.N. or NGOs to make decisions on:

- whether warfare is legitimate or not,[75]
- what action a national government must take against the so-called global warming "crisis,"
- whether deep seabed mining rights can be given to national liberation movements (the LOST or Law of the Sea Treaty),[76]
- whether gun control is necessary or not,
- whether the death penalty is appropriate or not, and
- family rights issues.[77]

To some global socialists, the self-defense of one nation against attack by another nation might not be allowed.[78] They see national sovereignty as being secondary to the U.N.'s unique, international sovereignty. They see the U.N. as a world government with a member nation's constitution as irrelevant to the U.N.'s greater moral authority and legitimacy.

Some global socialists even believe that not following U.N. dictates might constitute a criminal act. For example, if America did not choose to limit its carbon dioxide emissions to certain levels (to alleviate the so-called global warming "crisis"), America and its leaders might be subject to international criminal proceedings and penalties.

Some global socialists even want to impose international taxes to support the programs of the U.N. France has already begun a tax on international airline tickets purchased within France. The money is apparently earmarked for the United Nations.[79] If the U.N. were to impose international taxes on the world, where does its moral authority come from? Remember the Boston Tea Party and "Taxation without Representation?"

However, beyond the words in its feel-good charter, the United Nations has no claim to a superior moral authority or special legitimacy. In fact, a case can be made that it specifically does not have moral legitimacy in the areas that global socialists claim or imply. To illustrate, according to the 2009 Index of Economic Freedom, there are only seven "free" nations of the 179 nations ranked. There are also an additional 22 "mostly free" nations. One of the seven "free" nations is Hong Kong and one of the "mostly free" nations is Macau.[80] Neither Hong Kong nor Macau is a member of the United Nations.[81] So, if we assume there are about 27 free or mostly free member states in the United Nations, then we can conclude that only roughly 14% of the nations in the U.N. are free.

How can the remaining 86% of the nations in the U.N. (or their global socialist advocates) claim moral legitimacy in the matters of governance when these 165 or so nations are ruled by an elite (be they kings, emperors, dictators, ruling parties, fascists, communists, or other socialists) who limit, deny or destroy freedom. Were it not for the often-times violent power they hold over their people, they likely would not be in positions of political and economic power. The U.N. has little or no moral standing outside its very narrow scope.

For global socialists and other socialists to give the U.N. special moral legitimacy and to cite the U.N. as a superior moral authority is another deception of socialism.

Global Socialism, Norming, and Back-Door Socialism
American socialists also rely on the United Nations and Non-Governmental Organizations to promote socialism indirectly. Often, socialist programs are so obnoxious to the American people that there is no way Congress will approve the legislation necessary to enact the programs into law. In some cases, socialists will enlist their allies in the U.N. and NGOs to try to force these programs onto the American people. This back-door approach is called "norming."[82] How does it work?

Norming works by strong persuasion or even subtle intimidation. With norming, the U.N. adopts, or an NGO gets several nations to adopt, the socialist program in question. Then, socialists go back to key American leaders and the public trying to convince them it's the "normal" thing to do. It's the right thing because other nations have taken the lead. America must follow the lead, or be out of step, or be isolated from the world community.

The deception here is that getting the U.N. or several nations to agree to a socialist program by no means makes it "normal" or even, remotely desirable for America. It is also deceptive to use extra-Constitutional means to obtain a new program or major policy change.

America was founded on a Constitution. The Founding Fathers did not choose to emulate the British monarchy or any other system based on a ruling elite. America was not based on atheistic materialism or socialism. America was not based on allowing any non-representative authority to diminish our freedom or rule over our citizens. Why should America today give up its Constitution and forego its leadership to the U.N. or some Non-Governmental Organization likely run by a ruling elite, or even at best, run by a moderately benign and grossly ineffective, international bureaucracy?

To sum up, socialism uses deceit, deception and fear as weapons in America's Economic War. It distorts the meaning of important words and it camouflages its plans to control you and your family's lives and lifestyles. It also uses fear to prevent people from clear thinking and reasoning. Socialists have created many so-called "crises" and "scares" to frighten you into giving up your freedom. Global socialism also threatens America with its attempts to create socialism on a global scale and to back-door socialism into America through non-Constitutional means. Global socialism is a concrete danger to America's sovereignty.

America's Economic War is truly a danger to you and your family. But, America can still win the war. It is no longer conservatives vs. liberals. It's American Capitalists vs. socialists.

With an understanding of some of the dangers to you and your family, as well as an understanding of some of socialism's weapons, it is time to gain a better appreciation for American Capitalism and a deeper insight into the dysfunctional system known as socialism.

Part II

The Combatants

Chapter 3

American Capitalism is God-Inspired Freedom and Individualism

"For you, brethren, have been called to liberty; …
through love serve one another."
Galatians 5:13

Whether you are a believer in God or not, whether you are a Christian or not, American Capitalism is God-inspired freedom and individualism. While atheists and agnostics might not believe in or understand the spiritual and moral foundations of American Capitalism, they nevertheless exist. While those outside the Judeo-Christian faith tradition might not comprehend the linkage between belief in God and liberty, it nevertheless exists.

Indeed, it is possible to accept, live, and enjoy American Capitalism without ever realizing or knowing its spiritual and moral foundations, because Christian principles have been woven into the very fabric of American Capitalism. Christianity and its Jewish heritage are in the DNA of American Capitalism.

It is also possible to defend and promote American Capitalism from a purely economic point of view as many economists and some think tanks have done. After all, American Capitalism is undeniably the most powerful economic engine ever seen in the world.

But, to do justice to American Capitalism, and to defeat socialism in America's Economic War, it is necessary to bring all the forces and resources of American Capitalism to triumph over its enemy. To defeat the evil of socialism requires a spiritual as well as a political and economic battle.

Socialism claims the moral high ground. It wants to help all those "victims" they have created. It claims capitalism is all about money and greed. Nothing can be further from the truth.

American Capitalism is about faith and morality. Socialism is about atheism and immorality. American Capitalism is about freedom and peace. Socialism is about control and violence. American Capitalism is about free markets and prosperity. Socialism is about economic inefficiency and poverty. American Capitalism is about family and trust. Socialism is about groups of "victims" and distrust. American Capitalism is about spiritual and material human growth. Socialism is about moral decay and social disintegration.

American Capitalism is moral. Socialism is immoral.

Let's see why.

The Christian Foundations of American Capitalism

The foundations of American Capitalism are embedded in the Judeo-Christian principles found in the Bible, found in the natural law (that is written on the hearts of people), and found in the moral thinking of the Christian Church's theologians and philosophers developed over many centuries. While non-Christian philosophers have added to the body of moral thinking, clearly Judeo-Christian principles form the strong spiritual rock upon which American Capitalism was built.

Included in that thinking and reasoning was the concept that government is distinct from religion, and the two should peacefully co-exist without invading one another's legitimate territory. In the words of Jesus in Matthew 22:21, "Render therefore to Caesar the things that are Caesar's, and to God the things that are God's."

That's why American Capitalism has come to accept people of all religions and people of no religion. Yet, for those who espouse no religion, it is wrong to deny those who do believe in God their right to fully express their religious beliefs. It is also wrong to disassociate American Capitalism and the American Government entirely from God. To do so, is comparable to disavowing your grandparents from your family line. It is wrong. It is dysfunctional. It has broad and deep negative effects on one's psyche and one's life.

It is also quite foolish (in a pragmatic sense) to attempt to cut off the American Government from any mention of God or images of our Judeo-Christian heritage. Why? Because those symbols of our Judeo-Christian heritage, the Ten Commandments and the Christian Cross, as well as those words "In God We Trust" and "One Nation Under God" in the Pledge of

Allegiance, unite America in our common heritage. They are a "cultural glue" that reminds us of the Christian principles that brought us together over 200 years ago and still animate and give purpose to our nation today.

If socialism can effectively destroy the knowledge of our Judeo-Christian heritage, if socialism can sufficiently distance our government from its founding Christian principles, and if socialism can keep our young from learning about our cultural origins, America will cease to exist. America will fall into moral and economic bankruptcy, the eventual fate of any nation that adopts socialism as its guiding philosophy.

Fortunately, American Capitalism can win America's Economic War against socialism. Now, let's answer a key question.

How did Judeo-Christian principles give rise to American Capitalism? It's a truly remarkable story. It all starts with faith in God. Rodney Stark beautifully captures the essence of this journey from faith in God, to faith in reason, and then, to faith in progress:

While the other world religions emphasized mystery and intuition, Christianity alone embraced reason and logic as the primary guide to religious truth ... from early days, the church fathers taught that reason was the supreme gift from God and the means to progressively increase their understanding of scripture and revelation. Consequently, Christianity was oriented to the future, while the other major religions asserted the superiority of the past.[83]

The accompanying figures traverse the path from faith in God to some of the innovations that led to American Capitalism.[84]

To begin this faith journey, early Christians had faith in God. They believed in a God who created the universe, who created man and woman, and who set up natural laws. Early Christians believed in a Supreme Being who was both personal and rational. They believed God would reveal Himself as man and woman became able to comprehend His revelation. This was in sharp contrast to eastern religions such as Buddhism and Taoism that understood only a supernatural essence, a non-personal power. Early Christians also believed that because God was rational, he could be studied by using reason and logic. From this faith in God, came rational theology, the study of God, as well as faith in reason itself, as a means to better understand God.[85]

Christian Faith-Based Progress and Innovation

Faith in God

Faith in Reason

Faith in Progress

Optimism

Creativity

Innovations

Christian Faith-Based Innovations that Led to American Capitalism

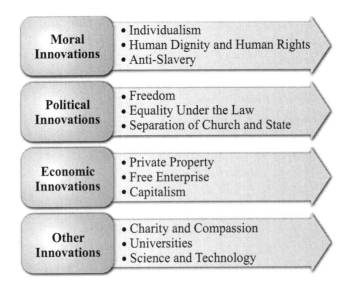

Moral Innovations
- Individualism
- Human Dignity and Human Rights
- Anti-Slavery

Political Innovations
- Freedom
- Equality Under the Law
- Separation of Church and State

Economic Innovations
- Private Property
- Free Enterprise
- Capitalism

Other Innovations
- Charity and Compassion
- Universities
- Science and Technology

In addition, underlying this faith in reason was a profound sense of the potential for human progress and the likely movement of mankind toward a deeper knowledge of life. Thus, the early Christian's faith in reason empowered a faith in progress. This faith in progress, in turn, created an unlimited sense of optimism for the future, an optimism that led to creativity and directly resulted in a myriad of moral, political, and economic innovations.[86] Indeed, optimism empowered creative reasoning that led to the application of human creativity to real world challenges, and ultimately, to stellar human innovations.

The early Christian faith in God and faith in reason spurred a deep confidence that people can improve life through thoughtful reasoning. The Christian Church inspired (and still inspires) people. The Christian Church was then (and still is) the true ally of liberty and freedom and optimism for the future. The Christian Church believed (and still believes) that people are made in the image of a Supreme Rational God and their fundamental nature is to reason. As Genesis 1:27 states: "So God created man in His own image." Indeed, the Christian Church has always been the opponent of fatalism,[87] hopelessness, and powerlessness. Socialism's creation, support, and promotion of victimhood stand in sharp contrast to the beliefs of the Christian Church.

The Christian Church believes people are freely called to use their reason to improve this world and are saved (from their own individual sins) by Jesus Christ. The quasi-religion of atheistic socialism believes people are helpless victims of this world and will be saved (from the sins of oppressive groups) by government.

Faith in God, faith in reason, and faith in progress led to an optimism of spirit. In the words of Jesus in Luke 17:21, "For indeed, the kingdom of God is within you." In Luke 21:31, Jesus said: "… know that the kingdom of God is near." These were positive, encouraging, faith-boosting words. This Christian optimism of spirit unleashed an intellectual freedom to pursue "right thinking," moral reasoning that sought good as an end. Some of the results of this right thinking were truly remarkable, culminating in innovative thoughts, brilliant new concepts, and eventually phenomenal human progress.

Individualism

In the area of spiritual and moral thinking, the early Christians created the concept of individualism. Unlike the Greek philosopher Plato and others that saw man as merely belonging to a group or city, Christians recognized that each person was an individual. Each person had free will and could commit sin. Each person is rewarded for good behavior and is punished for bad behavior. Individual human action has consequences. Individual responsibility for that action exists and is real. To Christians, salvation was (and is) an individual (not a group) matter.

Along with the view that man was created in the image of God, this individualism led quickly to the realization that people individually have a God-given human dignity with corresponding God-given human rights. This is the reason the Christian Church has a long history of opposing slavery, an evil practice eventually eliminated in many parts of the world largely because of Christian efforts.

The Christian Church's concept of individualism is a very important moral innovation in the road to American Capitalism.

Equality under the Law

From individualism sprang forth the Christian concept of the moral equality of all people under God and the legal equality of all people under the laws of a nation. Equality under the law forms a cornerstone of true justice in a nation and is another key innovation that led to American Capitalism. In Deuteronomy 10:17, we can see that God "shows no partiality" by these words:

For the Lord your God is God of gods and Lord of lords, the great God, mighty and awesome, who shows no partiality nor takes a bribe.

In the words of Jesus in Galatians 3:28, "There is neither Jew nor Greek, there is neither slave nor free, there is neither male nor female; for you are all one in Christ Jesus."

Indeed, the influence of the Christian Church's concept of equality under the law is visible today on the United States Supreme Court building in Washington, DC. Across the top of that building are inscribed the words: "Equal Justice Under Law."[88]

Closely related to equality under the law is the idea that "No Man is Above the Law." This dates back to the year 390 A.D. when the Roman emperor, Theodosius the Great, massacred seven thousand mostly innocent people. Bishop Ambrose, a proponent of liberty, challenged the emperor to repent for the massacre showing that no man, even an emperor, can be above the law. Eventually, Theodosius did repent in Ambrose's cathedral.[89]

Today, when people speak of the Rule of Law, they are really invoking the Christian Church's concept of equality under the law and the fact that no man is above the law.

Freedom

The Christian Church was also a pioneer in the development of freedom, an incredibly important foundation of American Capitalism. While freedom did exist at times in pre-Christian years, its existence was limited to just a few places, under a few circumstances, for finite periods of time. Freedom, while discussed by some ancient philosophers, was typically not permitted, or at best, it thrived for awhile and then was snuffed out by powerful dictators.

The most notable instance of freedom was the early Hebrew republic mentioned in the Old Testament. John W. Robbins describes it succinctly.

As for the form of government, God established a republic in Israel. The nation was divided into twelve tribes, much as the United States is divided into fifty states. Each tribe had its own territory and border; each had its own local government; and the nation as a whole had a national government. There was no king; there was no powerful central government. The government consisted mostly of judges; there was no legislature to create new laws each year, only judges to settle disputes in accord with the laws that God had already given ... Taxes were extremely low. Money, gold and silver, was provided by private merchants, not the government.[90]

This Hebrew republic was noted for its freedom. People were free to do as they pleased within the framework of God's laws including the Ten Commandments. It ended when the people requested a human king from God as recorded in the Book of 1 Samuel in the Bible. It is worth noting that God considered the request for a king to be a rejection of Him. Yet, God did grant the people's request and gave Israel a king, after Samuel first warned the people of the problems they would encounter with a human king.

The theme of freedom also appears in the New Testament and it led the Christian Church to its innovative thinking in the arena of liberty. From Scripture verses such as Galatians 5:13: "For you, brethren, have been called to liberty; ... through love serve one another" and 2 Corinthians 3:17: "Now the Lord is the Spirit; and where the Spirit of the Lord is, there is liberty," the Christian Church developed the concept of human liberty as a fundamental component of human dignity. At the same time, the Christian Church also saw tyranny as intrinsically evil.[91]

It is true that the Christian Church's concepts of individualism, equality under the law, and freedom are very important moral and political innovations in the development of American Capitalism. But, the Christian Church's impact and influence didn't stop there. The moral thinking and reasoning of the early Christian Church also led to innovations in economic thinking.

Private Property

Another major innovation of the early Christian Church was private property. Its role in laying the groundwork for American Capitalism was profound.

From the Ten Commandments came the admonishments: "You shall not steal" and "You shall not covet your neighbor's house" in Exodus 21:15 and Exodus 21:17 respectively. These commandments provided the moral foundations of private property. After all, if private property should not exist in the world, why would God create two commandments to protect it? Note that the quasi-religion of atheistic socialism preaches that private property should be abolished, running squarely against the long-standing moral position of the Christian Church on private property.

St. Thomas Aquinas, the great thinker of the Christian Church, stood solidly behind the concept of private property. He thought that "private ownership is both legitimate and necessary."[92] Aquinas believed that private property was good:

Firstly, because everyone takes more care of things for which he is privately responsible than of things held in common, the responsibility for which is left to the next man. Secondly, because human affairs are more efficiently organized when each person has his own distinct responsibility to discharge. Thirdly, because there is a greater chance of keeping the peace when everyone is content with his own matters.[93]

Pope Leo XXIII added to the support for private property (and the rejection of socialism's drive to eliminate private property) in these powerful words:

Hence it is clear that the main tenet of Socialism, community of goods, must be utterly rejected, since it only injures those whom it would seem meant to benefit, is directly contrary to the natural rights of mankind, and would introduce confusion and disorder into the commonweal. The first and most fundamental principle, therefore, if one would undertake to alleviate the condition of the masses, must be the inviolability of private property.[94]

Clearly, the Christian Church's concept of private property was an innovation in thinking. Monarchs and dictators of old knew nothing of private property rights when they taxed their people and looted their enemies. As we will see later, the Christian Church's concept of private property forms the basis of both a free market economy and American Capitalism.

Free Enterprise and Capitalism
Private property inevitably led to two other economic innovations of the Christian Church, the development of free enterprise and capitalism. Eventually, these innovations would blossom into American Capitalism.

Contrary to the popular belief of many people, free enterprise and capitalism did not begin with the Protestant Reformation and the thrift and frugality associated with it. While Max Weber's book, *The Protestant Ethic and the Spirit of Capitalism,* did a lot to popularize the myth that capitalism started at the time of the Protestant Reformation, the facts prove otherwise. Instead, free enterprise and capitalism really began around the ninth century in the monasteries of the Christian Church. There monks chose to support themselves by doing such things as farming; raising cattle, sheep, and horses; and producing wines. So, successful were the monasteries at selling their commodities, that they earned profits and could use those profits to purchase other necessities.[95]

In fact, as profits increased, the monks even learned to re-invest their profits in their own enterprises, thereby financing additional business growth.[96] The financial concept, to be known by accountants centuries later as retained earnings, now had been born on these Christian Church estates.

With investments and profits, the monks even became bankers to their customers, loaning them money and charging interest. It is worth noting that the Christian Church's early condemnation of usury (charging interest on loans) gave way to revised reasoning and thinking about the morality of interest.[97] Recall that the Christian Church's faith in God, led to faith in reason, and then, faith in progress as a path to a better understanding of God and the world. In this case, the Christian Church reasoned that charging interest was a moral practice. Thus, Christian faith empowered reason and reason generated enormous understanding and progress for people.

The Christian Church also initiated many other innovations such as using cash rather than barter and the use of professional administrators to oversee their smooth-running enterprises.[98]

With regard to the Christian Church's faith in reason, Rodney Stark wisely points out that: "capitalism is in essence the systematic and sustained application of reason to commerce."[99]

Besides these economic innovations, the Christian Church created many other innovations that positively impacted the world and set the stage for American Capitalism. These innovations spanned many fields including charitable giving, university education, as well as in science and technology. Let's review some of these other stellar innovations.

Charitable Giving and Compassion

Christianity forever changed the world with its emphasis on charity and compassion for the individual. In pre-Christian times, the Greeks and Romans typically gave charity only when they could reasonably expect a favor in return. In sharp contrast, Christians gave to help those in economic or physical need.[100]

Another key difference between Roman charity and Christian charity was that Christian charitable giving was up to the individual. It was not coerced. It was voluntary and done out of a sense of love. Roman charity was done on a whim or to seek a future gift or favor. Romans considered charity to be foolish and often a sign or weakness. To the average Roman citizen, it made little or no sense to be compassionate, especially to the weak and the poor.[101] Alvin J. Schmidt quotes the Roman philosopher Plautus on charitable giving in this way: "You do a beggar bad service by giving him food and drink; you lose what you give and prolong his life for more misery."[102]

But, then, where did Christian charity and compassion originate? It was certainly a stunning innovation to the world. The themes of loving your neighbor as yourself, feeding the hungry, and being a Good Samaritan to someone in need, all come from the Bible. Consider the powerful words of Jesus in Matthew 25:34-36:

Then the King will say to those on His right hand, 'Come, you blessed of My Father, inherit the kingdom prepared for you from the foundation of the world: for I was hungry and you gave Me food; I was thirsty and you gave Me drink; I was a stranger and you took Me in; I was naked and you clothed Me; I was sick and you visited Me; I was in prison and you came to Me.'

Jesus goes on to say in Matthew 25:40,

And the King will answer and say to them, 'Assuredly, I say to you, inasmuch as you did it to one of the least of these My brethren, you did it to Me.'

The Christian Church took these words and many other passages in the Bible to heart, and Christian charitable giving and compassion branched out in many directions. For example, Christian compassion not only was directed to the hungry and poor, but it also reached out to help widows, orphans, the sick and the old. Christians helped those in need with orphanages, institutions for the aged, institutions for the blind, hospitals for the sick, and places for the mentally ill.[103]

Today, we can see the same Christian compassion and charity in America. America is the most generous nation the world has ever known, rushing supplies and food to unknown victims around the world when disaster strikes without regard to ideology or religion. To illustrate, consider The President's Emergency Plan for AIDS Relief (PEPFAR). After three years of implementation, PEPFAR supported treatment for over one million Africans.[104]

Indeed, Christian compassion is built into the DNA of American Capitalism.

Universities

Still another innovation of the Christian Church that led to American Capitalism is the university. It might surprise some that universities are the invention of the Christian Church. But, it is true.

While Greek and Roman philosophers are sometimes credited with the first universities, the facts indicate otherwise. The Greeks and Romans only taught in small groups. They did not create on-going institutions. They did not create libraries. They did not engage in research. They did not systematically seek out new knowledge (preferring instead to focus on the past).[105]

In sharp contrast, the Christian Church created the first universities in the twelfth and thirteenth centuries. These were institutions devoted to the use of reason in the pursuit of truth, knowledge, and innovation. They were sometimes fairly large with enrollments that could exceed a thousand students. They amassed large stores of books into libraries of knowledge and they were not content to study just the ideas of past philosophers. Of interest too, nearly all faculty members held holy orders (meaning that they had official standing in the Christian Church).[106]

In America, the Christian Church is responsible for founding nine of our first ten universities. Harvard, Yale, Princeton, and Columbia were all founded by various denominations of the Christian Church.[107] In fact, prior to the American Civil War, 92% of America's 182 colleges and universities had been founded by denominations of the Christian Church.[108]

Thanks in large part to the Christian Church, America's colleges and universities were established and blossomed into institutions of knowledge, creativity, and innovation. Our system of higher education became known as the best in the world and it helped fuel our incredible economic growth. University education is pivotal in American Capitalism.

It is profoundly ironic that under the negative influence of atheistic socialism, many professors at many colleges and universities have substituted:

- atheism for Christianity,
- propaganda for truth,
- bias for reason,
- controlled speech for free speech,
- political indoctrination for education,
- ideology for research, and
- the pursuit of power for the pursuit of knowledge.

It is also tragically ironic that some of these same professors, at these same institutions of higher education (many founded by the Christian Church), limit the free exercise of religion and religious free speech on their campuses. What would the founders of these colleges and universities think today? Why do their trustees permit it?

Certainly, the Christian Church's invention of the university is an innovation that led to and helped fuel American Capitalism. The Christian Church's reasoning and thinking also spurred innovation in science and technology that had a similar positive impact on American Capitalism.

Science and Technology

The Christian Church's faith in reason and faith in progress created the intellectual climate for both science and technology to thrive. Let's see how.

While popular culture today often tries to portray a fundamental rift and animosity between science and religion, such a schism does not really exist. Indeed, Christianity and science both seek the truth, both seek knowledge, and both have faith in reason, as the means to achieve these ends.

The imaginary battle between faith and reason is strictly a myth! Those opponents of faith (who think they rely on reason alone) need to consider an important fact. Faith in a rational God empowers faith in reason itself.

Thomas L. Woods, Jr., quotes the Christian critic Friedrich Nietzsche as saying:

Strictly speaking ... there is no such thing as science 'without any presuppositions' ... a philosophy, a 'faith,' must always be there first, so that science can acquire from it a direction, a meaning, a limit, a method, a right to exist ... It is still a metaphysical faith that underlies our faith in science.[109]

Put simply. To have faith in natural science requires faith in reason. To have faith in reason requires faith in something metaphysical, that is, something *meta* or *above* the physical or natural world, something *super*-natural. To have faith in reason requires faith in God.

That's why the Christian Church is responsible for the rise of science and scientific innovation. Without faith in reason, science could never have been invented. Contrary to popular belief, faith and reason are not enemies. They are allies in science and in the pursuit of the truth.

From the Christian Church's faith in reason and from the universities it founded, science grew up, new scientists were educated, and innovative scientists pursued new knowledge and a better understanding of God's creation. Many of the great thinkers, philosophers, and scientists were Christians. Often, these thinkers were also both scientists and theologians.

A long list of Christian scientists and their inventions can be developed from reading history books.[110]

Besides creating an environment of reason and intellectual freedom, the Christian Church also empowered the rise of technological innovation. Why? Certainly, faith in reason was one part of it. But, in addition, private property played a big role in it as well. The reason why private property was a critical factor in technological innovation is that the inventor directly benefited (in a financial or economic sense) from the invention (much as an inventor holding a patent enjoys the financial rewards from his or her patent today).

It is worth taking a moment to distinguish between science and technology and their respective types of innovation to avoid any confusion in terminology. The purpose of science is to seek new knowledge about the physical world, while the purpose of technology is to solve existing problems in the physical world using existing knowledge.

Science relies on two activities to develop new knowledge: theories and experimentation. To be valid, a new theory (that attempts to explain the world better) must hold up under scientifically-controlled experiments. Some theories are rejected when experiments disprove them. Some older theories fall when a new and better theory is confirmed by scientific experimentation.

Technology uses existing scientific knowledge and typically relies on physical measurements to create new and better solutions to physical problems.

To illustrate, some socialists hold the theory that carbon dioxide emissions are the cause of the so-called global warming "crisis." But, since scientists have found that as carbon dioxide emissions increase, sometimes global temperatures increase and sometimes they decrease, many scientists believe carbon dioxide emissions are not the cause of global warming. Recall that Chapter 1 covers the so-called global warming "crisis" in more detail including reference to relevant scientific information.

In American Capitalism, both scientific and technological innovations abound. The Christian Church's faith in God and faith in reason led to faith in progress and optimism. All of these factors empowered a climate of intellectual freedom and creativity that spurred on numerous innovations in science and technology.

Thus, we can see the enormous impact the Christian Church has had on the development of American Capitalism. This impact ranges from the moral innovations of Individualism, Human Dignity and Human Rights, and Anti-Slavery, to the political innovations of Freedom, Equality under the Law, and the Separation of Church and State. It ranges from the economic innovations of Private Property, Free Enterprise, and Capitalism, to the additional innovations of Charity and Compassion, Universities, as well as Science and Technology. It is truly fair to say that the foundations of American Capitalism are embedded in the faith, thinking and teaching of the Christian Church.

Let's look next at the Architecture of American Capitalism.

The Architecture of American Capitalism

What is American Capitalism? What is its architecture? What are the building blocks of the greatest engine of human economic growth and prosperity ever known in the history of the world? What holds this system together? Why do economic experiments by other governments often fail? The answers to all these questions are summarized in the Architecture of American Capitalism.

American Capitalism is God-inspired freedom and individualism. It is a moral, political, and economic system that is based on freedom and individualism, operating within a minimal set of laws designed to maximize and protect that freedom and individualism. (Of course, with the increasingly negative effects of atheistic socialism, it is straying from its optimal design principles. In America's Economic War, this Architecture of American Capitalism is definitely threatened.)

American Capitalism stands on a foundation of key laws, key freedoms, key requirements, and key institutions. Taken together they create a distinct American Culture, a unique American Government, and the very powerful American Economy. This is our infrastructure. This is our American Civilization. Without one or more of the key building blocks in the accompanying table, American Capitalism will collapse. Let's look at the Architecture of American Capitalism in some detail.

The Architecture of American Capitalism			
Key Infrastructure	**American Culture**	**American Government**	**American Economy**
Key Institutions	Christian Church Family	Constitution Freedom	Free Market Free Enterprise
Key Requirements	Morality	Free Speech	Private Property
Key Freedoms	Religious Freedom	Political Freedom	Economic Freedom
Key Laws	Divine Law Natural Law	Rule of Law	Contract Law

Key Laws

At the foundation of American Capitalism are four key laws. These are the laws that empower our key freedoms and individualism. Divine Law is a set of primary moral principles revealed to us in the Bible. These are the Ten Commandments and the other Biblical principles that are woven into our culture. Many of these also appear in natural law, the laws written on our hearts. For example, most everyone believes in their hearts that murder and theft are wrong and should be against the law.

It is very interesting (and actually quite profound) to note that if you study natural law closely, you will see that you must either accept natural law in its entirely, or reject it totally and outright. There is no moral middle ground. Attempting to accept only a portion of natural law always results in moral and/or logical contradictions.[111]

Divine Law and natural law form the basis for morality. Morality, in turn, forms the basis for all human relationships and for civil society. If everyone felt free to kill their neighbors or steal their property as they pleased, chaos would ensue and civil order would collapse.

The Rule of Law is the third law at the foundation of American Capitalism. The Rule of Law simply means that all citizens must follow whatever civil laws are put in place to protect and promote freedom and individualism. No man or woman is above the law.

Many civil laws are directly taken from Divine Law and natural law. Civil laws against murder and theft, for example, are taken from the Ten

Commandments. But, in addition, many other civil laws expand on Divine Law and natural law. To illustrate, securities laws protect people from fraudulent activities in the purchase and sale of stocks and bonds. These laws are an off-shoot of the commandment against theft. Certainly, back in the days of the early Christian Church, you were not able to purchase 100 shares of common stock on NASDAQ or the NYSE.

Good civil laws promote and protect freedom and individualism. They empower people to grow individually and as a cooperative society. They do not limit freedom of human action. They do protect people from violence against themselves and their private property. They do protect people from crime and corruption. They do protect people from the arbitrary use of inappropriate police power by the government itself. Good civil government also protects people from the external threats of war, terrorism, and other attacks.

The fourth and final law that provides the foundation of American Capitalism is contract law. It is incumbent on government to enforce voluntary contracts among two or more parties. Otherwise, a reasonable level of trust is not possible, and the Free Market will not function smoothly. Business and commerce require agreements to be made in order to run efficiently. It is the role of government to enforce those agreements and to keep the Free Market operating effectively.

Key Freedoms

Closely related to the four key laws that form the foundation of American Capitalism are three key freedoms: religious freedom, political freedom, and economic freedom. For an individual to be truly free, he or she must be free to think, free to decide, and free to take action in those areas of life most important to people.

For American Capitalism to work, individuals must be free in a religious sense to choose the religion of their own choice (even if that religion is no religion at all, or the quasi-religion of atheistic socialism).

For American Capitalism to work, individuals must also be free politically. They must have freedom of speech, freedom of press, freedom of association, and freedom of thought (intellectual freedom). They must be free to question. They must be free to debate, discuss, and to disagree. They must even be free to be disagreeable, insulting, obnoxious, and/or downright nasty. They must also be free to choose their leaders in fair elections that are monitored to protect against fraud.

For American Capitalism to work, people must be free to buy, own, use, sell, or donate private property. People must also be free to do the work they choose, to engage in the free enterprise of their choice (if they so desire), and to operate freely within a free market. People should also be free to trade with individuals and companies outside America as well. In all of these endeavors, people should be free from excessive taxation and excessive regulation, as well as free from government-sanctioned or government-dictated centralized planning, control, coercion, compulsion and violence.

The role of government in American Capitalism is to protect and promote freedom and individualism. It is not to tax and regulate and control every action of every American. It is not to take away you and your family's freedom. It is not to control you and your family. It is not to control you and your family's lifestyles.

Within the four key laws, people are free to exercise their religious freedom, political freedom, and economic freedom in American Capitalism. Out of these key building blocks of the Architecture of American Capitalism come three key requirements.

Key Requirements
American Capitalism needs three other building blocks to function. Built on top of the four key laws and three key freedoms, these building blocks are morality, free speech, and private property.

Regardless of what religion each citizen adopts (or even if some citizens adopt no religion at all), American Capitalism requires morality to exist. This is an important limitation for socialists.

Since socialism is based on atheistic materialism and does not have God to rely on in its thinking, it does not believe in a moral or spiritual order. Therefore, socialism can't create an environment and climate of morality that is necessary to sustain American Capitalism. In fact, socialism in the long-run can't even sustain itself. Socialism is the black hole of philosophy, politics, and economics. It is self-destructive and suicidal. Socialism always leads to moral and economic bankruptcy.

American Capitalism also requires free speech. This is the most powerful and most important element of political freedom because it implies communication to the person next to you. The other political freedoms such as free press are all derived from free speech. Even free elections are a form of free speech. We freely inform everyone who we choose for elected office (albeit in a secret ballot).

The third and final key requirement of American Capitalism is private property. There are a host of theologians, philosophers, economists, and political leaders that over the centuries have trumpeted the close association between private property and freedom. Indeed, you can't have either economic freedom or political freedom without private property. In the words of the twentieth century philosopher and economist F. A. Hayek,

... the system of private property is the most important guaranty of freedom, not only for those who own property, but scarcely less for those who do not. It is only because the control of the means of production is divided among many people acting independently that nobody has complete power over us, that we as individuals can decide what to do for ourselves. If all the means of production were vested in a single hand, whether it be nominally that of "society" as a whole or that of a dictator, whoever exercises this control has complete power over us.[112]

When economists such as Hayek refer to the means of production above, they mean private property (i.e., the resources that people use to create goods and services and ultimately, new wealth). In addition, it is worth noting that excessive (or confiscatory) taxation is one way government can take away your private property. Also, excessive regulations are a means to limit your right to use your own private property as you see fit.

In America's Economic War, socialists are attempting to eliminate all three of these key requirements of American Capitalism. Socialists oppose morality, free speech, and private property. It is all part of socialism's larger attacks on the key institutions of American Capitalism.

Key Institutions

To organize our key laws, key freedoms, and key requirements into a strong and sustainable architecture, American Capitalism needs key institutions as well. Some of these institutions were created before American Capitalism; some of these institutions were refined by American Capitalism; and some of these institutions were created by American Capitalism. What are the key institutions in the Architecture of American Capitalism?

They are the Christian Church, the Family, the Constitution, Freedom, the Free Market, and Free Enterprise. Obviously, the Christian Church and the Family pre-date American Capitalism. The U.S. Constitution was created by the Founding Fathers of our nation at the beginning of American Capitalism. Finally, Freedom, the Free Market, and Free Enterprise all existed prior to American Capitalism, but were heavily influenced by and evolved under American Capitalism.

These institutions are essential to the health and well-being of American Capitalism. Each has been under heavy attack by socialists seeking to destroy American Capitalism. This is the essence of America's Economic War.

Key Infrastructure

The key laws, key freedoms, key requirements, and key institutions of American Capitalism are organized according to the Architecture of American Capitalism. Together, they create the key infrastructure of American Capitalism: American Culture, the American Government, and the American Economy. Together, they represent the best moral, political, and economic system the world has ever known. Together, they have out-produced and out-innovated every nation on the earth. Together, they have dispensed more charity and compassion around the world and at home than any other society in history.

American Capitalism is truly the greatest economic system ever developed. Unfortunately, it is under attack and is at risk of falling to socialism, a morally and economically bankrupt philosophy that has proven to be a dismal failure and the cause of about 50 million political murders during the twentieth century.[113] One estimate places the total death toll at more than 125 million deaths.[114] Fortunately, American Capitalism can win America's Economic War.

If you would like a simple formula for remembering the Architecture of American Capitalism, consider the accompanying figure. It covers the basics and is easy for all of us to remember, including children. Faith plus Freedom plus Free Markets equals American Capitalism.

A Simple Formula for American Capitalism

Faith **+** Freedom **+** Free Markets **≡** American Capitalism

Let's turn our attention to a description of American Capitalism. It will highlight the goodness of American Capitalism and will stand in very stark contrast to the evil of socialism.

The Characteristics of American Capitalism

Let's now look at what makes American Capitalism so incredibly special. What is the basis of American Exceptionalism? What are its identifying characteristics? The accompanying table sums up these characteristics. Let's start by looking at faith and morality.

The Characteristics of American Capitalism	
Summary	God-Inspired Freedom and Individualism
Spiritual and Moral, Cultural	Faith (and Morality)
Political	Freedom (and Peace)
Economic	Free Markets (and Prosperity)
Sociological	Family (and Trust)
Impact on Civilization	Spiritual and Material Human Growth

Faith (and Morality)

Understanding the Architecture of American Capitalism makes describing it very easy. Describing American Capitalism begins with faith in God. Faith in God empowers the rest of our American Civilization. For atheists and agnostics that don't believe in God, it might seem a bit awkward and uncomfortable. But, our American Civilization rests firmly upon and is based solidly on faith in God.

Interestingly, American Civilization has also been called Western

Civilization and the term Western Civilization was preceded by the term Christendom.[115] The Christian Church's faith in God is at the core of American Capitalism, despite all the arguments to the contrary.

Some say, for example, that American Capitalism is bad because some business people are greedy and corrupt. Some say, American Capitalism isn't moral because some people act immorally within American Capitalism. Some say, American Capitalism must be tightly regulated to avoid dishonest business practices. But, greed, corruption, and immorality will exist in any system. It's all relative.

It is true that under American Capitalism some greed, corruption, and immorality will happen. Yet, American Capitalism is basically a moral system with an embedded morality. Under socialism, greed, bribery, corruption, and immorality are much higher because socialism is a system not based on a spiritual and moral order. Recall the high levels of corruption in the "socialist utopias" of Zimbabwe and Syria cited in Chapter 1. Morality is built into American Capitalism. Immorality is built into socialism.

There is another reason why American Capitalism is moral. Morality implies choice. Morality implies that a person chooses between a good option and a bad option, a good decision or a bad decision. With American Capitalism and the freedom that goes with it, people have choices everyday and in all aspects of their lives. Hence, with freedom, individuals can make moral choices. (Of course, some individuals will use their freedom to make poor choices in a moral sense.)

With socialism, power rests with the government instead. In this case, the government elite make all the key decisions. Since socialism has no inherent moral system, it must rely on whatever it thinks is expedient, whatever makes sense at the moment to further its power and maintain its control over people. Individuals have fewer choices or possibly no choices at all (in some totalitarian forms of socialism).

With socialism, government operates without a moral system and therefore, its decisions are not moral. With socialism, individuals have little or no freedom, and therefore, they can't freely make moral decisions. A coerced choice is no choice at all. A coerced choice is certainly not a free and moral choice. Once again, we see morality is built into American Capitalism, while immorality is built into socialism.

Another moral dimension to American Capitalism is its purpose. American Capitalism is all about giving to others and serving others, while at the same time meeting our own needs. American Capitalism is the Biblical principle (that appears in Matthew 19:19 and earlier in Leviticus 19:18), "You shall love your neighbor as yourself" put into action. Each of us is called to love others in the same way as we love ourselves. Translated into economic terms, we are called to meet each other's needs, as we meet our own needs. American Capitalism is precisely about doing just that.

In George Gilder's perceptive words:

Capitalism begins with giving. Not from greed, avarice, or even self-love can one expect the rewards of commerce, but from a spirit closely akin to altruism, a regard for the needs of others, a benevolent, outgoing, and courageous temper of mind ... Not taking and consuming, but giving, risking, and creating are the characteristic roles of the capitalist, the key producer of the wealth of nations, from the least developed to the most advanced.[116]

American Capitalism focuses individuals' attention on "what they give" and then "getting something in return for their service."

Socialism is quite the opposite. It focuses people's attention on "what they get" and "getting something for nothing." After all, with socialism, resources are usually taken from the productive sector and given to preferred groups (even at the cost of weakening the productive sector and dissipating the productive capacity that creates new goods and services, and that generates new wealth for future growth).

American Capitalism is moral because its purpose is giving and serving. Socialism is immoral because its purpose is getting and taking.

Of course, socialists will jump in right now and say that their purpose is to give resources and help to the groups of victims that they have identified. They will say that they require power (and need to deny you freedom) to serve those victims in need.

But, the response to socialists is simple. American Capitalism with its Christian heritage of charitable giving and compassion will always be generous to those truly in need. American Capitalism, including individual Americans, individual Churches, individual religious charities, and individual private charitable associations, are the most generous people in the world.

Charity and compassion do not require socialism. Charity and compassion do not require government-dictated centralized planning, control, coercion, compulsion and violence. Charity and compassion do not require eliminating religious freedom, political freedom, and economic freedom. Charity and compassion do not require the elimination of the Christian Church, the Family, the Constitution, Free Markets, and Free Enterprise.

Also, American Capitalism attempts to lift people out of need. True charity and compassion empower recipients. Socialism seeks to maintain victims in their state of victimhood and their state of dependence on the government. After all, without victims, socialism loses its charity and compassion argument.

The "charity and compassion argument" is an excuse for socialism to take and exercise increasing amounts of power and control over you and your family's lives and lifestyles.

For all these reasons and more, we can say with certainty that American Capitalism is about faith and morality.

Without faith in God and the morality it engenders, American Capitalism would not exist. American Capitalism is faith and morality in action.

Freedom (and Peace)

American Capitalism is also about freedom and the peace that springs forth from freedom. Certainly, American Capitalism includes religious freedom, political freedom, and economic freedom. These freedoms also imply and include intellectual freedom, a type of freedom not all people choose to use. Philosophers, thinkers, and scientists value it, of course. Others use it as they wish. American Capitalism encompasses intellectual freedom as well.

What might not be so obvious, however, is that freedom is a component of love and is a necessary condition for peace. Freedom is a component of love because it fosters genuine acceptance of people. Freedom is acceptance of other people, their differences, their decisions, their actions, and their lifestyles. Freedom allows people to be themselves.

God, the author of liberty, has given mankind freedom and free will. Men and women can accept or deny God. They can sin or not sin. They can work hard or slack off. They can be generous or greedy. They can be kind or mean. God chooses to love us despite our choices, our imperfections, and our sins. He is always willing to forgive our mistakes and our sins.

In a similar way, just as God gives us the ability to accept or reject Him, we can accept or reject others. Individually each of us can accept others as they are or we can reject them outright. Acceptance is love. Rejection can be hate. Acceptance in no way means approval of what others choose or alignment with their values. It just means acceptance of their God-given freedom and their unique individuality.

Note that you can accept a person, but reject their choices and their lifestyle. This is love, not hate. Rejecting the person can be hate. Rejecting their choices and their lifestyles are typically value judgments. Individuals should always be free to make value judgments.

When people live in freedom, when people permit others to live in freedom, and when people accept other people's choices, the result is peace. This principle applies to nations as well. When nations live in freedom, when nations permit other nations to live in freedom, and when nations accept other nation's choices, the result is also peace.

Freedom, love and peace all go hand-in-hand. If we want to be have more peace in the world, we simply need more love and more freedom in the world.

American Capitalism is a moral, political, and economic system that is fundamentally peaceful in nature. This peace is a direct consequence of our freedom. However, we always need to be prepared to defend American Capitalism from nations that do not live under capitalism, that seek to take away our freedom and peace, and that seek to impose their way of life on us.

In addition, while America can choose to encourage other nations to adopt American Capitalism, it must never impose (directly or inadvertently) its way of life on others. This is the only policy consistent with American Capitalism.

If there is any doubt about the peacefulness of American Capitalism versus the violence associated with socialism, consider the 125 million deaths (mentioned above) that resulted from socialism and its policies of violence, control, compulsion, and coercion. Take one example to illustrate how socialism can work. In Archbishop Chaput's words:

In one winter alone, 1932-1933, the Soviets deliberately starved more than five million people to death in Ukraine for ideological reasons. The Communist party wanted to collectivize the farming. The peasants didn't. So, the party simply took their food and let them die.[117]

If these socialists permitted the Ukrainian peasants to live in freedom and to farm peacefully, five million people would not have starved to death. There are many other examples (both historic and more contemporary) of mass killings, torture, and violence associated with socialism. Socialism is about control and violence.

In contrast, American Capitalism is about freedom and peace.

Free Markets (and Prosperity)
American Capitalism is also about free markets and the prosperity they create. Chapter 1 highlights some of the many achievements of American Capitalism, the greatest economic system ever created in the history of the world. Our tremendous prosperity is the result of religious, political, and economic freedom. It rests squarely on our Christian foundations and on the Architecture of American Capitalism described earlier in this chapter.

But, what are free markets? Why do they create prosperity? Let's take a look at this incredible institution of American Capitalism.

A Cooperative Process to Meet Everyone's Needs
To begin with, a free market is not a grocery store, or a stock exchange, or a bank, or an auction site on a website. It is not a physical structure, a place, or a location in cyberspace. Rather, it's a process in which individuals cooperate together to meet each other's needs.[118] In the words of the renowned economist Ludwig von Mises,

Everybody acts on his own behalf; but everybody's actions aim at the satisfaction of other people's needs as well as at the satisfaction of his own. Everybody in acting serves his fellow citizens. Everybody, on the other hand, is served by his fellow citizens.[119]

In a free market, there is no violence, compulsion or coercion to act. There are no government-dictated minimum or maximum prices for goods and services. There is also no government-dictated minimum wages or maximum salaries. There are no government subsidies to help some suppliers and there are no government tariffs to inhibit other suppliers. Human action is free. Government action is strictly limited to protecting the free market's operation from foreign threats, domestic criminals, and individuals who fail to live up to their contractual obligations.

Freedom to Choose Your Work

With a free market, everyone is free to choose the employment of their choice. Since individuals differ in their knowledge and education, capabilities and skills, strengths and weaknesses, interests and preferences, as well as their stamina and endurance, individuals will be drawn to different professions and jobs. Not everyone will seek to be a doctor or lawyer. Not everyone will seek to be an electrician or a plumber. Not everyone will seek to be a teacher or professor. Neither will everyone have the requisite qualifications for these positions. Some will have natural talents for certain professions. Others will have innate skills for specific jobs.

Free markets have the unique quality of drawing each individual into that profession or job that best meets the needs of fellow citizens while still best meeting his or her own needs. To illustrate, suppose someone loves to write poetry but also has the ability to write computer software for engineering applications. The free market in poetry books might be very limited, since very few people probably require poetry to be fulfilled. Hence, the aspiring poet might find his compensation modest if he opts to write poetry books. If the poet has the need for a higher income to pay for a new sports car and vacations to tropical resorts, he might choose to write computer software instead. In American Capitalism, the aspiring poet is free to write poetry, or free to write computer software, or free to choose some other career. In American Capitalism, the aspiring poet is even free to write computer software during the day earning a higher income, and to write poetry at night until he is discovered (and can increase his cash flow from poetry book royalties).

With free markets, it is true that not everyone is able to get the precise job they seek, at the precise pay they seek, in the precise location they desire.

But, in a free market economy, everyone who wants to get a job is able to get a job, and in particular, a job that best matches their current qualifications with the current needs of all other individuals. Of course, in American Capitalism, individuals are free to improve their education and skills in order to eventually work their way into their ideal profession or job. They can also keep trying until a job opens up at the compensation level they seek and/or in the location they desire.

Freedom to be an Entrepreneur – Free Enterprise

There is another wonderful option open to those who live in American Capitalism. We call it Free Enterprise. Free enterprise goes hand-in-hand with free markets. Individuals who want to create a unique or ideal job (or who want to create a new business, or an entire new industry) can start their own business. These entrepreneurs can create a sole proprietorship, an LLC (Limited Liability Company), or a corporation, with just a modest amount of money.

Entrepreneurs have a unique, special and important function in free markets. It is a very different role from that of a CEO of a Fortune 500 company, or a department manager in a retail store, or a practice leader in a consulting firm. These individuals generally oversee existing businesses, although there can be entrepreneurial activities or elements in any business. Companies, for example, with solid Research and Development (R&D) budgets often bring out a steady stream of new products to meet customer needs.

The role of entrepreneurs is straight forward. Entrepreneurs observe the free market economy looking for opportunities to fulfill the unmet needs of consumers and businesses. When a need is detected, they start planning to meet that need. They determine the resources needed, pull together those resources, and typically create a new business to satisfy those unmet needs of individuals and businesses. The price system and profits guide entrepreneurs in their search for new unmet needs.

There are untold numbers of entrepreneurs who have started successful new businesses and were rewarded handsomely by the Free Market.

Freedom to be an Investor

In American Capitalism, individuals are also free to participate in the stock and bond markets, and also in the real estate market as investors. These markets create numerous millionaires and even billionaires as a result of smart investments in products, services, and real estate that best meet the needs of other people. Many people have started with nearly no financial resources and have parlayed these modest resources into small and large fortunes using their intelligence, intuition, and knowledge of the consumer.

Of course, many individuals who have chosen to work in various professions and jobs also start businesses on the side or become investors. In American Capitalism, there are many ways to participate in our free markets.

You Can't Have Prosperity without Capital Formation

An important aspect of free markets is capital formation, sometimes called capital accumulation. With capital formation, new businesses are easier to start and current businesses are easier to grow. With capital formation, technological and business model innovations can accelerate and impact business effectiveness and efficiency. With capital formation, labor productivity can increase to higher levels, while wages and salaries can increase correspondingly. With capital formation, our standard of living is likely to increase continually over time.

Capital formation takes place when individuals and businesses consume less money than they earn (in wages, salaries, and earnings) and then place that excess into savings and investments. The capital accumulated can then be invested in growing existing businesses, creating new businesses, or creating new technologies, or new business models. It can also be used to purchase technology or equipment that will increase worker productivity. Increasing worker productivity, in turn, means that a worker produces more goods and services; his or her time is worth more to the employer; and the worker's wages can be increased accordingly. With better businesses, new businesses, new technologies, higher worker productivity, higher wages and salaries, we can see how our standard of living increases over time.

Thus, free markets are able to continually and consistently create new wealth and prosperity and an increasing standard of living over time. One key to the success of American Capitalism is that excess earnings and profits are invested in the future. Without individuals and businesses that produce more than they consume, wealth creation would cease and our standard of living would flatten out and then decline. Because socialism consumes capital rather than accumulates capital, socialist economies devolve into bankruptcy. Socialism lives off the accumulated wealth of capitalism and eventually that capital is gone. Poverty-stricken and destitute "socialist utopias" are the outcome of socialism's faulty philosophy.

Note that since capital formation catalyzes economic growth, wealth creation, and on-going increases in our standard of living, it's important to eliminate or minimize taxes on capital gains that reflect successful capital formation and investment. Taxes on capital gains are a significant and direct disincentive to creating new wealth and a higher standard of living for a nation.

A general principle of economics is: (1) if government taxes something, then we will get less of it; and (2) if the government subsidizes something, then we will get more of it. In this case, if government taxes capital gains, we can expect less capital gains, less capital formation, less economic growth, less wealth creation, and lower (or no) increases in our standard of living.

Capital gains taxes do not hurt wealthy investors as much as they stifle the upward economic mobility of the poor and middle class who seek a higher standard of living. These taxes on capital formation inhibit the economy's ability to create new businesses, products and services. These taxes also tend to cut down on the number of new jobs, to cut down on the number of new, higher quality and higher paying jobs, to cut down on labor productivity, to cut down on wages and salaries, and ultimately, to restrain our economy and our standard of living from growing more.

Capital formation and capital gains are needed more by the poor and middle class than by the wealthy. The wealthy generally have their economic needs met. It's the poor and middle class who aspire to a better life economically that most require free markets, with capital formation fueling economic growth.

Capital formation is a very important component of free markets and the prosperity they generate for everyone. Another element of free markets that is crucial to their success is profits.

You Can't Meet People's Needs Efficiently without Profits

Contrary to the mixed-up thinking of socialists, profits have little (or nothing) to do with greed and everything to do with efficiency and a reward for that efficiency. In free markets, profits are a subtle, sensitive, and powerful signal to entrepreneurs to move resources into producing those products and services currently being demanded by other individuals or even other businesses, in the case of business-to-business markets (or B2B markets for short).

With socialism, governments have no incentive to meet people's needs (other than possibly to avoid a violent revolution). Even with welfare state socialism, there is little incentive to meet people's needs efficiently, since the governing elite can usually share (or in some cases, fake) their good intentions and tell the people that all will be well in the future.

Profits are a communications link among individuals freely operating within a free market. When profits start to increase in one area of the free market economy, entrepreneurs swing into action. As mentioned above, they pull together the critical resources necessary to create the goods and services consumers need. How does this happen?

Entrepreneurs might seek out investors to start new businesses. They might seek out financial help from banks, or from family and friends, or from angel investors, or from venture capitalists (who specialize in investing in and assisting start-up or early stage businesses). They might expand their current businesses or re-deploy resources from a less profitable product line to another product line in hot demand.

The beauty of profits is the clear and unambiguous signal they send to entrepreneurs and businesses. Solid profits mean individuals have a need that they want satisfied now. It's important to them. It's a priority. They are in effect saying to the rest of the economy move more resources over to meet our needs in a particular area.

On the other hand, if a product or service or business is not making a profit but instead is losing money, a different (but still quite clear) signal is sent from consumers. You are wasting resources. We're not interested in what you are selling. We want something else. We have others needs that are more important to us. We have higher priorities than this product or service. Stop wasting your time. Move resources to some other products or services.

Free markets are enormously and incredibly efficient. No matter how large or how rich a business is today, it can't continue to waste resources on products that people don't need and don't want. Sooner or later (and it's usually sooner) it will be forced to meet the needs of consumers. Otherwise, it will be lose all its resources and will find itself in bankruptcy. A free market is ruthless in eliminating waste and is quick to discipline the poor management of resources. A free market is the ultimate engine of conservation and the efficient use of scarce resources.

In American Capitalism, individuals acting freely are in charge and make critical resource allocation decisions by voting each day with their purchases. In socialism, the governing elite are in charge and make resource allocation decisions for everyone according to their own wishes.

No government can compare to the efficiency of a free market. No amount of good intentions on the part of government elites, no higher education degrees obtained by government elites, no number of supercomputer servers connected by high speed networks, and no combination of all these factors taken together can rival the efficiency of free market profits in effectively and efficiently utilizing economic resources to meet the needs of individuals.

Unlike free market economies, socialist economies don't have to be efficient. There is no powerful market force such as profit to make socialist governments operate efficiently. When a welfare state is wasteful and people's needs are not met, welfare state socialists simply use their inefficiency as an excuse to raise taxes once again, or to add more burdensome regulations. Of course, there is a day of reckoning for any "socialist utopia." Those nations that follow socialism always end up in moral and economic bankruptcy. In some unfortunate cases, only the power of a police state can keep individuals from revolution.

Thus, free market profits are a powerful signal in the most efficient use of limited economic resources. Profits direct entrepreneurs and businesses to move scarce resources to those areas of the economy that will meet the highest priority needs of individuals. In so doing, in meeting the needs of many consumers, these profitable businesses are rewarded. They are rewarded with profits and with the right to continue servicing consumers. Unprofitable businesses, in effect, lose their right to serve consumers. Financial resources are directed away from these ineffective businesses and are redirected to businesses that better serve consumers.

In summary, a quick example might be helpful. While some people in the recent past have criticized oil companies for their "excessive" profits on gasoline sales, these critics of the Free Market miss the point. Consumers vote with their wallets. Consumers consider gasoline for their cars, trucks, and SUVs a very high priority. They have bid up gas prices precisely because gasoline and the transportation it provides are important to them. The profits are telling the oil companies and entrepreneurs to invest more in gasoline and refineries and sources of oil. Consumers are telling the oil industry that we need gasoline. It's important to us.

If the oil industry is not thwarted by well-meaning (or hostile) government elites, they will likely use the profits from gas sales to seek out cheaper and better supplies of oil. They might seek out better domestic sources of oil, if socialists or extreme environmentalists do not get in the way. They might also seek to bring additional refinery capacity online. They might even seek out alternative forms of energy. The profits will also signal entrepreneurs to develop new businesses to meet the growing demand and needs of consumers.

Eventually, the Free Market will clear. That means that eventually gasoline supplies will increase, prices will decrease, consumer needs will be met, and consumer demand will be roughly equivalent to supply. At this point, "excessive" profits will return to a more normal level of profits consistent with whatever value is delivered by these businesses to their consumers. At this point, free market profits have accomplished their objective of directing more resources toward pressing consumer needs.

Instead of letting the Free Market clear, some socialists and others want to tax (and take away all) the so-called "excessive" profits from the oil companies. What would happen? Taxing profits would prevent the Free Market from working. It would mean businesses and entrepreneurs would not increase investment in meeting customer's needs for gasoline. Supplies would be less than required. Customer prices for gasoline would be higher. No one wins when the government interferes with the Free Market.

Note that in the above case, even the government is a loser. Despite the additional revenues generated by the increased taxes on the oil companies, the overall economy is weakened and in the long run, government receipts will decrease and its need to subsidize people and selected industries will increase.

Profits are a wonderful communications link in free markets. They are also a powerful incentive. Instead of being a sign of greed, they are a signal from consumers that resources need to be directed to meet particular needs. They are also a reward to entrepreneurs and businesses who effectively and efficiently serve consumers.

Let's look next at another element of free markets, competition.

You Can't Have Freedom without Competition

Competition is still another critical element of free markets. It results in faster, better, and cheaper products and services. It is also results in freedom in the marketplace. How does competition work within a free market?

With competition, individuals and businesses attempt to meet consumer needs with much faster products, with better products, and with cheaper products. The emphasis is on innovation that meets the needs of individuals. For an example of faster products, consider dial-up Internet services. Early 28K and 56K dial-up Internet services were surpassed in performance by cable and DSL Internet technologies. Loading pages from the Internet onto our home computers is now much faster and more enjoyable. If you use your home computer for work, it can also be much more productive as well.

To illustrate how competition led to better products, consider picture-tube TV technology giving way to flat panel LCD and plasma displays. The benefits to these technologies include crisper pictures, a smaller footprint in your living room, and lighter weight. In many ways, these newer TV technologies are a vast improvement over previous technologies. Of course, another related new technology, high definition technology (HD), is creating better flat panel TVs.

For an example of how competition creates cheaper products, just think about the declining cost of personal computers and computer storage over the past several years. With competition, these products continue to decline in price. Both individuals and businesses are the beneficiaries of competition.

Recall, too, the health care example from Chapter 1. In the two largely unregulated health care market segments of laser eye surgery and cosmetic surgery, prices have declined. The reason is competition. This runs counter to the general trend of increasing prices in the rest of America's health care industry. In those parts of America's health care industry that are highly regulated and tightly controlled by government, competition is thwarted, inefficiency is enhanced, and prices increase. In those few parts of America's health care system that are not highly regulated and are not tightly controlled, competition is free to innovate and to deliver higher value at lower costs. The result is greater economic efficiency and lower prices for everyone.

Interestingly, socialists call for a single-payer health care system where government is the single-payer and government regulates and controls the entire health care industry. As we saw in Chapter 1, this is a recipe for disaster. What our health care system needs today is much less government regulation and control. What our health care system needs today is a free market with healthy competition.

In the pursuit of profits, individuals and businesses enter free markets and compete with one another. The results are innovative products, products that are faster, better, and cheaper. In addition, competition creates choices. For example, if you don't like cable TV, you can order satellite TV instead. If you don't like attaching your notebook PC to a cable for Internet service at home, you can have a wireless Internet connection set up in its place. If you don't want to limit your notebook usage to be strictly from home, you can go to a neighborhood coffee shop and get wireless connectivity while sipping on your favorite warm beverage. Or, to take another example, if you don't like simple cell phones, you can buy cell phones with a host of useful services and apps. If you think about it, competition offers a seemingly endless array of choices in our lives.

Freedom without choices is empty. To be free to choose, implies you actually have some choices to make. Simply put, you need choices to be free. With American Capitalism, competition within a free market offers you many different choices across a wide spectrum of products and services. In so doing, it also offers you and your family economic freedom, that is, the freedom to choose and the freedom to select those products and services that best meet you and your family's needs.

Competition within a free market enables you and your family the "pursuit of happiness" that you alone define. No government-controlled "market" provides that same degree of freedom and that same latitude of choice.

In stark contrast, socialism does not believe in competition at all. With socialism, government chooses the "best way" for you and your family. There are no alternatives, no choices. Of course, with socialism there is little or no freedom in general.

As an aside, have you ever thought about why some teachers and schools are against teaching competition to children? Have you ever thought about how socialism's warped thinking has insidiously crept into our schools? Competition is good. It brings out the best in people. It should be taught in schools.

Just as you can't have freedom without competition, it is also true that you can't have free markets without one very critical component, private property. Why is private property so important?

You Can't Have Free Markets without Private Property

As we said earlier in this chapter, a free market is not a grocery store, or a stock exchange, or a bank, or an auction site on a website. It is not a physical structure, a place, or a location in cyberspace. Rather, it's a process in which individuals cooperate together to meet each other's needs.[120] It is (or should be) a process of free exchange between two individuals, or an individual and a business, or between two businesses. Sometimes, it can be between a business and a government as when a copier manufacturer sells a government agency new color copiers for their office. Let's think about some other quick examples.

You agree to buy your neighbor's used car for $1,000 and your neighbor agrees to sell you his used car for $1,000. That's a free exchange between individuals. You go to a favorite restaurant and buy lunch. The restaurant provides you with a tasty lunch and you pay the restaurant $15. That's a free exchange between an individual and a business. You pay an online retailer $150, the retailer ships you a new winter coat. Again, this is an example of a free exchange between an individual and a business.

All of the above examples are free exchanges taking place in a free market. All share some common characteristics. In each case, the individual or business gives some "thing" up and receives some "thing" else in exchange. In each case, one recipient receives a "thing" called money and the other recipient receives a "thing" called private property. While money doesn't technically have to be involved in a free exchange, barter is rarely used these days in a free market because it's simply not a convenient form of exchange.

Note that in every free exchange within a free market, each party believes they are receiving something that is of greater value than they are giving up.[121] One recipient believes the money they are receiving is more valuable than the private property they are relinquishing. The other recipient believes the opposite. The other party believes that the private property they are receiving is of greater value than the money they are spending for that private property.

Indeed, in every free exchange involving private property in a free market, it is a peaceful transaction in that both parties are cooperating to meet each other's needs, and in that both parties are peaceful and content with the fact that the transaction was good for them. No government-dictated centralized planning, control, coercion, compulsion and violence are required in a free market. Everyone is free to meet their own needs as they think best.

It is also very important to realize that private property is involved in every free exchange within a free market. If private property did not exist (as some socialists advocate), no free exchange can take place at all. If the government takes away all of you and your family's private property, you and your family can not exchange anything in a free market. In fact, if government controls everyone's private property, there can be no free market at all.

Because of this fact, socialists sometimes talk about a "social market." The concept of a "social market" put forth by some socialists is ludicrous. It is also meaningless. Either you have a market or you don't. It is either free or it is not free. A government can't simultaneously socialize (completely control) a market and claim that it is a free market.

If what these socialists really mean is to partially control a market, yet still retain some semblance of the benefits of a market, they are probably seeking a highly taxed and tightly regulated market. This approach results in an inefficient and an ineffective market at best. Such hampered capitalism, or the even more restrictive welfare state socialism, are economic theories and experiments that ultimately fail and collapse into moral and economic bankruptcy. Chapter 5 covers these topics in more detail.

But, back to you and your family. While totalitarian socialist regimes seize all private property outright, socialist proponents of hampered capitalism or welfare state socialism (the nanny state), take control more gradually and in a different manner. They steal away your private property by an ever-increasing tax and regulatory burden. How, you ask?

In effect, an increasing share of all goods and services produced, the Gross Domestic Product (GDP), is placed under the control of government. For example, if the average rate of taxes from all government bodies on all individual income is raised from 40% to 50%, and then from 50% to 60%, and later from 60% to 70%, a greater and greater share of your money is taken away from you and your family and is spent by government. Instead of you and your family spending the money you earned to meet your own needs, the government taxes away your earnings and spends it on whatever it chooses. In this way, an increasing share of GDP is controlled by government. In a complete socialist economy, the government controls all expenditures and all property.

By the way, while those average tax rates mentioned in the preceding paragraph might seem high to you, consider all the taxes you actually pay today and add up what percentage of all your income goes to government taxes at all levels of government, Federal, State, and local. You and your family might be very surprised at what percentage of your income actually goes to government taxes and what percentage of your earnings you actually get to keep and spend. Remember, it's not just income taxes. You and your family are probably paying most (if not all) of these taxes and possibly a few more:

- Federal Income taxes,
- State Income taxes,
- Local Income taxes,
- FICA taxes,
- Medicare taxes,
- Capital Gains taxes,
- State Sales taxes,
- County Sales taxes,
- City Sales taxes,
- City Occupation taxes,
- Hotel taxes,
- Property taxes,
- Phone taxes,
- Natural Gas and Electric taxes,
- Water and Sewer taxes,
- Gasoline taxes,
- Car Ownership taxes,
- Cable TV taxes,

- Airline Ticket taxes,
- Gift taxes,
- Estate (Death) taxes, and
- Many other taxes.

All of these taxes add up. Plus, as your taxes increase, your ability to purchase and keep private property decreases. How many families have had to sell off family assets or go into debt to pay a tax bill?

Without private property, you and your family can't freely exchange anything. Without private property, you can't have free markets and you can't have economic growth and prosperity. Private property is essential to free markets.

Let's turn our attention to one last critical component of free markets.

You Can't Have Free Markets without the Ability to Set Prices Freely

In order to have the free exchange of private property in a free market, individuals and businesses must be free to establish the prices at which they are willing to sell their private property. After all, it is their private property, and they should be free to decide the price at which they are willing to sell it.

If government sets prices, if government controls prices, or if government regulates prices, there is no free exchange and there is no free market. If government establishes prices in any of these ways, it is following socialist thinking. It is also limiting economic freedom, throttling back economic growth, and reducing prosperity. It is also unfairly hurting some individuals at the expense of others.

From a moral point of view, if government sets prices, it is forcing some people to sell their private property at prices lower than these individuals value their property. It is, in effect, a form of theft, robbing one person or business and unfairly benefitting another person or business. It is taking property away from individuals or businesses under the threat of government action. Such socialist policies are immoral.

In a free market, prices change continually, quite literally on a day-to-day basis. Within a free market for stocks and bonds, prices can change on a second-to-second basis. This is as it should be. One of the major reasons why a free market is so effective and efficient in meeting people's needs is that those needs are constantly changing and are being reflected in the prices for goods and services.

Both consumer needs and business needs change on an on-going basis. These needs translate into demand for products and services. The price system reflects these changing demands and balances them against the supplies of products and services. Increasing prices are the direct result of increasing consumer (and/or business) demand, all other things being held constant.

Note that increasing prices can also result from government monetary policy. This is known as inflation and is explained easily in Chapter 5's discussion on hampered capitalism.

Prices are closely related to profits and work in much the same way. Prices are also a communications link between consumers and producers. Prices signal to entrepreneurs and businesses that individuals need more of certain products and services (when prices go up) and that individuals need less of certain products and services (when prices go down). In fact, they are an early warning signal to entrepreneurs and businesses because prices flash immediately (or at least relatively quickly in most cases). Profits (or losses) take slightly longer to show up, but send an even more powerful message from individuals to entrepreneurs and businesses about demand for products and services.

To work properly, prices must be set freely. Let's consider what happens when a government adopts socialist policies and controls the market by setting prices.

Suppose, for example, the government decides that the prices of prescription drugs are too high and that the most any pharmaceutical company can charge a person for a month's supply of a prescription drug is $25. For purposes of this example, we will not consider the costs of distribution, transportation, and other costs. What's the impact of the government's decision to set prescription drug prices on pharmaceutical companies? What's the impact on consumers?

To begin with, by capping drug prices, the pharmaceutical company will likely not recoup its research and development (R&D) costs for producing some of its newer and more innovative drugs. With some other drugs, it will likely not recover most of its production and marketing costs. Overall, the company's earnings will decline substantially and in some situations, it might even become unprofitable.

The stock market will see the earnings weakness as a signal to withdraw capital from this company and probably the entire industry. The stock market will look for other growth companies and other growth industries to invest in. After all, investors want to earn the best possible return on their investment dollars. Remember, too, that investors include almost everyone directly as actual investors, or indirectly through 401K funds, IRAs, insurance policies, and savings accounts that individuals own.

At best, the drug company in this example will limp along manufacturing those drugs that are cheapest to make. It will likely eliminate or cut R&D on new and innovative drug therapies. At worst, it will go out of business completely. This is the impact on the producer side.

On the consumer side, supplies of drugs needed by consumers will be cut. Why? First, supplies will be cut because of the damage done to the drug manufacturers mentioned above. Manufacturers will need to cut costs by either cutting down the production of more costly drugs, or they will need to simply go out of business. In either case, drug supplies are cut. Second, supplies will be cut because the prices of drugs are artificially lower by government dictate. Doctors, who are aware of these lower government-controlled prices, will tend to prescribe more drugs to patients more often. After all, when the price for a product declines, demand for the product increases and supply of the product decreases. So, again, on the consumer side, there is a cut in drug supplies. Shortages and rationing ensue. Consumers will likely experience delays in receiving drugs as well.

In general, when government fixes prices at a level lower than the Free Market indicates is appropriate, demand increases and supply decreases. Government intervention in this way always leads to shortages and rationing, and to delays in meeting people's needs.

Ironically, in this example, government sought to provide lower cost drugs to consumers. Instead, it decimated drug companies, cut investments in the pharmaceutical industry, cut the supply of existing drugs, and potentially prevented new and better drugs from ever coming to market. It's no wonder why socialism always leads to economic inefficiency, economic dislocation, and eventually poverty.

Rather than looking at just this simple hypothetical example, let's consider a real-world example. Do you recall the various shortages for preventive vaccines that occurred in the recent past? For example, during the years 2000 to 2003, there were eight different vaccine shortages. These shortages were for flu, tetanus, diphtheria, chickenpox, and measles preventive vaccines. The reasons for these shortages include government intervention in the market that lowered prices artificially and impacted profits adversely. According to *The Wall Street Journal* and the National Academy of Sciences' Institute of Medicine study it cites:

In the 1970s, there were 25 vaccine makers; today – because of slim profit margins and legislative and liability issues – there are just five.[122]

The report concluded that the price squeeze, coupled with a heavy regulatory burden, has discouraged investment and driven drug companies out of the vaccine business.[123]

This actual example shows how government interference in free markets can impact you and your family. When a government adopts socialist policies and sets prices, you can expect shortages of whatever products and services are being controlled. Shortages also breed delays in satisfying the needs of individuals. You can also expect the decline of businesses and entire industries.

Just imagine what it would be like if socialists have their way and socialize the American health care system. If government can't even manage preventive vaccines, surely it can't manage our entire and much larger health care system. If our health care system is socialized into a single-payer, universal, government-controlled program, it will be plagued with across the board shortages and certainly will end up in shambles.

It's a fact. You can't have free markets without the ability to set prices freely. For government to set prices is a socialist recipe for creating widespread shortages of needed products and services, for delays in obtaining products and services, as well as for causing many profound economic disruptions to the economy.

Wages and Salaries are Prices Paid for Labor Services

A final point about setting prices. Wages and salaries are the prices paid for labor.[124] Individuals need the ability to set the prices at which they are willing to work, while entrepreneurs and businesses need the ability to set the prices they are willing to pay for work. In a free market, no individual should be forced to work at a lower price than they are willing to accept. To do otherwise, is a form of slave labor. On the other hand, no employer should be forced to pay any particular wage or a minimum wage. To do otherwise, is a form of coercion.

If a government sets a minimum wage for a particular job or for all jobs, the result is a shortage of jobs for those who fit into the category of job being regulated. When a minimum wage law is enacted, employers who can't afford to pay the minimum wage are prohibited from hiring the potential worker at the wage that corresponds to the potential worker's true value to the business. Once again, when government adopts the socialist policy of setting prices (in this case, wages, the price of labor services), shortages occur.

Just as with any other free exchange within a free market, both individual workers and employers need to agree to the terms of employment. When the terms of employment are mutually agreed upon, a free exchange of money for labor services can take place. The worker finds a job, the employer finds an employee. No government coercion is required.

Incidentally, in a free market, there is always a job for everyone that wants to work because there are always unmet needs.[125] However, an employer might have to pay more than they want for an employee. Or, the employer might have to forego hiring someone they can't afford. Similarly, an employee might not get paid what they want for their labor. Or, a person might forego working because they choose to wait to find a better paying job.

If a healthy individual seeks employment within a free market, they can always find it. It might not be at the pay they seek, or in their preferred line of work, or in their location of choice.[126] But, the Free Market always is ready to direct economic resources including labor to where there is the greatest need for those resources. Of course, there is always the special case of the individual with a disability that prevents them from working. But, this need must be addressed through public or private charity.

In all of these situations involving wages, salaries, and labor, there is nothing fundamentally different from any other free exchange taking place in any other free market. Both parties to a free exchange must agree on that exchange.

Just as you can't have free markets without the ability to set prices freely, so too, you can't have a free market in labor services without the ability to set wages and salaries freely.

Free Markets (and Prosperity) Summary

To sum up this section, let's look at the accompanying figure. It shows the various characteristics of free markets. These characteristics stand in sharp contrast to the economic policies of socialism that lead to moral and economic bankruptcy.

A free market is a cooperative process that meets people's needs without resorting to government-dictated centralized planning, control, coercion,

The Characteristics of a Free Market

Free, Cooperative, and Peaceful Process

Free to Set Prices

Free to Choose Your Work

Free to Buy, Own, Use, and Sell Private Property

Free Market

Free to Be an Investor

Free to Compete

Free to Be an Entrepreneur

Free to Earn Profits

Free to Create Capital Formation

compulsion and violence. A free market also allows individuals to choose their own unique role. Individuals are free to choose their own line of work, or they can save and become an investor, or if they believe they want to start their own business, they can become an entrepreneur.

A free market requires capital formation, the ability to bring together new capital for investment. It also uses prices and profits to direct economic resources into those products and services that individuals demand. Without these powerful communication signals, a free market would not be as efficient and effective at meeting individual's needs. Individuals and businesses, of course, must be free to set prices for their products and services. Otherwise, cooperative and peaceful free exchange is not possible.

Competition is an important element in a free market as well. Competition serves to bring out the very best in people. It is also instrumental in creating faster, better, and cheaper (less expensive) products and services, all to meet the needs of individuals.

Finally, private property is the very important cornerstone of a free market. Without private property, nothing can be bought or sold. There can be no free exchanges. Without private property, the idea of a free market makes no sense at all.

American Capitalism is truly about free markets and the prosperity it creates. As we will see shortly, it's also about family and trust.

Family (and Trust)
Faith and morality, freedom and peace, free markets and prosperity, all describe American Capitalism and all foster and support both the family and trust. In American Capitalism, the basic economic unit is the family. Family, in turn, is that special institution that first creates and then nurtures trust in both spouses and in their children.

American Capitalism is built around the family and the trust that results from families. This trust empowers and invigorates American Culture, American Government, and the American Economy. The importance of the family and trust can't be overlooked or downplayed. It is vital in the life of American Capitalism. It is essential for upholding morality. It is critical for creating economic growth and economic wealth. It is key to sustaining the American Economy. The Family is one of the key institutions of American Capitalism.

As the Bible describes in detail, God is the creator of the family and the moral rules surrounding and protecting the family. God is also the author of marriage. When two people in love choose to marry, they form a family through marriage.

Marriage is first and foremost a spiritual commitment of a man and woman to live together in love and faithfulness for the remainder of their lives. It is also a legal contract sanctioned by the State for purposes of dealing with the economic realities of that spiritual union of husband and wife, as well as a means for protecting the couple's offspring. The family then is a divine institution for which a parallel legal institution is established to promote and protect the economic vitality of all the family members. It is a rock-solid foundation of American Capitalism.

With marriage and the establishment of a family comes a deep level of trust. A husband trusts his wife to love him and be faithful to him; a wife trusts her husband to love her and be faithful to her. When children come into the family, they grow in the parent's love and they trust the parents to meet their spiritual, emotional, and physical needs. This mutual trust radiates outward and influences trust in all other areas of life. There is no question that the love and trust of a family has a powerful, positive, and profound impact on culture.

Tampering with the institution of family, in contrast, is immoral and has a particularly negative effect on culture. To illustrate, consider "no fault" divorces or as Maggie Gallagher calls them "unilateral" divorces.[127] No fault divorces permit either the husband or wife to obtain a divorce without the other party's agreement. In other words, the legal contract of marriage can be broken by either party at will. This is not much of a legal contract.[128] Instead of "until death do us part," we now have "until any whim do us part." No fault divorces are the result of socialist thinking as we shall see later.

Can you think of the economic chaos that would ensue if commercial business contracts could be broken in the same way as marriages can now be broken with no fault divorces? Suppose, for example, that you decide to buy a new car for $25,000 at your local new car dealership. The dealer and you sign the papers. You give them a check for $5,000 with the balance to be paid with a bank loan that has been approved and finalized. If the government had enacted a law that allowed for no fault contract dissolutions, the dealer might call you back a week later and say the following. "Our contract with you is over. Please return the car immediately. We found a buyer who will pay $28,000."

Surely, such a contract termination is absurd. Yet, that is precisely what happens with marriages and no fault divorces all the time. Spouses and very innocent children are hurt in the process. Undue economic hardships are the result in many cases.

Despite a lot of bogus arguments to the contrary, no fault divorce is definitely not a recipe for strong marriages and strong families. It is a direct assault on one of the key institutions of American Capitalism. It is also an assault on you and your family. It diminishes the emotional and economic security of everyone's family because no one knows what day they will wake up and find out their spouse wants to leave. It makes the dissolution of marriages and families much easier, with all the resulting negative effects on the other spouse and on the children of the broken home.

Consider these impacts of the breakup of traditional families on innocent children:

Children from single-parent families are more than five times as likely to live in poverty, nearly twice as likely to need psychological help, and two and a half times as likely to drop out of school, get pregnant before marriage, abuse drugs, and commit crimes as are children from intact families.[129]

On the positive side, Linda J. Waite and Maggie Gallagher offer a more comprehensive and detailed discussion of the benefits of marriage and family. To illustrate some of their findings, one report by economists Joseph Lupton and James P. Smith they cite indicates that the median net worth of married couples in their fifties and early sixties far exceeded the net worth of the typical divorced person ($132,000 vs. $33,670).[130] Another interesting statistic they cite is that when compared to married people, non-married women have a 50% higher mortality rate while non-married men have a 250% higher mortality rate. Marriage and family life can truly be much healthier than single life.[131]

While American Capitalism fosters and supports the family, socialism rejects the family, marriage, and even raising children within the family. Does that surprise you? Your typical socialist doesn't advertise their immoral philosophy directly. Battles against the institutions of American Capitalism including the Family are taking place now as part of America's Economic War. Let's take a quick look at socialist thinking in the areas of family and marriage to contrast it with American Capitalism.

To start, let's look at our example of no fault divorce above. Where and when did no fault divorce originate? While some might choose a different place or an earlier date, socialists proposed a type of no fault divorce in Russia during the Russian Revolution of 1917. Either spouse could initiate a divorce if they felt they were incompatible. In effect, this meant that anyone could get divorced easily. Up until that time, however, marriage was a matter for the Church. With their strong disdain for the Christian Church, socialists effectively mandated religious marriage out of existence in favor of civil marriages.[132]

In the United Sates, no fault divorce legislation was also created as an easy method to end civil marriages. In the U.S., no fault divorces began in California in 1970, eventually spreading around the nation as state after state adopted such legislation.[133] Remember, it's all part of socialist thinking.

But, socialism and its attacks on the family go far beyond no fault divorces. Karl Marx and Frederick Engels called for the "Abolition of the family!"[134] They believed family was a device to exploit women as property. They also believed in the abolition of religion and morality.[135] Because they were adamantly opposed to the Christian Church and the Christian Church was an advocate for the family as a divine institution, the family was also seen as a vestige of Christianity.

In place of traditional marriage and family, socialists believe that a marriage should last only for the duration of love. Hence, marriage was a temporary arrangement, certainly not a permanent commitment. In Frederick Engels' words:

... marriage is moral only as long as love lasts. The duration of an attack of individual sexlove varies considerably according to individual disposition, especially in men. A positive cessation of fondness or its replacement by a new passionate love makes a separation a blessing for both parties and for society. But, humanity will be spared the useless wading through the mire of a divorce case.[136]

Rather than a lifelong commitment, socialism proposes to replace traditional marriage with a series of passionate affairs that last as long as both "sexlove" partners want. Socialists believe in free love, not committed love.

With regard to children, socialists think it's best for them to be taken off and educated by professionals working for the State. Quite a difference from the approach taken within American Capitalism.

American Capitalism is about family and trust. It offers an enormously better alternative for your health and happiness than does the selfish, immoral, free love of socialism. Let's turn now to the last characteristic of American Capitalism.

Spiritual and Material Human Growth

American Capitalism is also about spiritual and material human growth. From its origin in faith in God and then faith in reason, to its faith in progress and then its inherent optimism, American Capitalism is about growth along all dimensions of human life.

With American Capitalism come faith and morality, freedom and peace, free markets and prosperity, as well as family and trust. Each of these attributes gives vitality to human life, human existence, and human growth. Together, they synergistically empower the human heart, soul, mind, and body.

With faith in God comes the courage to live and grow. With morality come the boundaries that nurture and protect us. With freedom comes the ability to explore, to create, and to become. With peace comes human harmony and compassion. With free markets comes human cooperation in meeting each other's needs. With prosperity comes spiritual and material human growth. With family comes the fulfillment of the deep longing in the human heart and soul for lifelong companionship, closeness, and intimacy. With trust comes faith in our fellow men and women.

Taken together, American Capitalism offers the best system for human life and human growth ever known in the history of the world. It's a system that offers men and women the opportunity to be "Fully Human, Fully Alive" to use the words in the title of a book by John Powell.[137] It's a system that offers unrivaled economic growth and prosperity without any need for government-dictated centralized planning, control, coercion, compulsion and violence.

Indeed, the prosperity that proceeds from American Capitalism provides the environment and support necessary to pursue and achieve spiritual and human growth. Not only does prosperity provide humanity with the capital to invest in improving our economic world, but it also provides the capital for enhancing and enriching our non-economic world.

Truly, many great achievements of humankind came as a result of the time, energy, and resources that were available once our physical and economic needs for water, food, heat, shelter, and security were met. In the absence of meeting these basic needs, higher needs and wants could not have been pursued, let alone achieved.

Prior to American Capitalism, a few elite lived well, while the peasant masses struggled to survive. Only the prosperity of American Capitalism allows significant investments in spiritual and human growth.

As a result of obtaining a certain level of economic growth and wealth, Americans can grow spiritually by spending more time and energy in prayer, Bible study, worship, and fellowship. Theologians and Church leaders can spend more time and energy in thinking through doctrinal challenges and in creating greater awareness and spiritual understanding. In other words, prosperity leads to spiritual growth.

As a result of obtaining a certain level of economic growth and wealth, Americans can also make investments in the arts, music, literature, education, science, engineering, medicine and health. So, prosperity also leads to human growth.

Without a doubt, American Capitalism leads to spiritual and material human growth.

American Capitalism – A Summary

As we have seen the foundations of American Capitalism are embedded in the Judeo-Christian principles found in the Bible, found in the natural law (that is written on the hearts of people), and found in the moral thinking of the Christian Church's theologians and philosophers developed over many centuries.

The early Christian faith in God and faith in reason spurred a deep confidence that people can improve life through thoughtful reasoning. Faith in God, faith in reason, and faith in progress led to an optimism of spirit that in turn led to creativity and to many moral, political, economic, and other innovations. Included among these innovations were: individualism, freedom, equality under the law, separation of Church and State, private property, free enterprise, charity and compassion, and universities. Numerous scientific and technological innovations also took place.

Upon its Christian foundation, American Capitalism was built. The Architecture of American Capitalism includes: key laws, key freedoms, key requirements, key institutions, and key infrastructure.

We have seen in this chapter how American Capitalism is about faith and morality, freedom and peace, free markets and prosperity, family and trust, and spiritual and material human growth. To summarize, American Capitalism is God-inspired freedom and individualism.

Let's next look at why socialism is power-based control and elitism.

Chapter 4

Socialism is Power-Based Control and Elitism

"To follow socialist morality would destroy much of present humankind and impoverish much of the rest."

F. A. Hayek[138]

The philosophy of socialism is the philosophy of evil. While American Capitalism is God-inspired freedom and individualism, socialism is precisely the opposite. Socialism is power-based control and elitism. No degree of stated good intentions to the contrary, the philosophy and practice of socialism is fundamentally evil and immoral.

Consider its origins. While American Capitalism is rooted in the Judeo-Christian principles found in the Bible, in the natural law written on the hearts of people, and in the thinking of Christian philosophers and theologians, socialism is founded on atheism and materialism. Socialism does not believe in God. Socialism does not believe in a spiritual or moral order. Socialism does not believe in religion. Socialism does not believe in morality. Socialism does not even believe in the truth. What, then, does socialism believe in?

Socialism believes in power. Socialism believes in getting power by whatever means is expedient. It can be through revolution or evolution. It can be through guns or through the ballot box. It can be through cleverly-contrived good intentions or through deeply-distorted lies. It can be through intellectual manipulations or through scientific falsehoods. It can even be through theological deceptions or faulty moral reasoning.

Once obtained, socialism believes in using power. The only purpose of power is control. Control over people's lives is the goal of socialism. This control means controlling what you can hear, what you can say, what you can think, and what you can do. This control means limiting, reducing, or destroying your religious freedom, political freedom, and economic freedom. In America's Economic War, socialism seeks to control all of our lives, including your life and your family's lives.

In socialism, only a small ruling elite (be they kings, emperors, dictators, ruling parties, fascists, communists, or other socialists) use this power to wield control over people's lives. Even though the ruling socialist elite claim to be concerned about people and often pretend to be the champions of the working person, socialism is all about getting and exercising power over the people. Socialism is power-based control and elitism, no matter how well socialists try to dress it up as something else.

This thirst for power-based control by a small ruling elite is evil and immoral. It runs totally contrary to the theological concept of individual free will and liberty that permeate the Bible. As we will see later in this chapter, even in the contrived variations of socialism known as Christian socialism and democratic socialism, socialism is still immoral.

Let's see why socialism is immoral and why it seduces so many good people.

The Seduction of Socialism – Part 1

What, then, is the allure of socialism? Why is socialist thinking so appealing to so many people and especially to so many of our intellectual elite? Why is socialism so tantalizing and tempting when it always leads to moral and economic bankruptcy?

The first answer is that socialism offers a powerful proposition, free money and free sex for all. That's quite a seductive combination. The carrot of endless government programs to take care of all of our material needs from "cradle to grave" holds incredible appeal. The idea of endless sexual encounters without the cares and responsibilities of marriage and family arouses the senses and ignites the passions. Taken together, free money and free sex are a powerful incentive to adopt any philosophy or any program, no matter how foolish and no matter how likely it is to fail.

If it seems a bit far-fetched that socialism holds out the inducement of free love and free sex to all, consider how our Christian-based culture has morphed in the last few decades under the influence of socialist thinking. Now, pre-marital sex is widespread and accepted. Sexual promiscuity and sexual deviations extend throughout our culture and our entertainment media. In the past, living together before marriage was discouraged. Today, it is encouraged. The traditional family, consisting of a husband and wife and children, is much less prevalent. Single parent "families" are epidemic.

Now, no fault divorces are much simpler to obtain and considerably more commonplace. The result is a fast and easy method to end the marriage commitment and break up families. Our declining culture has streamlined the family destruction process. How very sad.

Free love and free sex, or as socialist Frederick Engels called it "sexlove," is permeating American Culture. Truly, we can say that American Culture is being transformed from a moral Christian culture into an immoral culture and sometimes an amoral culture. Note that by an immoral culture, we mean a culture that chooses immoral behavior over moral behavior but still recognizes a moral code. By an amoral culture, we mean a culture that does not choose to have any moral code at all.

Indeed, free love and free sex have been a major reason for socialism's initial acceptance,[139] while free money, free love and free sex continue to make socialism popular in some circles. But, socialism is far more seductive, for far more reasons, than simply offering free money and free sex, appealing as that is for many people.

For the powerful and those who seek power, socialism offers unchecked power. For leaders and those who seek to lead others, socialism offers limitless control over people. For the corrupt and those who seek opportunities to be corrupt, socialism offers manifest corruption.

For government bureaucrats and those intellectuals who think they can plan an entire economy better than the Free Market, socialism offers the false pride of pretentious and empty plans and meaningless and useless programs. For the social planner and the social engineer, socialism offers the means and the excuse to create an on-going series of unrealized social plans and failed social experiments.

For the warm-hearted and those with good intentions, socialism offers the false hope of making a real difference in people's lives.

For the lazy and those that seek to avoid work, socialism offers a free ride.

Socialism offers all these "benefits" to all these people. Its price is your freedom, your money, and sometimes your life.

Socialism is an intoxicating philosophy that lulls the minds, hearts, and souls of many. It is a philosophy that is based on power, not God. It is a philosophy based on control and violence, not freedom and peace. It is a philosophy that is based on elitism, not individualism. It is a philosophy that is utopian, not based on reality or practicality. Unfortunately, for all its intelligent proponents, socialism simply does not work. Socialism always leads to moral and economic bankruptcy. It also leads to considerable violence and often many thousands or millions of deaths. Undefeated, it will lead to destitute poverty and the destruction of American Civilization.

Sometimes, socialism seduces even the best-intentioned Christians as we see below.

The Seduction of Christian Socialism

Since the nature of Christians is to trust God and think well of their neighbors, Christians often succumb to the allure of socialism. Christian socialists believe that socialism is a means for living a good Christian life. They see Christian socialism as a modified version of socialism that incorporates Christian principles into socialism. More specifically, they think it is possible to replace socialist atheism with Christianity and then, follow socialist thinking in other matters, including socialist economics. They stress helping the poor with money taken from the rich, that is, the forced redistribution of wealth through the tax system. They also stress the concept of "social justice" with equal outcomes for all regardless of effort and performance. Recall that in Chapter 2 we saw why the term "social justice" is so misguided, so misleading, and so deceptive.

The arguments for Christian socialism fall into two main buckets: (1) Christian socialism is moral – it's the implementation of the Christian Gospel by helping the poor and being a good steward of the environment; and (2) American Capitalism is immoral – it's all about profits and greed and the exploitation of workers. As usual, the socialists have it backwards.

Christian Socialism is Immoral

Christian socialism is a theological mistake and a moral distortion of Christianity. While American Capitalism is based on faith in God and faith in reason, socialism is based on faith in man and faith in man's power. Socialism rejects religion and morality. Socialism also often rejects reason. But, oddly enough, socialism sometimes takes on the qualities of a quasi-religion. Socialism in its basic form and even Christian socialism in its attempt at a spiritual version of socialism are both fundamentally evil and immoral. Let's look at the reasons why this is true.

While Christian socialism touts its "morality," it is not possible to be a Christian and a socialist at the same time. First, a Christian Socialist needs to disavow his faith in God because the first principle of socialism is reliance on power, not God. The entire "moral code" of socialism rests on raw power and choosing material means that promote socialist ends. Socialism relies on power exercised by human beings. With socialism, there are no eternal truths. In fact, there is no truth at all. This type of "morality" is entirely inconsistent with Christianity.

Socialism also is in conflict with both Divine Law and natural law written on the hearts of people. For example, with socialism, it is fine for the government to take away as much money from individuals (in the form of taxes) as it likes and give it to whatever groups it designates (in the form of subsidies). This is a violation of the Ten Commandments and specifically, the admonition against theft. As you remember, the fact that socialism is in conflict with both Divine Law and natural law was discussed in greater detail in Chapter 3.

Second, a Christian socialist must forego a Christian culture (such as the American Culture) to accept a culture based on socialism. This means accepting things like abortion, pre-marital sex, no fault divorce, the demise of the family and marriage, sexual depravity, the pagan ritual of cremation, and violence. How can a Christian accept immorality in the name of a socialist "morality" that is so distinctly opposed to Christian culture? Alternatively, if someone claims to be a socialist, how can they accept a Christian culture?

The unmistakable conclusion is that in the realm of morality, the term "Christian socialism" makes no sense whatsoever. If someone is a Christian, they can't be a socialist. If someone is a socialist, they can't be a Christian. Christianity is a philosophy that results in a moral system and a moral culture. Socialism is a philosophy that rejects a moral and spiritual order and results in an immoral or amoral culture.

Christians can't adopt a philosophical system that rejects both God and morality. Certainly, they can't adopt it on moral grounds.

But, for purposes of discussion, let's assume you can splice together

Christianity and its morality with socialism and its economic system. Is that moral? Is that more moral than American Capitalism?

Today's advocates for Christian socialism will be disappointed because this doesn't work either. Why? Well, recall from Chapter 1, Lameiro's First Law of Economics and Socialism's Chain of Control. Remember too, from Chapter 3, the Architecture of American Capitalism. Notice the important interrelationships among culture, government, and the economy. American Culture, American Government, and the American Economy are all inextricably linked together in one whole American Civilization. In general, for any nation and for any civilization, the culture, the government, and the economy, are all linked together into a sophisticated, multi-dimensional network that we call civilization.

It is simply impossible to disconnect morality from the economy. The immorality of socialism infiltrates into and infects the entire economy.

So, once again, we come to the conclusion that Christian socialism makes no sense whatever. It is a ruse and a deception. It's a way to get Christians to adopt an un-Christian philosophy. It is a means of fooling good people into accepting an immoral philosophy, socialism.

Two other points might be helpful here. Some socialists argue that Christian socialism is a way to help the poor or a means to be a good steward of the environment. These are not sufficient reasons to adopt socialism by Christians. Christians need to love their neighbors by directly being involved in private charity and compassion. Christians can also be involved in supporting government programs for the truly needy and destitute. Similarly, Christians need to be good stewards of all the resources entrusted to them. But, such efforts to help the poor or to be good stewards of the environment are not a license to use an immoral system to achieve these goals. The ends don't justify the means.

With regard to helping the poor, the Christian Church led the world in meaningful charity and compassion as was highlighted in Chapter 3. Indeed, private charity is much more humane and efficient than the cold-hearted "charity" of welfare state socialism. Finally, if a socialist government takes your money and redistributes that money to its favorite groups, that's not charity at all. Charity and compassion come from the heart, voluntarily. Charity should never be forced on the donor or on the recipient.

The notion of Christian socialism doesn't make sense. To the extent Christian socialism is actually just socialism disguised with misleading moral arguments and good intentions, it is immoral. Christian socialism is immoral.

American Capitalism is Moral

The second argument for Christian socialism is that American Capitalism is immoral – it's all about profits and greed and the exploitation of workers. Quite the contrary, American Capitalism is moral. Chapter 3 covered this topic in some detail. But, a few quick summary points here are probably helpful.

American Capitalism and the Free Market are all about individuals coming together freely, peacefully, and in mutual cooperation to meet each others' needs in the most efficient way possible. The Free Market does not require government-dictated, centralized control, coercion, compulsion, and violence. The Free Market operates most effectively and efficiently without interference by the government.

Prices and the resulting profits (or losses) are part of a powerful communications system that direct resources to the needs most demanded by consumers. Profits are moral because they assure the highest priority needs of individuals are met in the fastest and most resource-efficient manner. They are also moral because they reward those who produce the most products and services, they reward those who produce products and services in the most resource-efficient ways possible, and they reward those who do so in the least amount of time. Profits are also an incentive to meet consumer's needs.

Without profits, what is the incentive to work hard? Or, even what is the incentive to work at all? Under welfare state socialism, incentive diminishes. Under complete socialism, incentive disappears almost completely and destitution and poverty result.

Another subtle point that many critics of American Capitalism seem to miss is that the beneficiaries of profits are not just the entrepreneurs and businesses that produce the products and services in high demand. The beneficiaries also include the workers who consume the products and services. After all, every worker is not only a producer of products and services, they are also a consumer of products and services. So, in helping others, they are also being helped by others.

As was mentioned in Chapter 3, this is the Biblical principle (that appears in Matthew 19:19 and earlier in Leviticus 19:18), "You shall love your neighbor as yourself" put into action. Each of us is called to love others in the same way as we love ourselves. Galatians 5:13 tells us: "For you, brethren, have been called to liberty; ... through love serve one another." Translated into economic terms, we are called to meet each other's needs, as we meet our own needs. American Capitalism is precisely about doing just that. Of course, for those who are too poor or too ill or too disabled and are unable to meet their own needs, we are called in love and service to meet their needs through charity and compassion.

One final point about the morality of profits. Profits are very temporary.[140] An entrepreneur or a company only makes a profit for as long as they meet consumer needs. If an entrepreneur or business stops producing products and services that meet consumer needs, profits will evaporate quickly and the no longer effective entrepreneurs or companies will be forced out of business. In this case, profits will flow to other entrepreneurs or businesses that meet consumer needs faster, better, or cheaper.

As to the argument that American Capitalism is immoral because it exploits workers, that argument has been refuted quite vigorously by many economists over the years.[141] Socialists, like Marx, have long argued that capitalists make profits by exploiting the labor of workers.[142] The Marxist theory of the surplus value of labor is that workers create value above and beyond their wages and that capitalists keep that surplus value for their own.[143] What is missed by socialists is that in the Free Market, workers are paid their full value in the production of goods and services. Importantly, entrepreneurs also must be paid for their efforts.

The entrepreneurial function is vital in the Free Market. Entrepreneurs study the market and look for new opportunities to create faster, better, and cheaper products and services to meet consumers needs. Once possibilities are identified, entrepreneurs bring together the resources necessary to turn the possibilities into reality. Entrepreneurs line up investors, hire management teams, and secure office space, R&D labs, and/or manufacturing facilities. Eventually, workers are hired as well.

In the Free Market, everyone and every resource are paid for at its market price. This includes the salaries and wages for workers. Their compensation is determined by such factors as education, knowledge, skills, and related experience. Their compensation is commensurate with the value they create in the marketplace.

So, labor in general, and workers in particular, don't create surplus value and are not exploited by the entrepreneur or by the businesses that employ them. Once again, the moral arguments made against American Capitalism by socialists fail.

To sum up, American Capitalism is not immoral because of profits and it certainly does not exploit workers. While American Capitalism is in fact moral, Christian socialism is immoral despite its faulty moral arguments about helping the poor and being good stewards of the environment.

Socialism and Christian socialism both seduce many people. The idea of democratic socialism is also seductive and immoral, although sometimes for slightly different reasons.

The Seduction of Democratic Socialism
Everyone who thinks about political freedom probably associates democracy with freedom and American Capitalism. This, of course, is understandable since democracy and capitalism usually go hand-in-hand. But, recall that democracy isn't directly part of the Architecture of American Capitalism. The reason is that democracy is actually built into our Constitution and permeates American Capitalism.

Democracy usually involves the election of representatives to a government that makes laws to help run the nation. Most people automatically think of elections within a democracy as free and fair. Also, most people generally think of the election results as free and fair. Yet, we know this does not have to be the case.

Elections can be free and fair, or they can be rigged and unfair. Some people can tamper with election machines, election ballots, or the final election returns. So, simply holding elections does not give assurances of free and fair elections, even though the government in question might still appear democratic.

We know, for example, that some socialist countries have held elections in the past that didn't give the people a choice of outcomes. These elections were definitely not free and fair. Their governments were certainly not free either, despite the fact that they exhibited some sense of democratic participation. These socialist governments, in fact, might be considered one form of democratic socialism and might seduce some citizens into thinking they are living in freedom.

But, the real seduction of democratic socialism arises in another distinct way. Suppose that through lack of understanding, or lack of education, or deception on the part of candidates for office during the election process, people freely elect socialist leaders who are intent on creating a socialist system. Suppose citizens are deceived by clever rhetoric and catchy phrases that mask the socialist programs that they will be subjected to after the election. Or, suppose the process of deception takes place over a number of years and a number of election cycles? Is this form of democratically-elected government, what might be called democratic socialism, truly a moral system?

Some people might be seduced into thinking that this is a moral system. After all, the people elected the socialist leaders. Is it a moral system? No! It's not moral.

Indeed, if any deception took place (even over a period of years or decades), it is not a freely and fairly elected socialist government. People were deceived. They didn't know what they were voting for and they got something else. Since some socialists use deceit and deception as common practices, it is likely that some democratically-elected socialist leaders used deceit and deception to get elected.

Let's look at one last case of seduction related to democratic socialism. Suppose citizens understood they were voting for socialist leaders, socialist policies, and a socialist government. Is the freely-elected socialist government moral? Even in this unlikely scenario, the government is immoral for all the reasons that the philosophy and practice of socialism are immoral.

People are free to make mistakes in life. They are free to sin and free to live an immoral life. If people choose socialism in free elections with full knowledge of what they doing, they are free to choose such an immoral system. However, it does not make socialism moral. It also does not allow those citizens that voted against socialism to live in freedom. It is imposing government-dictated, centralized planning, control, coercion, compulsion, and violence on those individuals that do not want it. It is a violation of their God-given liberty and human dignity.

So, in all these three cases, democratic socialism is immoral and any attempts that succeed in persuading people about the morality of socialism, is seduction. Elections held for show with the outcomes fixed ahead of time are certainly not moral. Elections in which citizens are deceived into voting for socialist leaders and programs are also not moral. Finally, elections in which people freely and knowingly choose socialism do not result in a moral government because socialism is not moral and because those who vote against socialism are denied their God-given liberty and human dignity.

Democratic socialism like Christian socialism and other variations of socialism are all immoral. Unfortunately, many people have been seduced by socialism to the detriment of nations and the entire world. Chapter 5 and Chapter 6 present other examples of the seduction of socialism.

America's Economic War is an attempt to seduce you and your family and indeed, all Americans, into giving up their religious freedom, political freedom, and economic freedom. It is an attempt to substitute power-based control and elitism for American Capitalism. If socialism wins America's Economic War, we will lose our freedom and moral and economic bankruptcy will certainly ensue.

Let's turn our attention to a description of socialism. It will summarize this philosophy of evil.

The Characteristics of Socialism

As we will see, the characteristics of socialism stand in stark contrast to the characteristics of American Capitalism. Indeed, the arguments for socialism are seductive to many groups, but the realities of socialism are devastating to most individuals living under such a system. The accompanying table sums up the characteristics of socialism. Let's learn more now.

Atheism (and Immorality)
By now, an accurate picture of socialism should be crystallizing before your

eyes. Socialism is a philosophy and a way of thinking about life that is based on a rejection of God. It is atheism. It rejects faith in God. It rejects religion. It rejects a spiritual and moral order. It rejects morality and a moral code. It rejects faith in reason, except in some cases of expediency. It even rejects truth.

The Characteristics of Socialism	
Summary	Power-Based Control and Elitism
Spiritual and Moral, Cultural	Atheism (and Immorality)
Political	Control (and Violence)
Economic	Economic Inefficiency (and Poverty)
Sociological	Groups of "Victims" (and Distrust)
Impact on Civilization	Moral Decay and Social Disintegration

Besides rejecting God and morality and truth, socialism also rejects the Christian Church, the family and marriage. It believes that children should be raised by the state and not by the parents. It believes in pre-marital sex and quick, easy divorces. It believes in sexual promiscuity, sexual deviations, and sexual license.

Socialism rejects the Ten Commandments and rebuffs the morality that is a fundamental component of American Capitalism and its predecessors, Western Civilization and Christendom. Why does it reject these vital Christian principles? Because socialism doesn't believe in God or spirituality or morality or religion or the beliefs that have created centuries of spiritual and moral progress as well as our unprecedented economic prosperity.

Socialism rejects individualism and places people into groups. It treats people as if every member of each group thinks and acts monolithically. It does not comprehend or respect individual differences or individuality. Individuals are merely pawns of the State. They are dispensable and have no fundamental value, except to the extent that obey the State and provide value to the State or the socialist elite running the government.

With socialism's rejection of individualism, comes the rejection and denial of human rights and human dignity as well. This includes the very special right to life itself. That's why atheistic socialism is "pro-choice," a positive-sounding way to say that socialists are pro-abortion on demand. Indeed, socialists don't value life at all. If they did value life, socialism would not be responsible for 125 million deaths, as referenced earlier in Chapter 3.

Rather than faith in God, socialism is mistakenly founded on the notion of materialism. Materialism is the idea that there is no spiritual reality; rather, life consists of nature – the physical world, what we can see and hear and touch. In part, this is the reason why radical environmentalism allies itself so closely with socialism. To socialists, there is no spiritual world, only a tangible, physical world. To them, there are no eternal moral truths.

As an aside, in the mixed up world of socialism where truth is a victim, socialists sometimes claim that American Capitalism is immoral because it creates a materialistic, consumer-oriented economy. How can socialists with a straight face criticize American Capitalism for being too materialistic, when socialism rejects God and is based on materialism, and when at the same time, American Capitalism is based on faith in God with prosperity a byproduct? Recall the words of Jesus in Matthew 6:31-33 that speak to how our material needs are met after we first seek God in our lives,

Therefore do not worry, saying, 'What shall we eat?' or 'What shall we drink?' or 'What shall we wear?' ... For your heavenly Father knows that you need all these things. But seek first the kingdom of God and His righteousness, and all these things shall be added to you.

Truly, socialism is a worldly philosophy and practice that is characterized by its atheism and immorality. Despite its considerable effort to portray itself as moral, socialism is evil and immoral at its core.

Control (and Violence)

Besides being characterized by atheism and immorality, socialism is also described by control and violence. Socialism is power-based control and elitism. This means that a few people, a ruling elite (be they kings, emperors, dictators, ruling parties, fascists, communists, or other socialists), control the rest of the nation. This power-based control runs the gamut across the entire culture, government, and economy. Depending on the degree of socialism that is implemented, it can run from considerable control to complete dictatorial totalitarianism, from a nanny state to a ruthless dictatorship. In all cases, it involves government-dictated, centralized planning, control, coercion, compulsion, and violence. In all instances, religious freedom, political freedom, and economic freedom are curtailed or eliminated entirely.

You might be wondering now why it is necessary for socialism to rely on control and violence. The answer is simple, but it takes a few paragraphs to see the big picture. Let's see why socialism requires both control and violence.

By rejecting faith in God, socialists also reject the Divine Law found in the Bible. In turn, by rejecting the Divine Law found in the Bible, socialists also reject individualism, human rights, human dignity, human life, liberty, and private property. If the last three items seem familiar, they are found in the Declaration of Independence in these words,

We hold these truths to be self-evident, that all men are created equal, that they are endowed by their Creator with certain unalienable Rights, that among these are Life, Liberty and the pursuit of Happiness. – That to secure these rights, Governments are instituted among Men, deriving their just powers from the consent of the governed ...

Here the pursuit of happiness equates to having and holding private property. For example, if a couple owns their own home, it is a source of accomplishment, security, and happiness. Or, if a young engineer just out of college purchases a new car, it can give them a sense of freedom and happiness. Private property ownership (and the happiness often associated with it) seems to be built into human nature.

Consider next that any individual human action can be done voluntarily (in freedom) or involuntarily (by control, coercion, compulsion, and violence). It is either one or the other. It can't be both at the same time. Similarly, property can be owned individually (private property) or collectively (public property owned by the government).

By rejecting our God-given liberty and private property, socialists also reject the Free Market at the very same time. This means that for socialists all human action can't be voluntary, but instead must be involuntary (or coerced). This also means that for socialists all property can't be private, but instead must be owned publically (by the government). In the words of socialists Karl Marx and Frederick Engels, "... the theory of the communists may be summed up in the single sentence: abolition of private property." [144] Communism, of course, is just one version of socialism. But, all versions of socialism ultimately rest on the rejection of liberty and private property.

With socialism, there can be no private property and no free market. Hence, under socialism, freedom to exchange private property freely among mutually cooperating individuals make no sense whatsoever. In the view of socialists, only a controlled "market" makes sense. To control a market, socialists use government-dictated, centralized planning, control, coercion, compulsion, and violence.

Of course, to take away an individual's private property in the first place also requires control, coercion, compulsion, and violence as well. It is a natural right to hold private property and individuals often will fight (verbally or legally or even physically) to keep their property.

By rejecting our God-given liberty and by rejecting private property, socialists can only resort to control, coercion, compulsion, and violence to force human action. They can't rely on liberty and freedom. They can't rely on the Free Market. They can't guarantee the actions they seek without control, coercion, compulsion, and violence. Depending on the exact nature of a socialist government, this control and violence can take the form of high taxes, stringent regulations, burdensome mandates, imprisonment, beatings, torture, and even death.

By rejecting the *theory of contract* (voluntary actions among freely acting individuals within the Free Market), socialists are only left with the *theory of violence* (involuntary actions by people forced by government control, coercion, compulsion, and violence). [145] In socialism, the theory of violence trumps the theory of contract.

Contrast the control, coercion, compulsion, and violence of socialism with the freedom and peace inherent in the Free Market where everyone is free. There is an incredible difference. American Capitalism is far better for you and your family.

As we have seen, socialism is characterized by atheism and immorality as well as control and violence. What else differentiates socialism from American Capitalism?

Economic Inefficiency (and Poverty)

Since socialism rejects the Free Market, it is left with government-dictated, centralized planning, control, coercion, compulsion, and violence. Unfortunately, for citizens living under socialism, this equates to living without freedom and living with poverty. In "socialist utopias" (countries that live under complete or near complete socialism), the poverty and destitution is profound and the people live in misery. In countries that live under welfare state socialism (covered in Chapter 5), their economies are better off, but they are still moving steadily toward economic bankruptcy.

Let's dive deeper and consider some important findings. In a comprehensive study published in the Cato Journal (a publication of the Cato Institute), information and data from the Fraser Institute, Freedom House, the Heritage Foundation, the International Institute for Management Development, and the World Economic Forum were statistically analyzed. The results were striking. This study showed an incredibly strong relationship between economic liberty and prosperity. In the words of the study's authors, "Economic freedom and economic wealth are inextricably linked. All signs point in the same direction: *those who would like people to enjoy greater prosperity must work to assure greater economic liberty.*"[146]

Under American Capitalism, the economic efficiency of the Free Market results in enormous economic growth and wealth, as well as sustained economic prosperity. Under socialism, without the benefits of the Free Market, socialist economies are economically inefficient and destined to see little or no economic growth. What causes economies to fail under socialism? What's the economic problem with socialism?

The Fundamental Economic Problem with Socialism

F. A. Hayek describes socialism's fundamental economic problem in a book entitled *The Fatal Conceit.*[147] The title gives away the problem in a few simple words. Socialists believe that they are smarter than the Free Market. They believe that as elites they can make all the decisions necessary to run an entire economy and do it better than all the people in a nation freely acting within mutual cooperation. Socialists think they can make all the hiring decisions, allocate all the resources, make all the production decisions, set up all the distribution networks, and set all the prices for the entire economy.

Socialists believe they can make all these plans, and all these billions and billions of planning decisions better than the Free Market. How utterly foolish. Socialists are not only conceited, but they are also naïve and foolish and absolutely wrong!

No amount of good intentions on the part of socialist elites, no higher education degrees obtained by government bureaucrats, no number of supercomputer servers connected by high speed networks, and no combination of all these factors taken together can rival the efficiency of the Free Market.

Indeed, Free Market prices and profits provide the subtle and powerful communications system that produces the most efficient mechanism for the allocation of resources known in the history of this world. That's why the Free Market is such a strong and robust engine of economic efficiency, economic growth, wealth creation, and prosperity.

The fatal conceit is to think that one socialist, one person, one elite leader, one committee official, one party leader, or one government bureaucrat can plan an entire economy. It's simply not possible, no matter how educated, or how smart, or even how well-intentioned (assuming you want to ascribe good intentions to some socialists) that someone might be in the arena of economics. You might ask the question: Why does socialism require just one person to make all the decisions? That's easy.

Let's take a very straight forward example to see why all decisions under socialism eventually come to just one person. Suppose a new socialist government takes over America. This is actually not an unrealistic example. After all, that's why socialists are fighting America's Economic War. They seek to replace American Capitalism with socialism.

Suppose further that the socialists appoint 197 "smart" socialists to run America's approximately 197 distinct industry groups as defined by Investor's Business Daily.[148] Examples of these industry groups include:

- Medical – Ethical Drugs,
- Telecom – Wireless Services,
- Food – Meat Products,
- Internet – Content, and
- Household – Appliances.[149]

Assume for purposes of our discussion that the socialist elite leader for the Medical – Ethical Drugs industry thinks that it's best to invest $5.76B into his industry next year. Presumably, the other socialist leaders will make similar determinations. But, back at The White House, the president's staff compiles all the plans from all the industry leaders. They find that there is definitely not enough money for each industry leader to get what they want for their particular industry.

Note that with socialism, we can comfortably forecast that revenues will be down and that there will a major budget shortfall, because taxes are so high, because productivity will be so low, and because people don't have any incentive to work hard under socialism.

With millions and millions of small plans, medium plans, and big plans to be formulated and with billions and billions of economic decisions to be made about hiring, resource allocation, production, distribution, and pricing, there are bound to be a gigantic number of conflicts, trade-offs, and turf wars. There are also bound to be a lot of indecision, uncertainty, confusion, and chaos. We can also throw in that there will be lots of bribes and lots of corruption, as we generally find in socialist systems. The results of all of these problems are delays, shortages, inefficiencies, and government waste on a level never experienced under American Capitalism.

The bottom line for our example is that the 197 industry plans made by those 197 "smart" socialist leaders will be in conflict. Just one person at the top of this hierarchy, probably the socialist president (or dictator), will have to make the final determination on every plan and every economic decision throughout the American Economy. Some ultimate authority will have to referee the conflicts and make the final decisions. All those millions and millions of plans and those billions and billions off decisions will fall to one person to make.

Only a very conceited socialist can think that they can make billions and billions of economic decisions correctly and that they can outperform the Free Market. How conceited. How fatal (from an economic perspective).

The fundamental economic problem with socialism is that it can't accurately and efficiently make all the plans and decisions necessary to run an entire economy. It can't make all the calculations. It can't determine all the prices. It can't determine all the wages. It can't allocate all the resources. It can't make all the production decisions. It can't make all the distribution decisions. It can't do all these things, it can't make all these decisions, and it can't make all the many other related decisions efficiently, effectively, and in a timely manner.

There is no mechanism for socialists to accomplish these tasks. Socialism's only tools are power, control, coercion, compulsion, violence, guesswork, and corruption.

Without question, we can say that socialism is characterized by economic inefficiency and the poverty that results from its massive inefficiency. Example after example abound. The study published in the Cato Journal cited earlier, showing the strong correlation between economic freedom and prosperity, backs up this fact as well.

Truly, socialism is about atheism and immorality, control and violence, as well as economic inefficiency and poverty. What else can be said about socialism?

Groups of "Victims" (and Distrust)

Socialism is also characterized by groups of "victims" and distrust. While American Capitalism is about family and trust, socialism rejects the idea of family and its philosophy leads to distrust. Indeed, socialism is not concerned about families, except to the extent that socialism can weaken American Capitalism by reducing the family's influence on our culture.

However, of far greater importance to socialists than families, are groups of "victims." Socialists see the world in terms of raw power, groups (or classes) of "victims", and their struggles for power. In the words of Karl Marx and Frederick Engels: "The history of all hitherto existing society … is the history of class struggles … Freeman and slave, patrician and plebeian, lord and serf, guild-master and journeyman, … in a word, oppressor and oppressed …"[150]

In today's America, socialists divide up our nation into classes such as corporations vs. workers, men vs. women, and various racial and ethnic groups pitted against one another. Socialists promote and thrive on class conflict. It is part of their power-based, negative thinking. It is part of their rejection of individualism. Socialists see groups, where American Capitalists see individuals. Socialists see class conflicts, where American Capitalists see freely-chosen and mutually beneficial cooperation.

Where did socialists come up with their odd theory of class struggle? Some believe that it originated with the ideas of Charles Darwin and Herbert Spencer and the school of thinking that followed known as Darwinism.[151] Charles Darwin was the British naturalist and author of the book *On the Origin of Species*,[152] while Herbert Spencer was the philosopher who coined the term "survival of the fittest."[153] Darwinism first suggested that there were fundamental struggles between classes and between races.[154] But, regardless of the precise origin of this off-beat theory of class struggle, it does not describe reality.

In nature, classes of animals don't struggle with other classes of animals for their existence. Birds are not in a class struggle for existence with dogs. Fish are not oppressing flowers. However, individual animals sometimes struggle for their own individual existence. For example, a deer might struggle for its own food during a period of extreme drought. In nature, a struggle for existence is an individual matter and is definitely not a group concern.

In a similar way (and contrary to socialist thinking), groups of people don't struggle for existence against other groups of people. New Yorkers are not in a class struggle with Californians. Men are not in a class struggle against women. Of course, there might be some individuals in life that struggle with other individuals as, for example, when two people vie for a promotion at work. Yet, this type of situation is hardly a "class struggle for existence."

Indeed, civilizations are all about mutual cooperation. Wars and other acts of violence (including the acts of violence perpetrated in the name of socialist "progress") are anomalies within the history of human cooperation. Unfortunately, for all of us, wars and violence occur far too often.

While American Capitalism thrives on free, mutual, and peaceful cooperation among all people, socialism works hard to build artificial class struggles where they don't exist. In so doing, socialism sows the seeds of conflict and violence. Socialism, operating on an international level, also sows the seeds of armed conflict and war. In contrast, mutual cooperation among nations through free trade promotes peace and harmony as well as economic growth and wealth on a global scale. After all, free trade is simply free markets working across national borders. That's why the philosophy of American Capitalism believes in free trade among the nations of the world.

Creating groups of "victims" and class conflicts have another negative impact. These socialist practices lead to distrust among people. Thinking that one group is "after you" because you belong to a different group, a group of "victims," fosters a sense of alienation from other people. It also cultivates distrust. Being a "victim," means you might think people are "out to get you." You get more sensitive. You get more sensitized to potential and perceived insults.

None of these feelings are very positive or very healthy. Distrust doesn't promote internal peace and harmony within individuals. Distrust also doesn't promote external peace and harmony among individuals.

In addition to its philosophy of creating unnatural class struggles, another factor that leads to distrust within socialism is its rejection of truth and morality. When people know that their leaders and their government are immoral, when people learn that truth and morality do not exist, it is difficult to trust anyone. Society and civilization ultimately break down.

Without trust, it is difficult to sustain economic prosperity because individuals need to trust each other to function together in free, mutual, and peaceful cooperation. Francis Fukuyama, in his book on trust, explains,

... one of the most important lessons we can learn from an examination of economic life is that a nation's well-being, as well as its ability to compete, is conditioned by a single, pervasive cultural characteristic: the level of trust inherent in the society.[155]
.

Certainly, trust is important to American Capitalism. It is definitely a powerful factor in American Culture. American Capitalism is about family and trust, while socialism is about groups of "victims" and distrust. There is one final characteristic of socialism we should consider next.

Moral Decay and Social Disintegration

Socialism is also about moral decay and social disintegration. With the rejection of morality, socialism results in moral decay across the entire spectrum of culture. In Chapter 1, we saw how socialist immorality adversely impacts dating, relationships, marriages, and families. It also brings brutality and violence as well as sexual depravities to the arts, music, literature, and entertainment. Its negative influence extends from partial birth abortions to the meaninglessness of "anonymous death" (that we mention later in Appendix A).

From the heights of morality with Christian-based American Capitalism, to the depths of immorality under socialism is a long, tortuous, Road of Human Suffering and Indignity. It ends in moral and economic bankruptcy. It ends in the loss of religious freedom, political freedom, and economic freedom. It ends in human degradation, suffering, destitution, poverty, violence, and death.

The final result of socialism (in all its various forms) is moral decay and social disintegration.

Socialism – A Summary

Socialism is power-based control and elitism. It rejects God. Its rejects religion and morality. It even rejects the truth. In some instances, it rejects reason altogether. Socialism also rejects individualism, family and marriage. Socialism is immoral.

Despite its immorality, socialism seduces many intelligent people. For example, for the warm-hearted and those with good intentions, socialism offers the false hope of making a real difference in people's lives. For others, socialism offers unchecked power, manifest opportunities for corruption, and the chance for creating "social experiments." For the lazy and those that seek to avoid work, socialism offers a free ride.

For many, the seduction of socialism is free money and free sex. For these people, socialism offers the false promise of unlimited government programs to meet their material needs and unlimited sexual encounters without the cares and responsibilities of family and marriage.

But, socialism's false promises are grounded in immorality and can't be achieved. Instead, socialism always leads to moral and economic bankruptcy. Plus, socialism's insatiable power and control take away your religious freedom, political freedom, and economic freedom.

In contrast to American Capitalism, socialism is about atheism and immorality, control and violence, economic inefficiency and poverty, groups of "victims" and distrust, as well as moral decay and social disintegration.

The accompanying table summarizes the differences between American Capitalism and socialism. The differences are striking. Socialism is the exact opposite of American Capitalism. While American Capitalism is moral, socialism is immoral. Truly, the philosophy and practice of socialism are evil.

Summary of the Differences between American Capitalism and Socialism		
Characteristics	**American Capitalism**	**Socialism**
Summary	God-Inspired Freedom and Individualism	Power-Based Control and Elitism
Spiritual and Moral, Cultural	Faith (and Morality)	Atheism (and Immorality)
Political	Freedom (and Peace)	Control (and Violence)
Economic	Free Markets (and Prosperity)	Economic Inefficiency (and Poverty)
Sociological	Family (and Trust)	Groups of "Victims" (and Distrust)
Impact on Civilization	Spiritual and Material Human Growth	Moral Decay and Social Disintegration

With an understanding of American Capitalism and socialism, let's next look at various attempts to create a "third way," a hybrid system that combines American Capitalism and socialism.

Chapter 5

Hampered Capitalism and Welfare State Socialism – Attempts at a "Third Way"

> "The power to tax involves, as Chief Justice Marshall
> pertinently observed, the power to destroy."
> Ludwig von Mises[156]

Clearly, American Capitalism is superior to socialism in moral, political, and economic terms. In addition, from a practical point of view, we know that adopting socialist thinking always lead to moral and economic bankruptcy. Yet, despite the reasoned moral and intellectual case for American Capitalism and despite the hard practical evidence in the real world against socialism, socialists continue to seduce some people into thinking that socialism is better than American Capitalism.

The Seduction of Socialism – Part 2

One approach for seducing people is for socialists to argue for a so-called "third way" and then, to use the "third way" as a bridge to more complete socialism. Alternatively, some socialists recognize many of the severe problems associated with socialism and propose a "third way" in the hopes of getting a better form of socialism. They incorrectly think that they can mix and match features of American Capitalism and socialism into a workable, hybrid "third way" system. Such hybrids systems are simply not sustainable as we will see later in this chapter.

As you can probably imagine, a "third way" hybrid system can take a variety of different forms. In this chapter, we group these "third way" attempts into two major categories, hampered capitalism and welfare state socialism. We will also cover progressive socialism which is an attempt to "progress" toward welfare state socialism.

Regardless of the particular "third way" chosen, no hybrid "third way" is viable and sustainable. Each "third way" leads to increasing socialism and ultimately to moral and economic bankruptcy. The degree to which socialist thinking is adopted and practiced will determine the speed at which a civilization rushes toward moral decay, social disintegration, and abject poverty.

Indeed, the arguments for a "third way" are just another tactic for achieving socialism. In America's Economic War, you and your family not only face arguments for socialism outright, but you also face arguments for hampered capitalism and welfare state socialism. It's important to understand these arguments and to realize why they don't make sense.

Armed with knowledge about "third way" hybrid systems, you can better understand America's Economic War and the cultural, political and economic debates of our times.

Let's start by learning about hampered capitalism and then see, why it seduces many smart people.

The Seduction of Hampered Capitalism

Hampered capitalism is really what its name implies. Hampered capitalism is American Capitalism that is hampered by government intervention. The intervention can take the form of excessive taxation, heavy regulation, burdensome mandates, foolish subsidies, and any other actions, restrictions, and interference in American Capitalism. Hampered capitalism also includes any inappropriate limitations placed on your religious freedom, political freedom, and economic freedom. Hampered capitalism is, in effect, a limited form of socialism operating within American Capitalism.

Why are people seduced into thinking that hampered capitalism is better than American Capitalism? Usually, socialists argue that the Free Market doesn't work perfectly and it must be regulated and controlled. Or, companies need to be regulated to prevent them from selling inferior products or defrauding customers? Or, they say that the government needs higher taxes to finance some needs that are not being met.

Nothing in this world is perfect. We all know that fact. If we want per-fection, we need to wait until we are in heaven. Yet, the fact that American Capitalism is not perfect does not make socialism a better alternative. Socialism clearly fails in principle and in practice.

Yet, the idea of tweaking American Capitalism is seductive. Bright intellectuals and smart leaders think they can outdo Freedom and the Free

Market by government interference. But, socialism always fails to achieve its intended purposes. Plus, it always wastes economic resources in the process. Then, new socialist policies, programs, and plans must be invented to fix the original socialist policies, programs, and plans that failed. Of course, additional resources must be consumed and wasted.

With few exceptions, the Free Market sternly regulates entrepreneurs and businesses. A company does not need the government to direct its product development. A company that produces an inferior product, or that provides a terrible service, or that cheats consumers, will soon be out of business. Consumers will rapidly change their buying habits and individuals will quickly alter their purchasing decisions to best meet their own needs. The Free Market automatically moves resources to those best able to meet individuals' needs.

None of the socialist arguments for hampered capitalism hold up under close scrutiny. Instead, the drawbacks and costs to government intervention abound as we see below.

The Costs of Government Intervention

Ronald Reagan once said in describing government intervention that: "If it moves, tax it. If it keeps moving, regulate it. If it stops moving, subsidize it."[157] Indeed, this turns out to be a very apt description of government intervention under hampered capitalism.

Under hampered capitalism, overall wealth creation is cut dramatically and the economy does not reach its full potential.

Under hampered capitalism, tax and regulatory policies hinder the Free Market, causing it to be much less efficient and much less effective. Business and technological innovations are restricted and economic growth is throttled back. The costs to the economy in economic and financial terms are tremendous. The costs to you and your family are very significant.

Under hampered capitalism, you and your family pay higher taxes on your income, food, energy, and a myriad of other items. Under hampered capitalism, you and your family also receive lower salaries and wages because companies can't afford to pay you as much for your labor services as you are worth. Instead, employers pay you less than you are worth and use the money to pay their higher taxes and the costs associated with the numerous mandates placed upon their operation.

Under hampered capitalism, you and your family pay more for products and services, because businesses must pay for unnecessary regulations and mandates. Business need to pass along these costs of government intervention to their customers in the form of higher prices.

Remember a very important fact in economics. Businesses don't pay taxes and businesses don't pay for any other costs of government intervention (such as regulations, mandates, subsidies, and tariffs). Consumers pay for all taxes and all regulations and all costs of government intervention in the form of higher prices for the products and services they buy. So, in the end, you and your family are footing the bill for government intervention under hampered capitalism.

Plus, there are also opportunity costs that come with hampered capitalism. Economists and others often talk about opportunity costs. What are they?

Opportunity costs are the lost benefits of not choosing one option, when instead you choose a different, second option. For example, if you decide to attend graduate school for two years to get an MBA after graduating from college, you will lose two years of earning power. The opportunity cost for getting an MBA in this case is two years of income. Of course, you might choose to accept this opportunity cost in order to maximize your long term career prospects and earnings potential. That's an individual economic decision.

Under hampered capitalism, there are also many unknown opportunity costs. For every excessive tax, for every heavy regulation, for every burdensome mandate, for every foolish subsidy, and for every other action, restriction, and interference on American Capitalism, we can never know all the opportunity costs the American Economy has paid. Where would those tax dollars have gone? What would a corporation have done with the money it paid for a particular regulation? Where would the Free Market have directed those dollars to be invested that were siphoned off instead to a government mandate? How better might the Free Market have spent that subsidy money? What innovations were stifled? What new products and services never were brought to market? What companies were never started? What new jobs were never created? What suffering was not relieved? What needs were not met? How would you and your family's lives have been better? The opportunity costs for a highly taxed and tightly regulated economy are enormous indeed.

Inflation – An Insidious Tax

Another often overlooked cost of government intervention that can occur within hampered capitalism is the cost of inflation. Inflation is an insidious form of taxation that robs people who save of the value of their savings. It also cheats people who work of the value of their earnings. Inflation is a result of socialist thinking and socialist policies. It's an easy way for the government to raise taxes without individuals knowing that it's happening to them.

What is inflation? How does government intervention cause inflation? Why is it effectively a tax on you and your family? It's actually quite easy to understand as we will see.

Inflation, as you probably realize, is simply an overall increase in the prices we all pay for products and services across the entire economy. It is not just a price increase for one item, for a special reason and for a limited time. For example, if the orange crop in Florida is hurt one season by a severe frost and the supply of oranges is cut significantly, the price of oranges will likely go up for awhile. This is not inflation.

Let's consider a different kind of example. We saw in Chapter 1 that the government's ethanol biofuel policy has raised corn prices dramatically (by 70% in one six month period alone). This, in turn, is triggering major price increases in many food items such as meats, eggs, cheese, and soft drinks because corn is used for animal feed and for corn syrup. It is often true that government regulations and mandates can cause significant price increases for specific products and services. But, again, no matter how painful such spot increases are, this is not across-the-board inflation for most or all consumer prices.

Instead, inflation refers to the increase in the overall level of prices on most or all products and services. To illustrate, if you get a pen and pad out and list your family's expenses for a month, including mortgage payment or rent, gas and oil for your cars, groceries, restaurants, heat, electricity, phone, medical insurance, doctors and dentists, cable TV, entertainment, and all your other family expenses, you can add them up and learn your family's total expenses for the month. If you do this again in one year, you will probably get a different total for all of your family's monthly expenses. Assuming your lifestyle hasn't changed very much and your family is spending 5% more than last year, you have just experienced inflation.

What causes inflation? This is a topic that has been studied by economists and the evidence is very substantial and very conclusive. Inflation results from an increase in the supply of money over and above the increase in the output of the overall economy. In other words, inflation results from the government increasing the money supply too much. The government creates a greater amount of money than the amount of products and services that the economy is creating.

Think of it this way. The American Economy in a given year produces an incredibly large amount of goods and services. At the time of this writing, America's Gross Domestic Product or GDP is about an estimated $14T or $14,000,000,000,000.[158] We have a correspondingly large money supply to permit our economy to operate effectively and efficiently. But, if the government chooses to increase our money supply by a larger amount than the actual amount of output of additional products and services, there is more money chasing the actual products and services available to purchase. This means prices for those products and services are bid up. Eventually, these price increases permeate the entire economy and our cost of living increases.

In fact, the greater the increase in the money supply in proportion to the increase in products and services, the greater will be the rate of inflation and the greater will be the increase in the cost of living for everyone.

Indeed, the impact of this inflation is to debase or devalue the money we use. Simply put, inflation forces you to spend more money for the products and services you purchase. This is equivalent to the money in your wallet being worth less. In effect, your money is devalued.

It's important to note that socialists have long recognized the fact that inflation is an effective means to destroy American Capitalism. John Maynard Keynes wrote that:

Lenin is said to have declared that the best way to destroy the Capitalist System was to debauch the currency. By a continuing process of inflation, governments can confiscate, secretly and unobserved, an important part of the wealth of their citizens. ... Lenin was certainly right. There is no subtler, no surer means of overturning the existing basis of society than to debauch the currency. The process engages all the hidden forces of economic law on the side of destruction, and does it in a manner which not one man in a million is able to diagnose.[159]

Debauch means to devalue, debase, or degrade. In this context, it means to devalue the money supply.

But, how does the government actually increase the money supply and thereby cause inflation? That's easy to understand too, although probably very few people understand the process or even realize that the process is happening at all.

It starts with the federal government deciding to spend more money than it takes in from tax revenues. In any given year, Congress creates a budget. If that budget calls for a deficit, that is, for spending to exceed revenues, the government must find a way to cover its high expenditures.[160] While your family must live on a balanced budget or else face certain financial problems including potential bankruptcy, the government has no such limitation. It can effectively print more money whenever it chooses to.

Technically, the federal government can raise taxes or it can sell bonds to the public to cover federal deficits. However, increasing the money supply is an easier method politically. Voters don't like tax increases. Plus, consumers and businesses don't like higher interest rates generated when government borrowing competes with individual borrowing. So, inflation is a much easier approach for covering those federal deficits.[161]

To increase the money supply to cover the federal deficits, the U.S. Treasury sells bonds to the Federal Reserve System. The Federal Reserve System can pay for the bonds by either printing new Federal Reserve Notes or by crediting the U.S. Treasury on its books. Either way, by selling newly created bonds to the Federal Reserve, the U.S. Treasury has additional money that it can now spend. So, the federal deficits are covered.[162]

Incidentally, *monetary policy* is the government's strategy and plan for managing the nation's money supply. *Inflationary monetary policy* is a government's monetary policy that results in inflation.

With the power to create new money out of thin air, government officials can use the money for any number of social programs. But, of course, you and your family and all of us are footing the bill for these social programs through inflation and the increased cost of living. Inflation, then, amounts to nothing more than one more tax on all of us. It's an insidious and hidden tax that impacts those that work the hardest, save diligently, and invest prudently. Is it moral?

Inflation is Immoral

Inflation is immoral because it hurts so many and especially those that are least able to afford it, the poor and the elderly. These are individuals who have very little in the way of money and financial resources. To make their meager resources lose value through government-created inflation is cruel and tragic. To make the poor and elderly dependent on impersonal and bureaucratic government social programs is demeaning and dehumanizing.

Inflation is immoral because it saddles future generations with the costs of the current government's reckless spending. Our children and grandchildren and great grandchildren will have to pay the bill for today's social programs. They will be burdened with debt that they never voted for and that they never approved of. They will be burdened with debt that they never incurred and that they never received benefits for.

Inflation is immoral because it makes people think their wages and salaries are higher than they actually are. People initially feel good when they get a pay increase, only to realize later that sadly their money doesn't go as far as it used to go. Moreover, they find that they are now paying higher income taxes and possibly even paying the Alternative Minimum Tax (AMT) because their higher pay has pushed them into a still higher tax bracket. Such bracket creep is a means for the government to raise tax revenues without actually raising taxes in the usual manner.

Inflation is immoral because it makes people think that their homes are worth more than they truly are. Those equity increases are not as high as people might think. To find your real equity increase (if any), you need to subtract out the costs of inflation. Economists use the term inflation-adjusted to take into account the cost of inflation in various calculations.

Inflation is immoral because it helps people to become dependent on government social programs and because it causes people to stay dependent on government social programs. As socialist programs take greater control of the economy and the resources of the nation, the recipients of government social programs become increasingly dependent and increasingly poor.

Inflation is immoral because it makes a mockery of legal contracts. People are paid what they contractually agreed to accept in dollars. But, the dollars they accept are not as valuable when they receive the money, as when they originally signed the contract. The correct dollar value might be paid in full; but, the actual value promised is not paid in full.

Indeed, inflation is immoral because it destroys the value of the money that we use every day, in so many different ways.

Inflation is the product of socialism and its immoral approach to life. Inflation is truly one more cost of government intervention that can occur with socialist thinking.

Certainly, the allure of hampered capitalism is real. The idea of improving on American Capitalism sounds appealing to many at first. But, the cold, hard reality is that hampered capitalism doesn't improve American Capitalism. It hamstrings and retards the American Economy. It cuts economic growth. It wastes valuable resources. Plus, it leads directly to welfare state socialism by financing social programs with high government-imposed taxes and government-generated inflation.

Let's next turn our attention to welfare state socialism and see why it also seduces so many good people.

The Seduction of Welfare State Socialism

If government intervention under hampered capitalism continues to damage the economy with more and more, inefficient and ineffective social programs, economic growth languishes and the entire economy falters. At the same time, the government begins to resemble an enormous nanny state with promises of social programs for all. The nanny state is simply welfare state socialism in practice.

Indeed, welfare state socialism is a form of socialism that claims to focus on developing social programs to "help" people and bases its legitimacy on its so-called "good" intentions. It typically offers "cradle to grave" social programs for groups of "victims" and for people in general.[163] In fact, it's a close philosophical cousin to Christian socialism with a false appeal to the morality associated with helping people in need. In reality, welfare state socialism is still socialism. It is still immoral and it still fails for all the same reasons.

What are its "good" intentions? At a high level, welfare state socialism claims that it wants to "help" people. Of course, that's hardly an objective anyone can disagree with. More specifically, proponents of welfare state socialism criticize American Capitalism because there is some poverty within capitalism, because there is inequality in income and wealth among individuals, and because there is a lack of financial security.[164] So, the "good" intentions (or goals) of welfare state socialism can be summed up rather easily. They are: (1) the elimination of poverty; (2) the elimination of inequality in income; (3) the elimination of inequality in wealth; and (4) the elimination of financial insecurity.

While these goals might seem desirable at first glance, please look again more closely. Let's start by taking the intention of eliminating poverty. What does that mean?

Socialism Can't Eliminate Poverty

In life, there are two types of poverty: the *poverty of destitution* and the *poverty of comparison*. The poverty of destitution is a situation in which an individual can't meet their own basic physical needs for survival. They might not have adequate shelter or enough food to eat, for example. In contrast, the poverty of comparison is a different type of situation in which an individual doesn't have as many material possessions as some others do. Such a person in today's America might live in a small apartment and have only one older car to drive. They probably are not able to afford a vacation to a tropical resort or many other luxury items. So, in comparison to others who are better off financially, such a person might be said to be in a state of *comparative poverty*, but not in a state of *destitute poverty*.

Certainly, a poor person living in America today lives a far better life than a poor person did in the year 750 AD or even in 1750 AD. In fact, it's possible that a poor person in America today lives a far better life than even a rich person did in the year 750 AD or in 1750 AD.

So, while the intention of welfare state socialists might be to eliminate poverty, just what kind of poverty are they trying to eliminate? It must be the poverty of comparison. After all, with billions and billions of dollars being spent by government each year on poverty programs and additional dollars being donated by numerous private charitable organizations and millions of individuals, how can anyone be suffering from the poverty of destitution in America today?

Consider, for example, that Federal spending for Social Security, Medicare, Medicaid, and other entitlements (excluding net interest) in 2008 is estimated to be $1,551B. That's about 11% of America's Gross Domestic Product (GDP) and approximately 53% of all program spending.[165] If anyone is suffering from the poverty of destitution in America, it is difficult to blame it on a lack of Federal spending. (It's possible that quite a lot of money is being gobbled up by waste, fraud, and corruption, however.)

Also, think about the 1960's and the Great Society and the so-called War on Poverty. Why didn't those social programs end poverty? Again, it's hard to believe that the poverty of destitution exists in the United States today given the tremendous amount of money being spent by government and the large amount of money donated by private charitable organizations and compassionate individuals.

Instead, if it's the poverty of comparison that socialists seek to eliminate, then they must want everyone to have the exact same income and the exact same level of wealth. This way there are no economic differences among people and no poverty (or wealth) of comparison. If this is the case, then the goal of eliminating poverty is really the same as the twin socialist goals of eliminating inequality in income and eliminating inequality in wealth.

Of course, the result of achieving these twin goals will be for everyone to live in poverty, presumably at the exact same level of poverty. This makes sense since socialism always leads to moral and economic poverty.

It is also important to realize that over time we can expect some welfare states to devolve slowly into more complete socialist states and then, directly into destitute poverty. Some other welfare states might not go the route of complete socialism. These other welfare states might simply go bankrupt, when their people get tired of their government's bankrupt social programs, broken promises and unrealized goals, and when the people lose trust in their government altogether. Usually, when individuals lose trust in their government, a change in the government is inevitable by either ballots or bullets.

When thinking about wealth and poverty, it is important to remember that American Capitalism fosters capital formation (see Chapter 3) and creates economic growth and wealth. Socialism, on the other hand, consumes capital and destroys economic growth and wealth. It never promotes capital formation or capital accumulation (as some economists have called it). In the words of Ludwig von Mises: "History does not provide any example of capital accumulation brought about by a government."[166]

Socialists think that the economic growth and wealth created under capitalism will continue forever and will continue to fuel their social programs. Socialists don't realize that by destroying American Capitalism they are cutting off the economic growth and wealth they require to pay for welfare state social programs.

American Capitalism is not the cause of poverty. Socialism (in any of its various forms) is the cause of poverty.

In America and in other nations, socialist thinking has not eliminated the poverty of destitution. Around the world, socialism has instead been the cause of much destitute poverty. Socialism can't eliminate the poverty of destitution. Moreover, in seeking to eliminate the poverty of comparison, socialism is really pursuing the twin goals of the elimination of inequality in income and wealth. But, if socialism succeeds in reaching these two negative goals, it will create the poverty of destitution in the process. We will learn more about this outcome in the next section.

Socialism Can't Eliminate Inequality in Income and Wealth without Causing Poverty

In nature, differences and variations enrich life, empower life, and propel life forward. In contrast, uniformity is a close cousin of mediocrity.

Consider the atmosphere. As the earth rotates through its annual orbital trajectory, the sun unevenly heats the earth's atmosphere and surfaces. The earth's tilt and the very shape of the earth itself also contribute to this uneven heating. The temperature differences, or thermal variations as some might prefer to call them, generate powerful barometric pressure gradients. (Gradient is just another word for difference.) In turn, these pressure differences manifest themselves as *Highs* and *Lows* in the earth's atmosphere and big letter H's and L's on the weather maps you see on TV every night. These H's and L's drive our short term weather, our long term climate, and maintaining a healthy energy balance across the earth. The bottom line is that these temperature and pressure differences are built into the very fabric of our life and human existence.

Consider another example, integrated circuits and the electronic products you live with everyday. These rely on a natural phenomenon known as electricity. They are driven on differences. Physicists and electronic engineers (EE's) call these *potential differences*. Such differences in electric potential between two locations in a circuit drive electric current. Without these *potential differences*, your cell phone, your notebook computer, and your TV, not to mention hundreds of other electronic devices you own, would not function.

Finally, think about one last example, the differences between the sexes. Men and women are truly different; both sexes are unique, special, and different in their own God-created ways. Using John Gray's words to describe these dramatic differences: "Men Are from Mars, Women Are from Venus."[167] In fact, these differences enliven and enrich our lives. They make life more challenging and rewarding, and certainly more enjoyable.

Without the differences built into life by God, life would be rather dull, routine, and listless without the bright, colorful differences we see all around us in our lives and in nature.

The economics of life works much the same way. Income differences and wealth differences among businesses and individuals inspire entrepreneurs to create faster, better, and cheaper products and services. They also motivate individuals to improve their education and skills, to think smarter, to work harder, to save more, to invest wisely, and to shop prudently. These differences also encourage individuals to change jobs if they can get ahead faster, or if they can receive better pay or benefits. Income and wealth differences create healthy motivation for, and solid competition among, individuals, entrepreneurs, and businesses alike.

Ludwig von Mises reflects on the importance of income and wealth inequality for economic growth in these words:

Even those who look upon the inequality of wealth and incomes as a deplorable thing, cannot deny that it makes for progressing capital accumulation. And it is additional capital accumulation alone that brings about technological improvement, rising wage rates, and a higher standard of living.[168]

Indeed, it is income and wealth differences that drive economic growth and new wealth creation in our economy. It is socialists that deplore these differences.

It is vitally important to note that the American Economy is vibrant and is certainly not static. The dynamic nature of American Capitalism means that someone with a low or middle income can become a financial success overnight. There are countless stories of individuals with brilliant new ideas who became millionaires when their ideas were commercialized. In a similar way, many creative entertainers have become instant pop stars, amassing fortunes in just a period of a few months or years. With American Capitalism, upward economic mobility is not only possible, but it happens all the time.

The reverse is true too. Companies that were once great successes can get out of touch with their customers. They can move from profitability to lackluster performance in a short period of time. They sometimes are even forced to file for bankruptcy when their products and services don't meet the needs of customers.

Consider, too, some facts about upward economic mobility within American Capitalism. According to Arthur C. Brooks,

The U.S. Census Bureau, the Urban Institute, and the Federal Reserve have all pointed out that, as a general rule, about a fifth of the people in the lowest income quintile will climb to a higher quintile within a year, and that about half will rise within a decade. ... Millions and millions of poor Americans climb out of the ranks of poverty every year.[169]

In other words, if we break all incomes into quintiles (that is, five buckets with the same number of people in each bucket), 20% of individuals will move out of the bottom income quintile within one year and 50% of individuals will move out within 10 years. That's considerable upward income mobility. In America, individuals move out of poverty rather dramatically.

In his research, Arthur C. Brooks found that instead of income equality causing happiness, happiness is really caused when individuals think that have a chance of moving upward economically. Opportunity and upward economic mobility are the keys to happiness, as opposed to socialism's false promise of income equality.

So, both upward and downward economic mobility are possible in American Capitalism. Income differences and wealth differences drive the dynamic creation and destruction of products, services, jobs, professions, businesses, and sometimes entire industries. Joseph A. Schumpeter captured this dynamic nature of American Capitalism with the phrase "Creative Destruction." In his words:

Capitalism, then, is by nature a form or method of economic change and not only never is but never can be stationary. ... This process of Creative Destruction is the essential fact about capitalism.[170]

In contrast, socialists seek uniformity, not diversity. When you think of it, that's rather odd given the lip-service some socialists give to diversity. Their idea of diversity involves diversity only when it promotes class struggles and other politically-correct, socialist thinking.

In particular, socialists seek the elimination of inequality in income and the elimination of inequality in wealth among all people. But, without these differences, there is no motivation to create economic growth and wealth. Without inequality in income and wealth, the Free Market would collapse because these differences drive motivation, competition, and growth. If everyone received the same income, what incentive would people have to do better, or for that matter, what incentive would people have to do anything at all. Plus, what incentives would entrepreneurs and businesses have to create new, faster, better, and cheaper products and services. Subsequently, if no one worked at all and if nothing new were ever created, the entire economy would crumble.

Incidentally, because socialism destroys all economic incentives, that's the reason why socialism needs control, coercion, compulsion, and violence to force people to do what they want them to do. American Capitalism relies on economic incentives to achieve free, mutual, and peaceful cooperation. Without economic incentives, socialism relies on government-dictated control, coercion, compulsion, and violence to force human action.

Indeed, if welfare state socialists achieve their twin goals of the elimination of income inequality and the elimination of wealth inequality, the result will be the elimination of economic growth and the elimination of wealth creation. This will quickly lead to capital consumption, to a declining standard of living, to economic poverty, and eventually to utter destitution.

Socialism can't eliminate poverty. It also can't eliminate inequality in income and wealth without creating more poverty. Let's next look at socialism's fourth "good" intention.

Socialism Can't Eliminate Financial Insecurity

Socialism also seduces many intelligent people by criticizing the financial insecurity that exists under American Capitalism. Socialists cite the fact that businesses can close down. New technologies can destroy old jobs, causing people to become temporarily unemployed. Interest rates can rise causing people with adjustable-rate mortgages (ARM's) to have their payments increase. Some prices can go up, hurting consumer budgets. Some prices can go down, hurting profits and jobs.

Things change. With a dynamic economy under American Capitalism, change happens and some financial insecurity happens along the way. This is part of economic growth and wealth creation. The Free Market automatically re-directs resources to the places where they are most needed. This means changes are taking place constantly.

Individuals change. Needs change. Individuals change their minds too, and their needs change at the same time. Eventually, these needs propagate throughout the economy. Prices and profits change. Products and services change. Jobs and professions change. Businesses and industries change. Some old products, services, jobs, businesses, and industries are lost. At the same time, new products, services, jobs, businesses, and industries are created.

Why do socialists lament if gasoline prices go up one week? But, they don't celebrate if gasoline prices go down the next week? For that matter, why don't socialists celebrate if notebook computer prices or cosmetic surgery prices or other prices go down over time?

Why are socialists against change in the Free Market? Why do socialists think prices need to be frozen in time within the Free Market? Why do socialists think things always must stay the same? Or, is it that the only change socialists really seek is to replace American Capitalism with socialism?

Some financial insecurity is inherent with Freedom and the Free Market. In life, there is some insecurity in nearly everything we do. If you hop in your car and drive to the supermarket or drive to a baseball game, you might get into an accident. If you take a vacation and fly to a warm, sunny place, you might hit bad weather and waste your money, or worse yet, your plane might crash in route to your destination. If you buy a ticket to the movies, you might see it and then think it's a dud. If you quit your job and take a new position across town, you might just find out that your previous job was actually much better. Risk and insecurity abound in life.

Some financial insecurity is good in a sense too. Some financial insecurity pushes us to save and invest for a rainy day or for retirement. Some financial insecurity also encourages us to be careful with our money and to spend wisely. Plus, it motivates us to work hard and keep our jobs, in case sales drop and some individuals must be laid off.

But, socialism seems to reject the notion of financial insecurity. At least, it is willing to tempt you with the prospect of government-sponsored financial security, even though it recognizes that it can never guarantee you and your family any given lifestyle or any true financial security over the long run. Many people succumb to this temptation and foolishly believe it is worth giving up their freedom to obtain some semblance of financial security (even the security of being in shared, destitute poverty).

Indeed, welfare state socialism promises "cradle to grave" financial security. If any economic system could honestly offer such security, it would be a marvelous achievement. But, no economic system can. Socialism certainly can't deliver financial security. The problem with socialism is that it can't deliver on any of its empty promises. Yet, many people naively believe their phony story and socialism seduces them into supporting this evil and immoral philosophy.

Why can't socialism deliver on its "good" intention to eliminate financial insecurity? The answer is simple. It would have to eliminate change. To do this, it would have to eliminate Freedom and the Free Market. This, of course, would lead to moral and economic bankruptcy. Can you imagine living in a world that didn't change? It's surreal. Can you envision living in a nation that's economically bankrupt? Destitute poverty is definitely not a form of financial security. The bottom line is you and your family's financial security would go out the window under socialism.

As Ludwig von Mises bluntly pointed out: "what counts in life and reality is … not good intentions, but accomplishments."[171] With regard to the "good" intentions that welfare state socialism uses to seduce intelligent people, socialism can't deliver on their phony promises. "Socialist utopias" invariably turn out to be morally and economically bankrupt. Besides, their "good" intentions sound good at first, but really are deceptive in and of themselves. Specifically, welfare state socialism can't eliminate poverty. Welfare state socialism also can't eliminate income and wealth inequality without causing more poverty than already exists. Finally, welfare state socialism can't eliminate financial insecurity without eliminating Freedom and the Free Market and without destroying American Capitalism and the American Civilization in the process. Then, you and your family would be left in poverty and without any financial security.

Hampered capitalism and welfare state socialism seduce many people into supporting the bankrupt ideas of socialists. Let's look at one final attempt at a "third way" that seduces other good people into adopting socialist ideas.

The Seduction of Progressive Socialism
Progressive socialism is still another variation of socialism that seduces many forward-looking people. Its proponents often call themselves "progressives" implying that their socialist philosophy and programs would move America toward some positive goals. As we mentioned in Chapter 2, progressives believe that moving America toward a "socialist utopia" is progressive, as if working toward moral and economic bankruptcy is ever progressive.

Progressive socialism takes its name and its general direction from the progressive movement of the late 1800's and early 1900's. This movement largely consisted of a hodge-podge of cultural, political, and economic rhetoric calling for "reform" and various social programs. The reform, however, amounted to little more than socialism.

Over the years, progressives have come to promote a variety of different specific socialist policies and programs. Progressives, for example, often promote a government take-over of the health care system and the stringent regulation of the Free Market. Today, their advocacy includes programs for high taxation and the redistribution of wealth.

Sometimes, progressives incorporate Christian thinking and democratic principles into their calls for socialist programs. In this way, progressive socialism's allure is similar to Christian socialism and democratic socialism and many people can be mistakenly seduced into thinking it is moral and good. But, socialism in all its various manifestations, including progressive socialism, is still evil and immoral.

To illustrate progressive thinking and its negative impact on America, consider progressive socialist's long-standing efforts to change our educational system by incorporating concepts from "social psychology" into our schools. In the words of Mary Parker Follett:

Early psychology was based on the study of the individual; early sociology was based on the study of society. But there is no such thing as the "individual," there is no such thing as "society"; there is only the group and the group-unit – the social individual.[172]

Notice how this socialist philosophy is decidedly against individualism and intellectual freedom, and definitely focused on group-think and social consensus. In fact, progressives don't even recognize individualism at all. Mary Parker Follett goes on to say:

The acceptance and the living of the new psychology will do away with ... consent of the governed, majority rule, ... From the analysis of the group must come an understanding of collective thought and collective feeling, of the common will ... When we change our ideas of the relation of the individual to society, our whole system of education changes. ... It is at school that children should begin to learn group initiative, group responsibility – in other words social functioning. Individual competition must, of course, disappear. All must see that the test of success is ability to work with others, not to surpass others.[173]

Notice, too, how progressive socialism rejects consent of the governed and majority rule, both axioms of American Capitalism. Another vitally important point is that progressive socialism rejects competition, not only competition within the Free Market, but also competition among students in school. Presumably, if you can indoctrinate children in socialist principles early in life, they will more likely reject American Capitalism when they become adults.

Incidentally, when individuals stop trying to surpass one another (as Mary Parker Follett suggests above), innovation stops as well. Healthy competition leads to innovation and improvements in the world. Is it any wonder why "socialist utopias" stop growing and improving, but live on in poverty and destitution?

In the view of progressives, we are not individuals. Rather, we are just members of a group or in Mary Parker Follett's words, "social individuals" or in her even colder phrase, "group-units." Obviously, progressives utterly reject the Christian doctrines of human dignity, free will, and individualism.

If you study America's public school system today, you can see the signature of progressive socialism on education. You can also see socialist thinking cropping up in so many ways including the efforts to eliminate competition. But, in addition to its negative impacts on education, progressive socialism has also won a number of other battles too. Let's consider their impact on our Constitution.

Progressives have literally re-shaped the Constitution in an attempt to bring socialist thinking into American life. Because progressives recognized that the Constitution stood in the way of implementing their socialist philosophy, progressives attacked two major components of Constitutional law: Federalism and individuals rights. These two elements of our Constitution and Constitutional law had the effect of limiting the power of the Federal government and assuring individual liberties, especially in the areas of private property and contract law. Federalism specifically refers to the fact that the Constitution enumerates a few limited powers of the Federal government and leaves all else to the states or to the people.

Unfortunately for Americans, progressives as a result of a number of key judicial decisions have been able to erode the original protections of the Constitution, increasing the power of the Federal government and simultaneously, enabling the Federal government to restrict individual rights.[174] We will look at the Battle against the Constitution as Originally Written and related battles in Chapter 6 and Appendix A.

While the language of the early Progressive Movement sounded progressive and positive, it was just the same old socialist philosophy. Following in that tradition, today's progressives use even more upbeat and positive language to sell their form of welfare state socialism.

It's interesting to know that many progressives think the only reason their philosophy has been rejected by many Americans in recent years is that it is not marketed properly. They believe if you market socialism well, it will sell. They believe if you follow good public relations (PR), good promotional approaches, good packaging of the message, and good overall marketing, people will listen and follow their negative philosophy.

Progressives often point to Ronald Reagan and think that he was successful in promoting freedom and limited government simply because he was a great communicator. However, progressive socialists don't get it. Marketing can be helpful. But, the message is more important than slick delivery. Americans are very smart. Americans get it.

Indeed, American Capitalism is moral. Freedom resonates in the hearts, souls, and minds of men and women. Socialism, including progressive socialism, is immoral. Its ideas resonate in the minds of dictators and people who seek power and control.

So, the positive-sounding words and slick "social marketing" of progressive socialism often seduces forward-looking people. But rather than producing "progress" toward any positive goals, progressive socialism still leads to welfare state socialism and eventually, moral and economic bankruptcy.

Let's sum up the various attempts at a "third way" alternative to American Capitalism and socialism by considering how they all differ along three dimensions: freedom, peace, and prosperity.

Four Degrees of Freedom, Peace, and Prosperity

As we have seen earlier in this book, American Capitalism is characterized by faith and morality, freedom and peace, free markets and prosperity, family and trust, as well as spiritual and material human growth. Socialism, in contrast, is about atheism and immorality, control and violence, economic inefficiency and poverty, groups of "victims" and distrust, as well as moral decay and social disintegration. The accompanying table compares hampered capitalism and welfare state socialism with American Capitalism and socialism along three dimensions.

Four Degrees of Freedom, Peace, and Prosperity			
Economic System	Degrees of Freedom	Degrees of Peace	Degrees of Prosperity
American Capitalism	Freedom	Peace	Prosperity
Hampered Capitalism	Some Freedom	Some Peace	Some Prosperity
Welfare State Socialism	Least Freedom	Least Peace	Least Prosperity
Socialism	Tyranny	Violence	Poverty

How does progressive socialism fit in? Progressive socialism is a form of socialism that is trying to "progress" from hampered capitalism to welfare state socialism. It's most related to welfare state socialism in terms of its impact on American Culture, American Government, and the American Economy. So, think of it as fitting on the welfare state socialism line in the accompanying table.

With highly taxed and heavily regulated hampered capitalism, you can expect to have less freedom than American Capitalism. In addition, you can expect greater government control on you and your family's lives. You can also anticipate a less peaceful culture with more violence. Finally, it is probably obvious that you and your family will be less well off financially. With hampered capitalism, there is less capital formation, less economic growth, probably higher inflation, and a lower overall standard of living.

Moving down the accompanying table from hampered capitalism, you get welfare state socialism. You can think of welfare state socialism as hampered capitalism with more taxes, more regulation, and an economy that is more restricted. With welfare state socialism, you and your family's religious freedom, political freedom, and economic freedom are further eroded, limited, and restricted. Besides much less freedom, there is less peace. In addition, the Free Market is stunted considerably with even less economic growth and wealth creation than with hampered capitalism. Of course, welfare state socialism with its many social programs (and its meager economic incentives to create wealth) leads to ultimate moral and economic bankruptcy.

The accompanying table provides a convenient comparison among American Capitalism, hampered capitalism, welfare state socialism, and socialism. As you go down the columns from American Capitalism to socialism, you can see the slide from freedom to tyranny, peace to violence, and prosperity to poverty.

Let's next think about the reasons why attempts at a "third way," including hampered capitalism, welfare state socialism, and even progressive socialism, are not sustainable, but inevitably lead to moral and economic bankruptcy. It's a simple story to understand.

Three Reasons Why There are No Sustainable, Hybrid "Third Way" Systems

As we mentioned earlier in this chapter, one approach for seducing people into supporting socialism is for socialists to argue for a so-called "third way." A "third way" is a combination of some of the characteristics of American Capitalism with some of the attributes of socialism. Then, socialists can use the "third way" as a bridge to more complete socialism.

Alternatively, some socialists recognize many of the severe problems associated with socialism and propose a "third way" in the hopes of getting a better form of socialism. They incorrectly think that they can mix and match features of American Capitalism and socialism into a workable, hybrid "third way" system. But, such hybrid systems are simply not sustainable. Why isn't a hybrid "third way" system sustainable?

There are three main reasons why current and even potential new "third way" systems will not work and can't be sustained in the long run. These reasons are true regardless of what these "third way" systems are called or how they are marketed.[175] Let's look at all three reasons.

Reason #1 – "Third Way" Systems Lead to Bankruptcy Directly or into Socialism (and then Bankruptcy)

First, "third way" systems always destroy the effectiveness of the market and hence, can devolve directly into bankruptcy because they waste scarce economic resources. However, if they don't go into bankruptcy directly, then they devolve into socialism which always leads to bankruptcy. So, from an overall economic point of view, hybrid "third way" systems are not sustainable over the long run. But, let's take an even more detailed look.

All hybrid "third way" systems involve interference in the Free Market. If they didn't involve interference in the Free Market, they would be American Capitalism outright and they could not be called a "third way."

Assuming, however, we do have a hybrid "third way" system, the system will interfere with the Free Market. This interference can take many forms, including one or more of the following: high taxes, stringent regulations, high inflation, dollar devaluation, burdensome mandates, needless tariffs, wealth redistribution, bureaucratic social programs, etc.

Recall Socialism's Cycle of Increasing Regulations and Control from Chapter 1. Remember in that cycle when the Free Market is regulated, the effectiveness of the Free Market is reduced. The greater the interference due to regulations, the greater the negative impact on the Free Market.

Recall specifically how Socialism's Cycle of Increasing Regulations and Control works: (1) hamper the market with regulations, (2) the market reacts by becoming less effective at meeting people's needs, (3) criticize the market for not meeting everyone's needs, (4) claim the market is failing, and (5) use the complaints to call for more government regulations. The cycle continues. Each time through the cycle, the market becomes weaker and less efficient. Eventually, shortages and rationing occur. Eventually, poverty in that area of the economy results.

In general, the Free Market is unquestionably the best mechanism known for allocating scarce economic resources and for creating economic growth and wealth. Even some socialists will admit this obvious fact. But notice further that as the elite and other people become disappointed with the results of their regulation of the market, there invariably is further criticism of the market and there are calls for even greater regulation. As regulations increase, the market becomes less free and less effective. Eventually, socialism takes complete control of the market and the Free Market ceases to exist.

The accompanying figure generalizes Socialism's Cycle of Increasing Regulations and Control from Chapter 1 to include not just regulations, but the more general case of government interference of all types. Again, this interference can take many forms, including one or more of the following: high taxes, stringent regulations, high inflation, dollar devaluation, burdensome mandates, needless tariffs, wealth redistribution, bureaucratic social programs, etc.

Socialism's Cycle of Increasing Interference and Control

Socialism's Cycle of Increasing Interference and Control works in precisely the same manner as Socialism's Cycle of Increasing Regulation and Control. Interference with the Free Market always leads to more interference and more control, because the intended goals of the original interference can't be achieved. Socialists, who are frustrated that the market does not perform as they want, push for greater interference. As interference increases, the market becomes less free and less effective. Ultimately, socialism takes total control of the market and the Free Market ceases to exist. Of course, the "good" intentions and goals of socialism are never met.

Hybrid "third way" systems always fail to meet their goals. Their attempts to regulate or in other ways interfere with the market always fail. These failures lead to calls for additional interference that result in still deeper failures. Systems based on hampered capitalism, welfare state socialism, progressive socialism, and other hybrid "third way" approaches always either go into bankruptcy directly (due the fact that they can't pay their bills) or they devolve into socialism (which lead to moral and economic bankruptcy).

Reason #2 –
"Third Way" Systems Lead to Capital Exhaustion

The second reason why all current and potential new, hybrid "third way" systems are not sustainable in the long run is that eventually capital is exhausted. All "third way" systems consume capital. The greater the interference of the hybrid "third way" system in the Free Market, the faster capital will be consumed.

Remember as we said earlier, no government in history has ever created capital. It is a Free Market function. Hampered capitalism, welfare state socialism, and progressive socialism all consume current capital and all prevent some new capital formation. In complete socialism, no capital formation takes place at all. This, of course, helps explain the destitute poverty associated with "socialist utopias."

All "third way" systems must pay for their government growth, and often a myriad of social programs. Some "third way" systems have to pay for an enormous military budget too. These expenses consume capital at a time when the "third way" systems are preventing additional new capital from being accumulated and formed. This is not a sustainable phenomenon.

You know that if you put $5,000 in your family's checking account, make no new deposits, and continue to write checks, then sooner or later, your checking account balance will hit zero. But, you ask: "Can't the government just print more dollars?" Yes, but there are problems too – inflation, dollar devaluation, etc. There is always a day of reckoning. Even a government can effectively go bankrupt. Unfortunately, individuals suffer the consequences and must deal with the destitution and poverty caused by socialist capital consumption.

Since hybrid "third way" systems consume so much capital and lead to capital exhaustion, they are not sustainable in the long run.

Reason #3 –
"Third Way" Systems Lead to Political Strife and Upheaval

A third reason why all current and potential new, hybrid "third way" systems are not sustainable in the long run is that "third way" systems create a climate of political strife and discord. Political upheaval and turmoil are the result. Why does this happen?

Hybrid "third way" systems work by taking wealth from the successful and the productive, and then spending that wealth on government and its many inefficient programs. Successful entrepreneurs, smart investors, effective corporate executives, industrious small business owners, intelligent professionals (doctors, dentists, accountants, others), popular entertainers, skilled sports players, very hard workers, and very frugal savers – in short, productive individuals – foot the bill for hampered capitalism, welfare state socialism, and progressive socialism. They create the capital. It's their wealth, produced by their labor – both intellectual and physical.

When a hybrid "third way" system taxes the "rich," they are really taxing those who create capital and wealth. Or, when a hybrid "third way" system interferes with the Free Market, they are interfering with the engine of optimum economic resource allocation and the engine of capital formation.

Government, in turn, spends this money on running itself and also re-distributes this wealth to specially-designated groups of "victims" through various social programs. Since all economic resources are scarce, these groups of "victims" will likely clamor for more and more resources from government. (Incidentally, we wouldn't call resources *economic* if they were not scarce. The air we breathe is not an economic resource because it is not scarce. It is a physical resource, however.)

So, with groups of "victims" demanding more and more from government, and productive individuals giving up more and more of their hard-earned cash, income, and wealth through taxes, redistribution, and interference in the Free Market, the situation is likely to cause political friction, strife, and discord. In the end, it can lead to political upheaval, turmoil, and even violence.

Forced redistribution of wealth from groups of productive individuals to groups of government-designated "victims" is not a recipe for free, mutual, and peaceful cooperation as the Free Market and American Capitalism offer us instead. It is not a formula for political stability. Instead, it is a formula for resentment, distrust, and political strife. For this reason too, hybrid "third way" systems are not sustainable. They will inevitably lead to political discord, instability and sometimes violence.

Regardless of the names we give to them or the marketing approach that we take to make them more palatable, hybrid "third way" systems are simply not sustainable over the long run. Hybrid "third way" systems lead to bankruptcy directly by not being able to pay for all their expensive programs, or to bankruptcy indirectly by devolving into socialism. Hybrid "third way" systems also lead to significant and costly capital consumption that ultimately results in capital exhaustion with no further capital available for expensive government spending and social programs. Finally, hybrid "third way" systems lead to political strife and discord, turmoil and upheaval, and sometimes political instability and even violence.

Hampered Capitalism and Welfare State Socialism – A Summary

While hampered capitalism and welfare state socialism seduce many intelligent and well-intentioned people into championing socialist thinking, they nevertheless are doomed to end without achieving their goals or their so-called "good" intentions.

With hampered capitalism, the direct costs and the opportunity costs of government intervention are enormous. Tax and regulatory policies hinder the Free Market, causing it to be much less efficient and much less effective. With hampered capitalism, you and your family pay higher taxes on your income, food, energy, and many other items. With hampered capitalism, you and your family also receive lower salaries and wages because companies can't afford to pay you as much as your labor services are worth. In addition, under hampered capitalism, government can create inflation by increasing the supply of money over and above the increase in the output of the overall economy. In the end, inflation turns out to be an insidious tax and a hidden tax that raises your cost of living.

With regard to the "good" intentions that welfare state socialism uses to seduce people, socialists can't deliver on their promise of "cradle to grave" security. While socialists "good" intentions sound positive at first, they really are deceptive. Welfare state socialism can't eliminate poverty. Welfare state socialism also can't eliminate income and wealth inequality without causing more poverty than already exists. Plus, welfare state socialism also can't eliminate financial insecurity without eliminating Freedom and the Free Market and without destroying American Capitalism and our American Civilization. Then, you and your family can expect only poverty with no financial security.

Let's next put our knowledge of American Capitalism, hampered capitalism, welfare state socialism, progressive socialism, and socialism into understanding the American Political Landscape today.

The American Political Landscape – A New Way to View It

With over three hundred million citizens, America consists of a large variety and mix of cultural, political, and economic viewpoints. To navigate this vast spectrum of ideas and opinions, it is helpful to break down the American Political Landscape into belief segments, each of which simply describes the major core beliefs of a different group of individuals. The accompanying tables present today's American Political Landscape and a brief description of each belief segment. Note that the belief segments are not meant to be mutually exclusive, so some individuals might fit into more than one belief segment.

In the first accompanying table, there are seventeen distinct belief segments representing different individuals grouped by their typical characteristic beliefs. In this segmentation model, a "Yes" indicates that a belief segment has a strong belief in, or emphasis on, Faith, Freedom, or Free Markets (depending on the column in which the "Yes" appears). Similarly, a "No" means that a belief segment has a strong belief against, or emphasis against, Faith, Freedom, or Free Markets. If a particular cell in the model has a blank space, that belief segment does not indicate or emphasize a strong belief for or against Faith, Freedom, or Free Markets (again depending on the column in which the blank space appears). For the Hampered Capitalists belief segment, the table lists a special entry, namely "Limited Free Markets." This indicates that Hampered Capitalists are primarily concerned with limiting Free Markets with high taxes and tight regulations.

To illustrate how this table works, consider the belief segment "Christian Capitalists." The three "Yes" entries in the table show that Christian Capitalists are generally in favor of Faith being an integral part of the American Culture; are usually in favor of Freedom being an important component of American Government; and, are typically in favor of Free Markets as the basis of the American Economy. In stark contrast, the "Progressives" belief segment has three "No" entries indicating that Progressive Socialists are generally against Faith being an integral component of American Culture; are usually against Freedom being an important part of American Government; and, are typically against having Free Markets as the cornerstone of the American Economy.

Combatants	Belief Segments	Faith	Freedom	Free Markets
American Capitalists	Christian Capitalists	Yes	Yes	Yes
	"Ronald Reagan" Conservatives	Yes	Yes	Yes
	"Classic" Liberals (True Liberals)	Yes	Yes	Yes
	Cultural Conservatives	Yes		
	Neoconservatives ("Neocons")		Yes	
	Economic Conservatives		Yes	Yes
	Libertarians		Yes	Yes
	Agnostic Capitalists		Yes	Yes
	Hampered Capitalists			Limited Free Markets
Socialists	Christian Socialists	Yes	No	No
	"New Deal" Liberals		No	No
	Progressive Socialists ("Progressives")	No	No	No
	Democratic Socialists	No	No	No
	Welfare State Socialists	No	No	No
	Environmental Socialists		No	No
	Global Socialists	No	No	No
	Atheistic Socialists	No	No	No

The table title: **The American Political Landscape - American Capitalists vs. Socialists**

Combatants	Belief Segments	Brief Descriptions
American Capitalists	Christian Capitalists	Christians who support the expression of faith within American Culture and who support traditional American religious, political, and economic freedoms and American Capitalism.
	"Ronald Reagan" Conservatives	Conservatives who support President Ronald Reagan's conservative principles that were based on his strong faith in God, his belief in freedom and individualism, his belief in limited government, his belief in a strong national defense, his optimism, and his love for America.
	"Classic" Liberals (True Liberals)	Liberals who support "liberty" in the sense of the classic liberals of the eighteenth century that include religious, political, and economic freedom.
	Cultural Conservatives	Conservatives who focus primarily on cultural and social issues.
	Neoconservatives ("Neocons")	Former "New Deal" Liberals (see below) and other socialists who became disillusioned with socialist cultural and economic thinking and failed social programs. They emphasize strong foreign policy and freedom.[176]
	Economic Conservatives	Conservatives whose focus is primarily on economic issues and the political and economic freedom that supports the Free Market.
	Libertarians	Classic liberals whose emphasis tends to be on political and economic freedom.
	Agnostic Capitalists	Those who do not believe in God, but do believe in economic freedom and the Free Market.
	Hampered Capitalists	Those who belief in free markets, but believe that strong government action along the lines of higher taxation and tighter regulations will improve the Free Market.

Combatants	Belief Segments	Brief Descriptions
Socialists	Christian Socialists	Those who believe in integrating Christian principles into socialism, despite the fact that socialism can't be reconciled with Christianity from a moral point of view.
	"New Deal" Liberals	Socialists that focus on creating new social programs in line with the thinking of President Franklin D. Roosevelt.
	Progressive Socialists ("Progressives")	Socialists that focus on making "progress" toward socialism. Progressives typically support such things as limiting individual freedom, increasing the power of the Federal government, nationalizing the health care system, and the redistribution of wealth.
	Democratic Socialists	Socialists that promote socialism as the "democratic" expression of the people.
	Welfare State Socialists	Socialists that focus on "cradle to grave" social programs.
	Environmental Socialists	Socialists that focus on "saving the planet" by controlling energy, the environment, and the economy, and by limiting freedom.
	Global Socialists	Socialists that seek to promote socialism throughout the world and/or socialists who seek to have one socialist government for the entire world (for example, by an expansion of the power of the United Nations).
	Atheistic Socialists	Socialists who don't have faith in God and who reject Freedom and the Free Market.

In a more concrete sense in the above example, the accompanying table indicates Christian Capitalists will more likely support such things as:

- the religious freedom to show the Christian symbols of a Christmas Tree, the Christian Cross, and the Ten Commandments in public; the
- religious freedom to allow a high school senior to mention Jesus Christ in her valedictorian speech;
- the political freedom to permit a college student to write an essay on "Why America is Great;"
- the political freedom to allow a talk radio station from airing whatever views they choose without being forced to air views they disagree with;
- the elimination of capital gains taxes and estate (death) taxes; as well as
- lower taxes, fewer regulations, and much smaller government.

This list, of course, is just a sample of the kinds of issues and positions Christian Capitalists are likely to take.

In a similar manner, the table indicates that Progressive Socialists will more likely support such things as:

- the prohibition of displaying the Christian symbols of a Christmas Tree, the Christian Cross, and the Ten Commandments in public;
- the elimination of any reference to God or Christianity in the public square or in schools;
- the elimination of free speech on college campuses (unless it supports socialist thinking);
- the elimination of free speech on talk radio (replacing it with the so-called "Fairness Doctrine");
- the elimination of free speech in general (replacing it with regulated, politically-correct speech);
- the elimination of a free market in health care (replacing it with a government-dictated and government-controlled single-payer, universal health care system);
- the elimination of a free market in energy (replacing it with very high energy and carbon taxes);
- the elimination of freely-set wages and prices (replacing it with government wage and price controls, shortages, rationing, and high unemployment);

- increased capital gains taxes and estate (death) taxes; as well as
- higher taxes, more regulations, and much larger government.

These issues and positions, too, are simply a sampling of what "Progressives" might support in practice.

The point of the accompanying table is to identify major belief segments to better understand how individuals agree and disagree on the three fundamental components of American Capitalism and American Civilization, namely, Faith, Freedom, and Free Markets. Note that with any segmentation model, this table does not capture every potential combination of ideas or every possible belief segment. It also can't capture all the sub-segments or all those individuals who straddle belief segments. But, it does help give us insights into the American Political Landscape today.

Overall, this table shows us that the first nine belief segments listed generally support American Capitalism, while the remaining eight belief segments generally support socialism. When discussing America's Economic War, the two primary combatants are American Capitalists vs. socialists. American Capitalism with its various capitalist and conservative allies are in a war with all those different elements of socialism. It is this war American Capitalism must win to retain our religious, political, and economic freedom. It is this war American Capitalism must win to grow that marvelous engine of economic growth, the wonderful American Economy. It is this war American Capitalism must win to preserve our American Culture.

With a solid understanding of the dangers you and your family face in America's Economic War in Chapter 1 and Chapter 2 of this book, we moved to Chapters 3, 4, and 5 to gain an understanding of the combatants in the war. Now, we have obtained a comprehensive knowledge of American Capitalism and socialism as well as various attempts at hybrid "third ways" that invariably are not sustainable. We have also viewed the American Political Landscape from a new perspective: American Capitalists vs. socialists, seeing the distinct belief segments and their relationship to one another. Let's next turn out attention to the war itself in Chapter 6 and Chapter 7, looking at the strategies that socialism is using against American Capitalism every day. Let's also review the actual battles in progress.

Part III

The Strategies and Battles

Chapter 6

Socialist War Strategy #1 – Attack and Destroy the Institutions of American Capitalism

"For You have armed me with strength for the battle;
You have subdued under me those who rose up against me."
Psalm 18:39

Make no mistake about it, America is at war today. Socialism is fighting hard to destroy American Capitalism and our American Civilization. It is attacking American Capitalism on many fronts. It has many allies in the political arena as well as in our government infrastructure. It has supporters in our news media and in our universities and schools. It has help from entertainers and the entertainment industry that thrive on denigrating American Culture and our way of life. It also has support from millions of good Americans who inadvertently support socialism by succumbing to the false promises, false hopes, and phony programs socialists continually offer (but never deliver). Finally, it has the tacit support of millions of other good Americans who recognize the negative impacts of socialism, but who fail to take action against socialism.

In Chapters 6 and 7, we will look at the two major strategies that socialism is currently using against American Capitalism in America's Economic War. In Chapter 6, we will see the 47 major battles and three special battles that are raging today. Chapter 7 details the second strategy socialists are using against American Capitalism. It describes how socialism seeks to control you and your family. With knowledge of these strategies and awareness of the many battles in progress, you can better understand what's going on in America today and how it directly impacts you and your family.

American Capitalism can win America's Economic War. Remember that you and your family's religious freedom, political freedom, and economic freedom are at stake. Remember, too, that you and your family's economic prosperity and lifestyles are at stake. In fact, even you and your family's lives are potentially at risk as well.

What is socialism's first strategy to defeat American Capitalism? It is simple. Attack and destroy (or at the very least, make ineffective) the institutions of American Capitalism, namely: the Christian Church, the Family, the Constitution, Freedom, the Free Market, and Free Enterprise. Each of these key institutions plays a critical role in American Capitalism. Recall that each is a vital component of the Architecture of American Capitalism. Without these institutions, American Capitalism will fail to exist.

Socialists are attacking all of the institutions of American Capitalism today. In battle after battle, as we will see below, socialists seek to destroy these key institutions and what they stand for. Taken together, these battles constitute America's Economic War.

American Capitalism must win these battles and defeat socialism for our generation and for the generations of Americans to come. Otherwise, socialism will bring with it the destruction of religious freedom, political freedom, and economic freedom. It will also usher in an age of power, control, violence, illness, poverty, and destitution. It would be the ultimate human tragedy for America and the world that looks to us for hope.

Let's start by surveying the battles taking place against the institutions of American Capitalism.

The War Room – A Quick Listing of All 47 Major Battles and 3 Special Battles

This section lists all 50 battles taking place in America's Economic War. It is organized into groups of battles that correspond to the particular institutions of American Capitalism that are being attacked. These groups are:

- 9 Major Battles against the Christian Church and Religious Freedom
- 6 Major Battles against the Family and Religious Freedom
- 13 Major Battles against the Constitution and Religious Freedom, Political Freedom, and Economic Freedom
- 1 Special Battle against The Declaration of Independence and America's Sovereignty
- 19 Major Battles against the Free Market, Free Enterprise, and Economic Freedom

- 2 Special Battles against the Free Market, Free Enterprise, and Economic Freedom

For readers who choose to delve into more detail about any or all of the above battles, Appendix A provides more detailed battle summaries. For each group of battles above, Appendix A contains a corresponding summary with information on each battle, battlefront examples, and over 365 reference notes for further study or research.

9 Major Battles against the Christian Church and Religious Freedom
- Battle against Faith in God
- Battle against the Bible
- Battle against Christian Symbols
- Battle against the Free Expression of Christianity
- Battle against Prayer
- Battle against Christmas and Easter
- Battle against Christian Churches
- Battle against Other Traces of Christianity
- Battle against Tolerance for Christianity

6 Major Battles against the Family and Religious Freedom
- Battle against Traditional Marriage
- Battle against Family Life
- Battle against Family Values
- Battle against Parenting
- Battle against Children
- Battle against Homeschooling

13 Major Battles against the Constitution and Religious Freedom, Political Freedom, and Economic Freedom
- Battle against the Constitution as Originally Written
- Battle against the First Amendment and Religious Freedom
- Battle against the First Amendment and Free Speech – Religious Freedom, Political Freedom, Economic Freedom
- Battle against the Second Amendment and Guns
- Battle against the Fourth Amendment and Warrantless Searches
- Battle against the Fifth Amendment and Private Property
- Battle against the Ninth Amendment and Freedom
- Battle against the Tenth Amendment and Freedom
- Battle against the Fourteenth Amendment and Freedom

- Battle against Article 1 Section 8 (Clauses 1, 3, 18) and Economic Freedom
- Battle against Article 1 Section 8 (Clauses 11, 12) and the Military
- Battle against Article 1 Section 10, Contract Law and Economic Freedom
- Battle against Article 2 and the President

1 Special Battle against The Declaration of Independence and America's Sovereignty

- Battle against The Declaration of Independence and America's Sovereignty

19 Major Battles against the Free Market, Free Enterprise, and Economic Freedom

- Battle against Private Property – Personal Taxes
- Battle against Private Property – Personal Taxes (Newer Taxes and Proposed New Taxes)
- Battle against Private Property – Personal Taxes (by Other Names)
- Battle against Private Property – Inflation
- Battle against Private Property – Corporate and Business Taxes
- Battle against Private Property – Regulations and Mandates
- Battle against Private Property – Environmental Regulations
- Battle against Private Property – Environmental Regulations that Hurt America's Energy Supplies
- Battle against Private Property – Eminent Domain (and *Takings*)
- Battle against Private Property – Usage Controls and Lack of Protection
- Battle against Private Property – Excessive Legal Judgments
- Battle against the Freedom to Set Prices – Wage and Price Controls
- Battle against the Free Market – Voiding Voluntary Private Contracts
- Battle against the Freedom to Choose Your Own Work
- Battle against Investors
- Battle against Entrepreneurs
- Battle against Venture Capitalists and Capital Formation
- Battle against Profits
- Battle against Competition

2 Special Battles against the Free Market, Free Enterprise, and Economic Freedom

- Battle against a Free Market in the Energy Industry – The So-Called Global Warming "Crisis"

- Battle against a Free Market in the Health Care Industry – The So-Called Health Care "Crisis"

Again, for more information on any or all of these battles in America's Economic War, please see Appendix A. For now, let's look at the most important battles and why they are so critical in winning America's Economic War.

Critical Battle #1 – Battle against Faith in God

Of the 50 battles against the institutions of American Capitalism, the first and most important battle is the Battle against Faith in God. This might be surprising to you at first. But, it's true. The reason this battle is so critical in America's Economic War is simply that faith in God is the starting point for American Capitalism. Appendix A provides information on this battle.

The Battle against Faith in God is actually a vitally important spiritual, philosophical, and intellectual battle at the very heart of America's Economic War. While it might seem far removed from the day-to-day concerns of buying groceries at the supermarket and the price of gasoline for our cars (or from the political issues relating to Freedom and economic issues dealing with the Free Market), it is still the core battle of our times. Indeed, it is the core battle of human existence. But, that's a topic beyond the scope of this book.

As we saw in Chapter 3, the origins of American Capitalism can be traced to the Christian Church's faith in God. From both faith in God and faith in reason as a way to understand God, faith in progress and optimism developed. In turn, from faith in progress, optimism, and creativity, a number of crucial Christian principles and innovations emerged. Recall that some of these principles and innovations included: Individualism, Human Dignity and Human Rights, Anti-Slavery, Freedom, Equality under the Law, Separation of Church and State, Private Property, Free Enterprise, Capitalism, Charity and Compassion, Universities, as well as innovations in Science and Technology. These pivotal Christian principles and innovations later set the stage for American Capitalism to emerge, to grow, and to flourish.

As we also saw in Chapter 3, the foundations of American Capitalism are embedded in the Judeo-Christian principles found in the Bible, found in the natural law (that is written on the hearts of people), and found in the moral thinking of the Christian Church's theologians and philosophers developed over many centuries. The Christian Church and its thinking form the spiritual and moral bedrock upon which American Capitalism is built. It also forms the basis of American Culture and the morality necessary to support American Civilization.

If the Battle against Faith in God were won by socialists and if individuals no longer believed in God, the results would be tragic and profoundly negative. The Christian Church would collapse, Christian principles would disappear, Christian morality would no longer exist, and American Culture would precipitously decline. In fact, there would be widespread moral decay and social disintegration.

The subsequent decline in American Culture would result in a cascading decline in both American Government and the American Economy. Our religious freedom, political freedom, and economic freedom would all be lost in the process. Moral and economic bankruptcy would ensue. Recall Socialism's Chain of Control in Chapter 1 and the clear and direct linkages among culture, government, the economy, and freedom.

For socialists who want to destroy American Capitalism, Strategy #1 is to attack and destroy the institutions of American Capitalism. In particular, this means attempting to attack and destroy the Christian Church. The Battle against Faith in God is the first step in such an attack against the Christian Church. With this battle and the other related battles presented in Appendix A, socialists seek to destroy the Christian Church. But, socialists are wrong again.

Certainly, the Christian Church is under attack by both atheistic socialists and other socialists today. It is important, however, to recall the words of Jesus in Matthew 16:18,

And I also say to you that you are Peter, and on this rock I will build My church, and the gates of Hades shall not prevail against it.

Socialists will never destroy the Christian Church. But, it is still important to understand the attacks on the Christian Church, so that American Capitalism will understand these battles. It will also facilitate understanding the many other battles American Capitalism faces with socialism's attempts to attack and destroy all the institutions of American Capitalism.

Appendix A provides more information on this battle and its various battlefronts such as attacking faith in reason, attacking the existence of truth, and promoting postmodernism and its socialist philosophy of atheism, nothingness, rage, and power. All of these battlefronts (and some additional related ones listed in Appendix A) comprise the Battle against Faith in God.

The Battle against Faith in God is crucial in America's Economic War. It is the first and most important battle. If American Capitalism loses this battle, the other battles would be moot and American Capitalism would lose the war. But, this battle will not be lost to the socialists. Indeed, the Battle against Faith in God will not be lost because the Christian Church will not be destroyed.

Next, let's look at another empty argument that is used to attack the Christian Church. It does not rise to the level of a battle and is not included in the battle summary tables. However, it is another socialist deception. It's worth understanding the argument and knowing why it is false.

American Culture is Based on Christianity, But America is <u>Not</u> a Theocracy

Today, one of the arguments used directly against the Christian Church (and indirectly against traditional American Culture) is that Christians, who speak out and express moral beliefs on public policy issues, seek to make America into a Christian theocracy.[177] While you can usually find individuals that believe almost anything (and you might even find a few who do seek to live under a theocratic government), the Christian theocracy argument is definitely <u>not</u> true in general.

Consider some facts. First, the concept of the separation of Church and State was developed within the Christian Church as explained in Chapter 3. Why would Christians that believe in the separation of Church and State seek to make over America into a Christian theocracy? (Incidentally, this is the same separation of Church and State concept that socialists often use to suppress the free expression of Christianity. Please see the Battle against the Free Expression of Christianity in Appendix A for more information on this point.)

Second, the concept of theocracy itself does not fit the current situation. A theocracy is a government in which civil and religious authority are essentially identical. For example, suppose Catholics sought a Catholic theocracy in America. They might try to elect the Pope as President. (For purposes of this example, we will overlook Article 2 Section 1 of the Constitution that requires the President to be a natural born citizen of the United States.) This person might then appoint Catholic Cardinals to his cabinet and major appointive positions. In addition, bishops and priests could fill all the remaining offices. Catholic Church doctrine would substitute for any legislation not deemed to fit in with the Church's teaching. This example represents a true theocracy. Obviously, this is not what Christians are striving to achieve in America.

If a Christian today opposes abortion because they believe it is killing an innocent human being before birth, this is expressing a moral position. Yes, it might be based on the Christian Church's teaching and the Bible. But, this does not constitute an attempt to create a Christian theocracy.

Similarly, if a Christian today chooses to wear a Bible verse on her shirt or a Christian Cross necklace on her neck while attending public school, this is certainly not an attempt to convert America into a Christian theocracy. Rather, it is an individual decision and a personal expression of her religious beliefs. It should not be prohibited by an inappropriate interpretation of the First Amendment.

The Christian theocracy argument is an empty argument used to shut off debate. Socialists want no part of Christian morality (or any morality that gets in the way of wielding the power they seek). This argument is a convenient means to eliminate Christians from entering into moral debates or public policy debates that raise moral questions.

True, American Culture is based on Christian principles and morality. But, American Government is not a Christian theocracy. It is also highly unlikely that any major movement will ever emerge that attempts to make America into a Christian theocracy.

Let's turn our attention to the second most important battle of the 50 battles in America's Economic War.

Critical Battle #2 – Battle against the Constitution as Originally Written

Just as the Battle against Faith in God is a profoundly important battle that represents an attack on the Christian Church, one of the key institutions of American Capitalism; so too, the Battle against the Constitution as Originally Written is a crucial battle against another institution of American Capitalism, the Constitution. This battle sometimes will be called a debate over *Originalism* or *Original Intent.* Regardless of the name for the battle, it is the second most important battle in America's Economic War. Appendix A provides information on the Battle against the Constitution as Originally Written.

The reason this battle is so pivotal in America's Economic War is that the Constitution guards all of our freedom – our religious freedom, political freedom, and economic freedom. Socialists, over the years, and progressive socialists, in particular, have sought to re-write the Constitution, attempting to thwart the original intent and the original language of the Constitution in ways that significantly restrict and limit our freedom.[178] In some cases, socialists have prevailed and our freedom has already been diminished.[179]

Our Constitution is worth fighting for and it is worth defending. The Constitution is that magnificent political document that joins all Americans together in a political union based on mutual liberty. It functions by declaring and protecting each American's individual religious freedom, political freedom, and economic freedom. It is an exceptional political document that must be defended for all of us to remain free.

In speaking of the Constitution, President Ronald Reagan said:

So, our protection is in the constitutional system; and one other place as well. Lincoln asked, "What constitutes the bulwark of our own liberty?" And he answered, "It is in the love of liberty which God has planted in us." Yes, we the people are the ultimate defenders of freedom. We the people created the government and gave it its powers. And our love of liberty and our spiritual strength, our dedication to the Constitution, are what, in the end, preserves our great nation and this great hope for all mankind. All of us, as Americans, are joined in a great common enterprise to write the story of freedom – the greatest adventure mankind has ever known and one we must pass on to our children and their children – remembering that freedom is never more than one generation away from extinction.[180]

Even though we have lost ground in this battle, many Americans are working toward regaining lost freedom. Appendix A lists many other battles that are spin-offs from this crucial battle.

By not interpreting the Constitution as originally intended by the Founding Fathers, many other battles have been spawned as well. For example, consider socialist's Battle against the Fifth Amendment and Private Property. Specifically, socialists have been trying to re-interpret the meaning of the *Takings Clause* in the Fifth Amendment of the Constitution. The Constitution states:

No person shall ... be deprived of life, liberty, or property, without due process of law; nor shall private property be taken for public use, without just compensation.

In essence, the Takings Clause means that an individual's private property (such as a home or small business) can't be taken away by the government unless there is a *public use* – such as the need to build a public highway or bridge, <u>and</u> there is *just compensation* paid to the private property owner.

Yet, in 2005, in a Supreme Court decision in *Kelo v. City of New London*, the Supreme Court ruled against private property owners in this landmark case over the interpretation of the Takings Clause. The story is straight forward. The results are troubling for proponents of freedom.[181]

Susette Kelo's nicely-kept home in New London, Connecticut was condemned in 2000. Why? Because the New London Development Corporation (a private, non-profit corporation), whose Directors and employees were not elected, decided to use its power of eminent domain (granted by the City of New London) to condemn a working class neighborhood in order for a private developer to build a hotel, condo's, an office building, and related developments. Susette and some of her neighbors went to court to prevent this taking of their private property. Unfortunately, the Supreme Court ruled against Susette Kelo and in favor of a very broad extension of eminent domain.[182]

The issue in this case is simple and easy to understand. Does the government have the Constitutional right to take private property from one individual and give it to another individual (a private developer), enriching the second party in the process, for purposes of economic development –

namely, for more jobs and higher tax revenues?[183]

Eminent domain, of course, is the long standing tradition of government having the right (under some limited circumstances) to take an individual's private property.[184] But, in this expansive interpretation of the Takings Clause, private property (one of the key requirements for a free market and economic freedom) is now at grave risk.

Justice O'Connor in her dissenting opinion to *Kelo v. City of New London* captured the significance in these serious words: "The specter of condemnation hangs over all property. Nothing is to prevent the state from replacing any Motel 6 with a Ritz-Carlton, any home with a shopping center, or any farm with a factory." Justice O'Connor also said: "Any property may now be taken for the benefit of any private party ..."[185]

But, how would the Founding Fathers react to the *Kelo v. City of New London* Supreme Court decision? James Madison, the author of the Takings Clause, would probably agree with Justice O'Connor's dissenting opinion. James Madison linked the purpose and role of *a just* government directly to the protection of private property in these words:

A Government is instituted to protect property of every sort ... This being the end of government, that alone is **a just** *government, which* **impartially** *secures to every man, whatever is his own.* [186]

Kelo v. City of New London is a battlefront example of the Battle against the Fifth Amendment and Private Property. It is one of many. Unfortunately, in this case, some of our economic freedom was lost. New legislation within the States as well as additional litigation in State courts might help restore some of our economic freedom. Ultimately, if the original intent of the Founding Fathers is to be restored, the Supreme Court needs to overturn *Kelo v. City of New London.*[187]

As mentioned earlier, by not interpreting the Constitution as originally intended by the Founding Fathers, many other battles have been spawned. In another example, socialists are constantly attacking the Constitution by trying to set limits on free speech. One battlefront in the Battle against the First Amendment and Free Speech is "campaign finance reform." This effort places a variety of restrictions on campaign finances, making it more difficult to raise money, and making it more difficult for political candidates to get their messages out to voters. Such political messages are clearly a form of free speech. After all, if we don't have unrestricted political free speech, how can we hope to have political freedom in America? Once you restrict free speech, you eliminate a key component of freedom.

Obviously, "campaign finance reform" is a roadblock to political free speech and political freedom. A strict interpretation of the First Amendment will make "campaign finance reform" a footnote in Constitutional Law textbooks and a topic for law student seminars. It certainly ought to be ruled unconstitutional.

Speaking of free speech, let's turn our attention to the issue of offensive speech, another means to silence individuals.

The Freedom to Speak and the Freedom to Offend

Where is it written in the First Amendment to the Constitution that Americans are not allowed to say things that are offensive, or nasty, or mean, or discriminatory, or even downright hateful? It's not written in the Constitution. The Constitution gives all Americans the right to freedom of speech in the First Amendment.

In our day-to-day lives, do most individuals go around insulting others? Probably not. Also, do most people verbally attack ethnic and racial groups with hateful comments? Probably not. Do most individuals try to create a "hostile environment" in their workplaces? Again, probably not. Yet, socialists feel compelled to regulate Americans' freedom to speak and freedom to offend others.

The result of socialist's on-going Battle against the First Amendment and Free Speech is that many Americans avoid saying anything that might remotely offend anyone. In a sense, they are afraid to offend anyone. Why are individuals so afraid to speak their minds?

For one thing, if you say something offensive at work, you can lose your job. If you are a college student, you can fail a class. If you take up certain political causes (such as moving an affordable housing project to another neighborhood), you can be fined.[188] Sadly, for Americans, socialists have made progress in limiting our free speech.

Besides the fact that the Constitution positively permits free speech without any limitations, another issue related to offensive speech is readily apparent. Who decides what speech is offensive, or nasty, or mean, or discriminatory, or hateful? Must Congress or the States create laws and regulations to set the standards for acceptable speech? In theory, nearly any speech can be offensive to some group, or some person.

Also, how about simple misunderstandings that come up on a day-to-day basis? Will they be forbidden by government laws or regulations? Will they become crimes that are punishable by fines or imprisonment? For example, suppose Bob tells Sue: "You look great. I think you must have lost 10 pounds this summer." Bob (and many other individuals) might consider this a real compliment to Sue. But, maybe Sue is battling anorexia and feels this simple comment is very offensive. Or, maybe Sue believes Bob is teasing her and engaging in offensive humor.

A problem with offensive speech is that the process of *taking offense* (of *being offended)* is in the mind of the person offended. Quite literally, anyone can take offense at nearly anything. If we never know what will offend someone <u>and</u> if we wish to avoid offending everyone, we can't ever speak freely at all (out of fear of offending someone at sometime). Limiting free speech to avoid offending others is futile because some people will always take offense. Limiting free speech to avoid offending others is also foolish because open and honest communications is essential in human relationships.

Christians might recall St. Paul's guidance in these profound words of 1 Corinthians 13:4-8,

Love suffers long and is kind; love does not envy; love does not parade itself, is not puffed up; does not behave rudely, does not seek its own, is not provoked, thinks no evil; does not rejoice in iniquity, but rejoices in the truth; bears all things, believes all things, hopes all things, endures all things. Love never fails.

In one translation of the Bible, the phrase "is not provoked" in 1 Corinthians 13:5 above is translated "it does not take offense."[189] Put directly, love does not take offense; it does not take offense at the many negative things people say. The Bible is guiding us to be accepting of others and not take the words and actions of others in a hurtful way.

It's true that the Bible includes much practical wisdom for our day-to-day lives. Three important themes in the Bible are: (1) God gave us liberty, (2) Love God and your neighbor, and (3) don't be afraid. Applied to the subject of free speech, the first theme teaches us we have freedom of speech. Yet, with our freedom of speech, comes responsible use. We should use it wisely to love our neighbor (second theme), rather than using it in an offensive way. From the third theme, we should also speak without fear of offending others. We need not, and should not, live in fear and anxiety. We were not created by God to be afraid. In 1 Corinthians 13:4-8, the Bible is guiding us to accept and overlook other people's mistakes, when others misuse their freedom and say offensive things to us.

When socialists try to legislate morality, it is as if they are trying to create the religion they so adamantly reject as atheists or agnostics. It is true that in many ways, socialism appears to be its own quasi-religion.

To summarize, there are three issues with prohibiting even the most offensive speech. First, the Constitution gives us the right to free speech. It is a Constitutional freedom. Second, if socialists make "offensive" speech illegal (or even unacceptable), government gets to determine what speech is legal (or what speech is acceptable) and you and your family lose your unrestricted right to free speech. Third, it is both futile and foolish to restrict free speech.

In addition, for Christians and for those who seek wisdom from the Scriptures, the Bible appears to support and endorse free speech, and counsels us to avoid taking offense at the negative words and actions of inconsiderate people.

Americans should have unrestricted Constitutional freedom of speech and the freedom to offend. Yet, the Battle against the First Amendment and Free Speech rages on today as one of the 50 battles in America's Economic War. Some of our free speech seems to have been lost. We need to get it back.

Before moving past some key topics related to the Battle against the Constitution as Originally Written, let's consider *judicial activism,* an important factor in America's Economic War.

Two Different Types of Judicial Activism – What's the Difference?

As with many terms in America's Economic War, language can be confusing.

Judicial activism, and its opposite, *judicial restraint,* are two critically important terms in America's Economic War that both are easily confused. Many of the 50 battles in America's Economic War hinge on Constitutional issues, Constitutional interpretation, and whether or not the justices and judges on critical cases believe in judicial activism. Let's look at the two ways the term *judicial activism* is used and the two ways that its opposite, *judicial restraint* are used.

The most common use of the term *judicial activism* is to designate justices and judges that use their judicial role to legislate from the bench and to modify the original meaning and intent of the Constitution from the bench. This is the first type of judicial activism listed in the accompanying table. President Ronald Reagan opposed this type of judicial activism. [190]

Two Different Types of Judicial Activism			
Type of Judicial Activism	Judicial Activism Definition	Characteristics of this Type of Judicial Activism	Proponents of the Constitution as Originally Written view this type of Judicial Activism as ...
#1	Justices and judges function as legislators	Justices and Judges can • Give new and unintended meaning to some parts of the Constitution, • Ignore other parts of the Constitution, and • Legislate from the bench. Justices and judges are *active* in the sense that they make new laws or change the Constitution.	Negative, because it overrides the Constitution's original meaning and intent.
#2	Justices and judges function as protectors of the Constitution and the Rule of Law	Justices and Judges can • Strike down legislation that is unconstitutional using the original meaning and intent of the Constitution as the standard. • This Constitutional test is known as *strict scrutiny.* Justices and judges are *active* in the sense that they overturn unconstitutional lower court decisions or unconstitutional legislation. • They actively enforce the Constitution.	Positive, because it supports and upholds the Constitution's original meaning and intent.

The opposite of the first type of *judicial activism* is *judicial restraint* in which justices and judges interpret the law, don't legislate from the bench, and attempt to uphold the Constitution's original intent. It is the type of judicial restraint of which President Ronald Reagan supported and spoke in these words:

The judicial branch interprets the laws, while the power to make and execute those laws is balanced in the two elected branches ... the Founding Fathers recognized that the Constitution is the supreme and ultimate expression of the will of the American people ... the Founding Fathers designed a system of checks and balances, and of limited government, because they knew that the great preserver of our freedoms would never be the courts or either of the other branches alone. It would always be the totality of our constitutional system, with no one part getting the upper hand. And that's why the judiciary must be independent. And that is why it must exercise restraint. [191]

The second usage of the term *judicial activism* turns the first definition on its head. It has the reverse meaning. With the second definition of judicial activism, justices and judges are judicially active when they overturn unconstitutional lower court decisions or legislation judged to be unconstitutional. These activities can take place under a standard of *strict scrutiny* that relies on the original meaning and intent of the Constitution.

Under the second definition of judicial activism, the term *judicial restraint* refers to an inactive judiciary that permits the legislature to get away with almost anything, including unconstitutional usurpations of power and limitations on freedom. Richard A. Epstein, a proponent of this second definition of judicial activism (and an opponent of its corresponding version of judicial restraint), writes about the *Kelo v. City of New London* Supreme Court decision in the words below. (Recall the *Kelo v. City of New London* case from earlier in this chapter.)

The decision has had odd consequences for a confused public. Judicial activism is still the enemy, and one heartfelt letter in the Wall Street Journal denounced Kelo as yet another instance of judicial activism, which gets matters 180 degrees backward – the villain of the case is excessive judicial restraint. [192]

Thus, Richard Epstein uses definition #2 for judicial activism. He believes that justices who overturn unconstitutional lower court decisions are showing judicial activism, while justices unwilling to overturn unconstitutional lower court decisions are exhibiting excessive judicial restraint.

As with other battles in America's Economic War, if you get involved in a discussion (or even just listen to those fighting the battles), it's important to understand what's being said. To understand the debates, discussions and arguments, it's vitally important to understand the definitions of the language being used. So, don't just listen to the terms used in the arguments. Be sure to understand what people mean by the terms they use.

Indeed, there is widespread confusion over some language used in America's Economic War. Just as American Capitalists sometimes disagree in terminology with other American Capitalists, socialists sometimes disagree in terminology with other socialists. Plus, of course, American Capitalists frequently disagree in terminology with socialists. In some cases, some socialists have also grossly distorted the meaning of words just to help attack and destroy the institutions of American Capitalism.

The key is straight forward. You need to be alert and cautious when it comes to language in America's Economic War. Note that in this book, we use definition #1 for *judicial activism*.

As we have discussed above, the first and most important battle in America's Economic War is the Battle against Faith in God. If socialists win this battle, American Culture and its morality will be destroyed. The second most important battle of the 50 battles in America's Economic War is the Battle against the Constitution as Originally Written. Without our Constitution intact, our freedom will be lost. Now, let's turn our attention to the third most important battle, the Battle against Private Property. If socialists win this battle, our economy and prosperity will be severely damaged and ultimately destroyed.

Critical Battle #3 – Battle against Private Property

The Battle against Private Property is the third most important battle among the many battles in America's Economic War. Actually, this very large battle is so extensive that it is broken down into a number of separate, smaller battles in Appendix A to better organize and understand America's Economic War. Appendix A presents considerable information on these battles against private property. Why is the Battle against Private Property such an important battle in winning America's Economic War?

Recall from the Architecture of American Capitalism that private property is the key requirement of the American Economy. Quite literally, the Free Market can't exist without the free exchange of private property. Without private property, economic growth comes to an abrupt halt, the economy declines precipitously, and eventually, economic bankruptcy results.

Socialists also see private property as crucial to American Capitalism. Recall the socialist perspective on private property from Chapter 1. In the words of socialists Karl Marx and Frederick Engels, "... the theory of the communists may be summed up in the single sentence: abolition of private property." [193] Communism, of course, is just one version of socialism. But, all versions of socialism ultimately rest on the rejection of liberty and private property.

Appendix A summarizes the various battles and battlefronts associated with the larger Battle against Private Property. Many of the additional economic battles in Appendix A not directly against private property are battles still being fought to destroy the Free Market.

Socialists are attacking American Capitalism on many battlefronts with:
- Very high taxes;
- Proposed new taxes, including Carbon Taxes, Global Taxes, and Internet Taxes;
- Taxes under a variety of names and taxation methods, such as *Imputed Income;*
- The insidious, hidden, and very immoral tax of government-caused inflation;
- Government taking private property away from private property owners with greatly expanded powers of *eminent domain;*
- Very high regulatory burden that adds enormous costs to the economy;
- Very high mandate burden that adds enormous costs to the economy;
- Very high environmental regulatory burden (outside the energy sector) that adds enormous costs to the economy;
- Very strong opposition to conventional energy sources, including,
  - Attacking nuclear energy,
  - Attacking nuclear power plants,
  - Attacking uranium mining,

- o Attacking coal mining,
- o Attacking coal-fired power plants,
- o Attacking large-scale hydropower,
- o Attacking liquefied natural gas,
- o Attacking oil-sands,
- o Attacking oil shale,
- o Attacking oil drilling,
- o Attacking oil refineries, and
- o Attacking power transmission lines;

- Very high environmental regulatory burden that attacks America's energy industry directly and makes America dependent on foreign energy supplies (enriching foreign countries at the expense of American consumers);
- Proposed Windfall Profits Taxes on oil companies to further hinder investment in critically-needed oil supplies and infrastructure;
- Very burdensome controls over if and how private property can be used; and
- Very costly and excessive legal judgments against private property owners.

All of these attacks are against private property. Most transfer private property from individuals, small businesses, and corporations to the government, either directly through taxation, or indirectly through regulations, mandates, controls, restrictions, and policies. Most of these attacks tend to increase the government's share of Gross Domestic Product (GDP). All of these attacks are forms of confiscation of private property and redistribution of that private property.

In addition, all of these attacks tend to diminish your share of the nation's economic pie. All of these attacks tend to diminish your economic freedom. Plus, all of these attacks tend to diminish your economic prosperity. All of these attacks tend to hurt you and your family, you and your family's lifestyle, and possibly even you and your family's lives.

If we lose the Battle against Private Property, America's strong engine of economic growth will break down. Then, we would suffer the eventual fate of all "socialist utopias." America would fall into moral and economic bankruptcy.

All of the above attacks on private property and the Free Market share one particular quality in common. They are incremental assaults on our economic freedom. They are measured. They usually occur one step at a time. They generally take time to have their impact. For example, consider the act of preventing an oil refinery from being developed. It takes years before the economic impact is noticed and your family's checkbook is hit hard by sky-high gasoline prices. But not all the battles result in slow, measured impacts. Some damage American Capitalism in a profound way.

Besides the Battle against Private Property, there are two special battles raging today that are major assaults against the Free Market. Losing these battles will have debilitating and devastating impacts on the American Economy. Losing either battle is a giant step toward socialism. Losing either battle is a giant step toward government-dictated centralized planning, control, coercion, compulsion and violence. These two special battles are the battles over the socialization (or nationalization) of the American energy industry and the socialization (or nationalization) of the American health care industry. Socialists are seeking both of these convoluted and complex, nationalization schemes in response to so-called "crises" that socialists have created.

Let's look at both of these so-called "crises" and the proposed socialization of two vital American industries. They both represent special battles against the Free Market.

The Seduction of Socialism – Part 3

Recall from Chapter 1 that the apocalyptic myth of an impending global warming "crisis" is another tool of socialism. Its purpose is to wrest economic power from your hands and give it to socialists who will run your life for you. The so-called global warming "crisis" is about controlling energy and controlling the economy. It's about power, socialists' power to control the American Economy. It's also about controlling you and eliminating your economic freedom.

Socialists can accomplish this, in part, by convincing you to alter your lifestyle or risk the survival of the planet. They also can accomplish this, in part, by creating major, new burdensome taxes, such as the proposed Carbon Taxes, and/or by creating massive, new government bureaucracies, such as the proposed "cap and trade" programs. These programs might better be termed as "tax and regulate," or "cap energy supplies and ration what's left," or "take-over and run the entire show" programs.

The Seduction of Environmental Socialism – Battle against a Free Market in the Energy Industry

This Battle against a Free Market in the Energy Industry (using the so-called global warming "crisis" as the motivation) is an attempt to socialize America's energy industry with all the negative ramifications and negative impacts that socialism has on an economy. Appendix A provides more information on this battle.

As is often the case, socialists attempt to use "crises" to gain power. They can't gain power in America, the greatest nation on the face of the earth, without convincing the American people something is terribly wrong. They can't wrestle freedom from the minds, hearts, and souls of Americans without claiming there is literally an earth-threatening disaster waiting to happen. By convincing you and your family that the earth is in jeopardy, they seek to socialize the energy industry.

Environmental socialists and their supporters are trying to convince all of us that drastic action must be taken to save the earth from the so-called global warming "crisis." Of course, the drastic action they propose is socializing America's energy industry, including:

- Taking control of the energy industry with a "cap and trade" program,
- Controlling the use of energy by individuals,
- Controlling the use of energy by small businesses,
- Controlling the use of energy by corporations,
- Taxing the use of energy,
- Taxing the energy industry,
- Regulating the energy industry,
- Attacking energy supplies,
- Attacking energy development,
- Attacking energy infrastructure development,
- Attacking energy transportation and transmission,
- Creating energy shortages,
- Rationing the energy that's left,
- Attacking your energy usage,
- Attacking your lifestyle,
- Raising your taxes, and
- Raising your energy prices.

The seduction of environmental socialism is simple. Socialists want to fool you into accepting socialism. They want you to think by socializing the energy industry you are doing something great. They want you to think you are saving the environment, saving various animal species, and saving the planet, all from the so-called global warming "crisis." Socialism also seeks to seduce you by using unwarranted fear and unfounded guilt to make you and your family change your lives and lifestyles.

In addition, the seduction of environmental socialism entails selling the American people into accepting the unnecessary suffering and bitter economic hardships that will result from the socialization of our energy industry. Unfortunately, for many Americans, unfamiliar with the complexities of climate science, physics and computer modeling, they are not in a position to debate socialists who are intent on creating a "crisis" to gain power and control over the American Economy.

Energy is the lifeblood of the American Economy and American Capitalism. American Capitalism literally runs on energy. Without energy, nothing works. If socialists gain control of our energy industry, they also gain control of our economy. That's why socialists are so eager to promote the so-called global warming "crisis" and are so hesitant to allow any debate on the topic. If socialists have their way, you and your family's lifestyle will be dramatically altered, your personal finances will be hit hard, and your economic freedom will be severely restricted.

Today's high energy prices are the direct result of attacks on the energy industry made years ago. Today's attacks on the energy industry will be felt hard in the future. If socialists have their way and socialists win the Battle against a Free Market in the Energy Industry, we will all be paying very high energy prices in the future. We will also live in cold houses in the winter and hot homes in the summer (because heating and cooling costs will soar). Travel costs will rise dramatically as well.

Socialism will exact a high price on America, if environmental socialists seduce the American people and win the Battle against a Free Market in the Energy Industry.

Let's look at another so-called "crisis" and another Battle against the Free Market.

The Seduction of Universal Health Care Socialism –

Battle against a Free Market in the Health Care Industry

The Battle against a Free Market in the Health Care Industry is a direct attempt to socialize (or nationalize) America's health care industry. This industry represents an estimated 16.3% of America's Gross Domestic Product (GDP).[194] This means if socialists get their way, the government will immediately take over more than 16% of the American Economy with one single program. This will move America much closer to complete socialism. It will also move America much closer to moral and economic bankruptcy, the eventual outcome all socialist nations face. Appendix A concisely summarizes a great deal more information about this battle, with references for further study.

In Chapter 1, you will recall our discussion on why your economic freedom and even your life are at risk with socialized health care. A snapshot of that discussion bears repeating here.

Under socialist thinking, America's health care system is increasingly over-regulated. Unfortunately, there is no longer a free market in health care in America. The American health care system is a hampered market, throttled back from reaching its full potential. You and your family are paying more for insurance, assuming you even have insurance. Plus, your choices of doctors and medical procedures are restricted by government interference in the market. Quality is down; costs are up. Government controls and regulations are the economic villain. Your economic freedom is limited in this important area of your family's life.

Two Cato Institute researchers sum up the situation succinctly:

... in America's health care sector, a dense thicket of laws and regulations disables the competitive process ... Government discourages patients from shopping for value and encourages them to disregard costs. It pays doctors and hospitals according to volume with no regard to quality. It restricts the choices available to patients and blocks competition among providers of medical goods and services. Through tax policy, subsidies, and regulation, government reduces patients' freedom to choose, reduces competition, and obstructs the market processes that deliver higher quality at lower prices.[195]

But, as bad as America's health care system is under a hampered market (at the time this book is being written), things will get worse if American Capitalism loses the America's Economic War. For a taste of complete socialized health care, Britain and Canada gives us some awful food for thought. Recall from Chapter 1 that Rush Limbaugh cites the case in Britain of Elizabeth Jones that was twice turned away from a hospital on the date of birth of her baby. The hospital was full and was not able to accommodate Elizabeth. Elizabeth finally delivered at home without help from the local British National Health Service maternity ward.[196]

In discussing Britain's socialized health care system, Michael Tanner writes:

Waiting lists are a major problem. As many as 750,000 Britons are currently awaiting admission to NHS hospitals. These waits are not insubstantial and can impose significant risks on patients. For example, by some estimates, cancer patients can wait as long as eight months for treatment ... Delays in receiving treatment are often so long that nearly 20 percent of colon cancer patients considered treatable when first diagnosed are incurable by the time treatment is finally offered ...[197]

Michael Tanner continues with some additional statistics on diagnostic testing and care under Britain's National Health Service:

The government's official target for diagnostic testing is a wait of no more than 18 weeks by 2008. In reality, it doesn't come close ... The latest estimates suggest that for most specialties, only 30 to 50 percent of patients are treated within 18 weeks. For trauma and orthopedics patients, the figure is only 20 percent. Overall, more than half of British patients wait more than 18 weeks for care ...[198]

Also, recall from Chapter 1 that other horrifying stories and statistics abound. Under socialism, British patients with dental problems sometimes can't find a dentist. Some patients even resort to pulling out their own teeth. In Canada, wait times for medical care can be staggering. Wait times for emergency heart surgeries range from five to six weeks, while wait times for emergency neurosurgeries are 10.7 weeks.[199] Emergencies can't wait. Lives are at risk. Patients are stuck under socialism. Yet, socialists in the United States look to Britain and Canada as models for America's health care system.

Socialists promote false hope, when they promise universal health care for everyone in America. Socialists, once again, have no way to deliver on their phony promises. Sure they can promise everyone government-provided health care. Words are cheap. Actions cost money, however. If America's health care industry is nationalized, you and your family can expect little innovation, poor quality, shortages, delays in receiving care, and long waits for services.

You can also expect under a socialized health care system that some drugs and treatments will be deemed too expensive and some people will have to go without care. Health care for older Americans might be significantly restricted to save money too. Plus, you can expect widespread rationing of health care to try to keep costs down.

You or your family members might even die while waiting for treatment.

Truly, without the powerful engine of economic growth and prosperity known as the Free Market, our health care industry will decline into inferior mediocrity (at best).

As an economic philosophy, socialism is a proven theoretical failure. As an economic system used by actual nations, socialism is a proven practical failure. We don't need to destroy America's innovative and strong health care system, the best in the world, with another socialist experiment doomed to failure.

Clearly, if socialists win the Battle against a Free Market in the Health Care Industry, the quality of American health care will decline. You and your family's lives might be at risk as well.

The Battle against a Free Market in the Health Care Industry is one of the 50 battles raging today in America's Economic War. All of these battles are part of socialism's first strategy to defeat American Capitalism by attacking and destroying (or at the very least, making ineffective) the institutions of American Capitalism.

Let's look next at socialism's second strategy. It impacts you and your family in very personal ways. Let's see why in Chapter 7.

Chapter 7

Socialist War Strategy #2 –
Control You and Your Family

> "For God has not given us a spirit of fear,
> but of power and of love and of a sound mind."
> 2 Timothy 1:7

In America's Economic War, Strategy #1 for socialists is to attack and destroy the institutions of American Capitalism, namely, the Christian Church, the Family, the Constitution, Freedom, the Free Market, and Free Enterprise. With this strategy, socialists are also attacking individuals and the very idea of individualism.

Indeed, socialist's first strategy is a direct attack on individual Americans. In particular, Strategy #1 is a direct attack on you and your family's religious freedom, political freedom, and economic freedom. It is also a direct, frontal attack on you and your family's finances and prosperity, and even your lives. That's why this war is vitally important to you and your family. That's why the outcome of America's Economic War today is so very important for generations of Americans to come.

But, socialists are not just waging war on the institutions of American Capitalism and they are not just targeting your freedom, your money and you life, in a general way. This leads us to socialist Strategy #2.

For their victory to be complete, not only must socialists destroy the institutions of American Capitalism, they must also control you and your family. Individual Americans and American families are extraordinarily powerful. No group of socialist elite can defeat individual Americans and American families intent on living in freedom. That's why socialist Strategy #2 is to control you and your family.

The accompanying table summarizes the six areas in which some socialists are trying to control you and your family. Specifically, some socialists are attempting to:

Examples of How Some Socialists are Attempting to Control You and Your Family	
Some Socialists are Attempting to …	**By Trying to …**
Control the Message (What You Can Hear)	• Control the language you hear and use (by distorting the meaning of words). • Control the news you see on TV. • Control the news you hear on talk radio. • Control the news you read in newspapers and magazines. • Control K-12 schools and what your children can learn (by substituting indoctrination for education). • Control colleges and universities and what college students can learn (by substituting indoctrination for education). • Control the entertainment you see and hear on TV, on DVDs, on music files, and in the movies.
Control the Conversation (What You Can Say)	• Control your speech. • Control your intellectual freedom. • Control your right to participate in the free market of ideas. • Control your right to participate in free and open debates. • Define what speech is permissible for you to use. • Attack you if you openly disagree with socialists. • Intimidate you (into self-imposed silence) if you want to openly disagree with socialists.

Control the Agenda (What You Can Think)	• Discuss socialist topics constantly that deal with –
	  ○ Attacking America.
	  ○ Attacking the institutions of American Capitalism.
	  ○ Creating false "crises" such as –
	    ▪ The so-called global warming "crisis."
	    ▪ The so-called health care "crisis."
	  ○ Creating false expectations such as –
	    ▪ Socialism and big government will solve your problems.
	  ○ Creating the impression that everyone is just a member of a social group, not an individual or a member of a family.
	    ▪ Destroying individualism.
	    ▪ Destroying the Family.
	  ○ Creating groups of "victims."
	  ○ Creating a welfare state mentality where "victims" think they are permanently dependent on government.

Examples of How Some Socialists are Attempting to Control You and Your Family	
Some Socialists are Attempting to …	**By Trying to …**

Control the Mood (What You Can Feel)	• Create fear in you and your family such as –
	  ○ Telling your children the earth will be destroyed by the so-called global warming "crisis."
	  ○ Telling you and your family that the economy is doing very poorly.
	• Create a sense of helplessness in you and your family.
	• Create a feeling of victimization in you and your family.
	• Create a welfare state mentality in which you think you are permanently dependent on government to help you.
	• Create a feeling of depression in you and your family.
	  ○ Telling you and your family that things are bad and will get worse without more socialist programs.

Control the Economy and Your Life (What You Can Do)	• Control you and your family's lifestyle by creating fear and guilt over the so-called global warming "crisis." • Control you and your family's health care by taking over the health care industry because of the so-called health care "crisis." • Control what you and your family eat by creating fear over certain foods. • Control what you and your spouse can do for a living (with a myriad of economic regulations). • Control what you and your spouse can earn and how much you and your spouse can keep (with a myriad of taxes and economic regulations). • Control how much you and your spouse can invest for retirement and how much you and your spouse can spend during retirement (with a myriad of economic regulations). • Control what you and your family can buy and sell (with a myriad of economic regulations). • Control <u>if and how</u> you can use your own private property.
Control the Election Process (What Type of Leaders You Can Elect)	• Make it harder to detect voter fraud (by allowing mail-in registrations, prohibiting Voter ID rules and prohibiting double registration database checks).[200] • Block the use of new technologies that can cut down on voter fraud by screening out phony registration addresses.[201] • Win elections by campaigning as an American Capitalist (but after elections, governing like a socialist). • Win elections by campaigning as a socialist with unrealistic promises (but after elections, not keeping those promises). • Win elections by running negative campaigns that smear opponents (and by discouraging voters from voting). • Win elections by casting doubts on the election process and challenging the results (when some socialists don't win).

- Control the Message (What You Can Hear)
- Control the Conversation (What You Can Say)
- Control the Agenda (What You Can Think)
- Control the Mood (What You Can Feel)
- Control the Economy and Your Life (What You Can Do)
- Control the Election Process (What Type of Leaders You Can Elect)

The accompanying table also presents examples of how some socialists are trying to gain control over you and your family in each of the six areas of control. Since many of these examples represent a synthesis of factors, forces and events of our times, no attempt is made to provide one or two quick references that capture these complex examples in a simple manner. In this sense, the accompanying table is a summary of what some socialists are attempting to do (control you and your family) and how they are trying to accomplish that strategy (by creating a *socialist zeitgeist* or what might be called a *prevailing socialist mindset for our times*). The examples are components of such a *socialist zeitgeist* that some socialists are fighting to create in America.

Let's quickly scan each of the six control areas in which some socialists seek to control you and your family.

Control the Message (What You Can Hear)

The negative socialist message is pervasive and pernicious. It's dark and deadly. It's boring and repetitive. It's 365 x 24 x7. What is it? It consists of thoughts such as these:

America is bad. The military is bad. American foreign policy is bad. The economy is bad. American Capitalism is bad. Wall Street is bad. Corporations are bad. CEOs are bad. Business is bad. Profits are bad. Competition is bad.

The economy is in a crisis. Foreclosures are up. Bankruptcies are up. Interest rates are up. Inflation is up. Prices are up. Food prices are up. Gasoline prices are up. Energy prices are up. Health care costs are up. Unemployment is up.

Jobs are down. Stocks are down. Bonds are down. 401(k)'s are down. IRAs are down. Consumers are down. Real wages are down.

Global warming is a crisis. There is a climate crisis. The earth is doomed. We don't have much time to save the planet. It's America's fault. We use too much energy. Our carbon footprints are too large.

Health care is in a crisis. Health care insurance is broken. Health care is broken.

America is broken. America is racist. America is sexist. America is homophobic. America is an awful country. America is bad.

We need government. Only government can fix the problems.

Is it any wonder that atheistic socialism is so negative? Without the God of love, peace and mercy, how can any group see things in a positive way? Even the so-called "Christian socialists" (a contradiction in terms) seem to be very deeply engulfed in the bleak philosophy of socialism. With this miserable mindset, it's no wonder that socialism always leads toward moral and economic bankruptcy.

The message of socialism is the message of gloom and doom. It's so negative because socialists are trying to convince you to abandon American Capitalism. Socialists want you to give up – give up your religious freedom, political freedom, and economic freedom. They want you to give up – give up control of you and your family's lives to a government that they control. They want power. They seek control over American Culture, American Government, and the American Economy. Without your acquiescence or complacency, socialism will fail to defeat American Capitalism in America's Economic War. Without your acquiescence or complacency, socialism will fail to take control of America.

Socialism's negative message is directed to you and your family. It's meant to chip away at your enthusiasm for America and for life. It's meant to cripple and disable you and your family.

While socialism offers such an incredibly negative message, American Capitalism provides a positive, uplifting vision for America. That's why American Capitalists tend to be more optimistic, upbeat, and thankful for living in America, the greatest nation in the history of the world.

Incidentally, the reason why some socialists attempt to control various media outlets; attempt to control indoctrination in schools, colleges, and universities; and attempt to script the entertainment industry, is precisely to limit other messages from reaching your eyes and ears. With a steady drumbeat of vitriolic messages, with a continuous streaming of pro-socialist propaganda, and with a constant theme that America and American Capitalism are bad, some socialists seek to convince you that we live in an immoral country and we must adopt socialism. (Of course, American Capitalism is moral and socialism is immoral. As is often the case, socialists have it totally backwards.)

Besides controlling the message and what you can hear, some socialists also want to control the conversation and what you can say. Let's look at this second area of control in which some socialists seek to control you and your family.

Control the Conversation (What You Can Say)

As part of Strategy #2, some socialists also seek to control the conversation. Specifically, they want to control what you can say. They do this in a growing number of ways. For example, in Chapter 6, in the sub-section on the Freedom to Speak and the Freedom to Offend, we saw that some socialists label certain kinds of speech as offensive. In effect, some socialists are telling Americans what they can and can't say. Some topics are strictly forbidden. Limiting free speech as offensive is one tactic that some socialists use to control what you and your family can say.

There are other more insidious means to control the conversation, and to restrict what you and your family can say. In Appendix A in the Battle against the First Amendment and Free Speech, we see how socialists have sought to limit free speech in many other ways. To illustrate, socialist efforts to block the free expression of Christianity is an attempt to control the conversation. Also, the so-called "Fairness Doctrine" and the so-called "Web Fairness Doctrine" are two related tactics to restrict free speech. If the so-called "Fairness Doctrine" results in radio stations taking your favorite talk radio program off the air, you are no longer able to call in and voice your opinions. Both you and the talk show radio host lose their freedom of speech in this communications venue. Plus, both Federal and State campaign finance reform laws are still other examples of attempts to control the conversation we can have in America.

Shutting down debate and discussion is one more socialist tactic. For example, as we have indicated elsewhere in this book, some socialists typically do not want any debate on global warming. Or, for that matter, they do not want debate on other issues as well. Often, those who disagree with socialist positions are shouted down on campuses in a show of rudeness and lack of tolerance. Yet, these same socialists will demand and expect tolerance for their ideas, no matter how offensive they seem to proponents of American Capitalism and our American Civilization.

As you might have realized too, hiring and firing decisions can be impacted dramatically by socialism's desire for uniform thinking. *Persona non grata* means the welcome mat is not out for American Capitalists in many college and university departments, in many newsrooms and editorial boardrooms, and on many TV program sets and in many movie studios across America today.

You can sometimes see socialist orthodoxy at play in who gets invited to professional and personal get-togethers. Both formal dinners and even casual events can be the means of enforcing socialist thinking. If you hold opinions that support America and American Capitalism, don't expect to be on the *A List* and get an invitation to most elite parties.
It even shows up in dating. Some socialists won't consider dating an American Capitalist. Socialists do not seem to tolerate American Capitalists and their views very well.

In some professional and personal circles, individuals actually feel intimidated to express their Christian morality, their pro-American views, or their pro-American Capitalist ideas. Sometimes individuals think there will be retribution, subtle or overt, if they speak openly and honestly. It has even been suggested that some skeptics of the so-called global warming "crisis" are committing a crime by promoting a different point of view on global warming.[202] If dissent and disagreement are actually criminalized in America, we are no longer free. We will have slipped into a socialist dictatorship. At that point, free speech will be non-existent and intimidation will be rampant.

In all these ways, some socialists are attempting to control the conversation and attempting to control what you can say.

Control the Agenda (What You Can Think)

Some socialists not only want to control what you can hear (by dominating the news media, schools, colleges, universities, and the entertainment industry) and some socialists not only want to control what you can say (by limiting your free speech with a variety of restrictive tactics), but some socialists also want to control the agenda. They seek to control what you can think. Controlling what you can think is the third control area in socialist's strategy to control you and your family.

Socialists are aggressive and persistent propagandists. They want to control the agenda. They seek to set the list of topics for national discussion. In part, they accomplish this by dominating the news media, the "education" establishment, and the entertainment industry. Of course, their dominance is not complete. Yet, they hold a powerful sway over these communication channels that "inform" America.

By setting the agenda, some socialists want to get inside your mind and control what you can think. They want their issues in front of you. They want their ideas to "inform" your thinking in such a way that you will agree to their viewpoints. Ultimately, they want you to relinquish your freedom and your power to them. Socialists seek power and control. They need your acquiescence, your complacency, your compliance, and your submission to destroy the institutions of American Capitalism, to control you and your family, and to gain the power and control they seek so badly.

The earlier table lists (in the Control the Agenda section) the themes and topics that socialists are using to set the national agenda. Of course, the list includes attacking America and attacking the institutions of American Capitalism. This is to be expected. But, in addition, it includes other common socialist themes such as the so-called global warming "crisis" and the so-called health care "crisis." Still other themes revolve around:

- Setting false expectations that socialism and big government can solve our problems,
- Creating the impression that everyone is just a member of a social group, not an individual or a member of a family,
- Destroying individualism,
- Destroying the Family,
- Creating groups of "victims," and
- Creating a welfare state mentality where "victims" think they are

permanently dependent on government.

These are the themes and topics some socialists are using to control the agenda and to control what you can think. Not surprisingly, some socialists seek to control the national mood as well. They want to control what you can feel as we will see in the next section.

Control the Mood (What You Can Feel)

Socialist's Strategy #2 to control you and your family also includes a fourth area of control, controlling what you can feel. If you and your family feel miserable and depressed, or worried and fretful, or anxious and fearful, socialists believe that you are more likely to give up on America, give up on American Capitalism, give up your freedom, and give up your power and control to them.

A depressed person is not a healthy person psychologically. They are more inclined to make poor decisions and more likely to make bad judgments. If socialists can change you and your family's mood from enthusiastic and optimistic, to depressed and pessimistic, they can control you and destroy American Capitalism. If socialists can depress you, they can win America's Economic War.

Recall from Chapter 3, the discussion on the Christian foundations of American Capitalism. A key point in that discussion was how faith in God led to faith in reason, then how faith in reason led to faith in progress, then how faith in progress led to optimism, then how optimism led to creativity, and finally how creativity spawned a myriad of moral, political, and economic innovations. From these innovations, came considerable moral, political, and economic growth. In addition, from these innovations, American Capitalism eventually sprang forth. With American Capitalism, came enormous economic growth and tremendous economic prosperity, flourishing under liberty and freedom.

Our faith in God generates hope. Optimism springs forth from that hope. Optimism is the lifeblood of America, American Capitalism, and American prosperity. It generates enormous energy for a new and better life for you and your family. Optimism is a spiritual virtue.

In sharp contrast, socialism offers pessimism as its overwhelming emotion.

Optimism has no place in an atheistic philosophy. Socialism sometimes tries to offer a glimmer of optimism and hope (especially when it tries to convince you it's going to solve your problems). You hear it now and then from socialists. But, socialism's moral bankruptcy greatly restricts socialism to just a few momentary embers of a dismal and dying socialist optimism. In either case, socialism can only deliver emptiness. It's a vacuous philosophy. In space, a vacuum takes up space and contains a void. In philosophy, socialism takes up thoughts and delivers little to mankind.

Some socialists are attempting today to control the national mood and to control what you can feel. It's all part of socialist Strategy #2 to control you and your family.

Control the Economy and Your Life (What You Can Do)

Socialists seek to control what you can hear, what you can say, what you can think, and what you can feel. In addition to all of that, socialists want to control the economy and your life. This means they want to control what you and your family can do in life. Wow! Talk about control.

When you think about the enormity of the American Economy, socialism's desire to control the economy, staggers the imagination. If socialists win America's Economic War, they will control the entire economy. They will destroy your economic freedom along with your religious freedom and political freedom.

Recall Socialism's Chain of Control in Chapter 1. It shows how American Culture, American Government, and the American Economy are all linked inextricably together, along with religious freedom, political freedom, and economic freedom. Controlling the American Economy also means controlling the culture, controlling morality, and controlling the government. Controlling the entire economy is equivalent to complete socialization of the economy, to complete socialism, and to a ruthless totalitarian dictatorship.

The earlier table shows some examples of how socialists want to control what you can do in your life. They include:

- Control you and your family's lifestyle by creating fear and guilt over the so-called global warming "crisis,"

- Control you and your family's health care by taking over the health care industry because of the so-called health care "crisis,"
- Control what you and your family eat by creating fear over certain foods,
- Control what you and your spouse can do for a living (with a myriad of economic regulations),
- Control what you and your spouse can earn and how much you and your spouse can keep (with a myriad of taxes and economic regulations),
- Control how much you and your spouse can invest for retirement and how much you and your spouse can spend during retirement (with a myriad of economic regulations),
- Control what you and your family can buy and sell (with a myriad of economic regulations), and
- Control _if and how_ you can use your own private property.

The battle summaries in Appendix A provide many specific examples of how socialists are attempting to control the economy and your life and what you can do in your life.

There is one final area in which some socialists want to control you and your family. This is in the area of elections.

Control the Election Process (What Type of Leaders You Can Elect)

In a democracy, free, fair, and honest elections confer power and control on elected leaders. The integrity of the election process is vital to a healthy democracy. In their quest for power over the American Economy, some socialists seek to control the election process. They want to control what type of leaders you can elect. It's all part of socialist Strategy #2 to control you and your family. It's all part of America's Economic War.

Unfortunately, it's true today that many Americans do not believe our elections are free, fair, and honest. According to John Fund:

... the level of suspicion has grown so dramatically that it threatens to undermine our political system. A Rasmussen Reports survey found early in 2008 that when it comes to concern about vote fraud, 17 percent believe that *large numbers of legitimate voters are prevented from voting. A slightly larger number, 23 percent, believe that large numbers of ineligible people are allowed to vote.*[203]

It's also true that the easiest way for socialists to obtain power is through various manipulations of the election process. If they can control the type of leaders you are able to elect, it's a simple road to victory in America's Economic War. If they can assure that socialists are elected to as many offices as possible, they can effectively destroy American Capitalism and replace it with socialism. In what ways are some socialists trying to control the election process?

Some socialists support policies that make it easier for voter fraud to go undetected. For example, by allowing mail-in registrations as well as by prohibiting voter identification (voter ID) rules and *double registration* database checks, voter fraud can take place with less detection.[204] Similarly, by blocking the use of new technologies that can screen out phony registration addresses, it is reasonable to expect more voter fraud will go unnoticed.[205]

In a vibrant and advanced democracy such as in America, using innovative, new technologies and straight forward procedures for voter registration and validation are appropriate measures to take to assure the integrity of our election processes and election results. Nearly 100 democracies around the world require photo identification to vote.[206] Why shouldn't voter ID rules be used in America?

Socialists also can try to control the election process by campaigning as American Capitalists (that is, by taking positions that support Freedom and the Free Market). But, after their election, they can govern as socialists (by attacking Freedom and the Free Market). In the language of the past, how often did you see candidates for office who sounded conservative when campaigning, but who governed like a "liberal" after being elected?

Another technique that socialists (and others) can use to win elections is to make unrealistic promises to voters during the campaigns and then not deliver on those promises. Of course, socialists can't deliver on an endless list of giveaway programs. The reason for their failure to deliver on promises is simple. There's never enough money to pay for their promises.

Socialist programs cost money and thus, consume capital. But, socialism has no mechanism to create capital and economic wealth. American Capitalism (through the Free Market) is able to create capital. Socialism relies on previously-created capital and then, consumes that capital. This reason also helps to explain why socialism always leads to moral and economic bankruptcy. When a nation consumes capital exclusively and does not have a mechanism to create new capital, bankruptcy eventually ensues.

Still another example of how socialists can attempt to control the election process is by running negative campaigns that smear their opponents. Negative campaigning discourages all voters from participating in elections. After all, why should voters take the time to vote when the candidates are such "awful" people? In particular, negative campaigning probably discourages the opponent's voters the most. Why vote if you don't like the socialist and your candidate is a "scoundrel" too?

Another benefit of negative campaigning is that it represents a big distraction. Instead of challenging socialists and their terrible ideas and flawed programs, campaigns degrade into smear campaigns and defensive reactions to those smears. Rather than focusing on ideas, policies and potential solutions to real problems, socialists can run negative campaigns and often, their challengers simply go along with their own subsequent negative campaigns in self-defense.

If this negative campaigning approach seems new, consider the past. Socialism has a long history of attacking its opponents personally. Economist and philosopher, Ludwig von Mises, wrote about this aspect of socialism (originally published in a 1922 book that was later revised in 1932 and 1936 with additional material) with these instructive words:

> ... *Marxism protects itself against all unwelcome criticism. The enemy is not refuted ... Marx and Engels never tried to refute their opponents with argument. They insulted, ridiculed, derided, slandered, and traduced them, and in the use of these methods their followers are not less expert. Their polemic is directed never against the argument of the opponent, but always against his person.*[207]

Precisely, because socialism is indefensible morally, politically, and from an economic point of view, it is forced to avoid debate and discussion. Then, socialists can run campaigns strictly on personal attacks against its opponents, American Capitalists.

Finally, some socialists can attempt to control the election process by casting doubts on the election process and challenging the results when socialists don't win. Socialists do what they can to win elections. But, if they can't win, then can always claim the election results are not accurate. Contesting election results that appear to be fair and honest is another example of how some socialists can attempt to control the election process and what type of leaders you can elect.

The earlier table summarizes the various ways some socialists attempt to control you and your family. They try to:

- Control the Message (What You Can Hear)
- Control the Conversation (What You Can Say)
- Control the Agenda (What You Can Think)
- Control the Mood (What You Can Feel)
- Control the Economy and Your Life (What You Can Do)
- Control the Election Process (What Type of Leaders You Can Elect)

All six areas of control stem from socialist Strategy #2 to control you and your family.

With an overall understanding of socialism's battles against the institutions of American Capitalism in Chapter 6 and socialism's six areas for attempting to control you and your family in Chapter 7, it's time to think about what life will be like in America after America's Economic War is over. Chapter 8 will provide two distinct visions for America. One vision assumes American Capitalism wins America's Economic War; it's upbeat, positive, and optimistic. The other vision is pessimistic. It describes what America might be like if American Capitalism loses to socialism.

Chapter 8 also discusses some political and economic consequences of America's Economic War, including will the American economy turn-around quickly, or get bogged down in a bad recession, or worse, collapse into a ten-year depression? Finally, Chapter 8 predicts when America's Economic War will probably end and which side will likely win.

Let's jump into Chapter 8.

Part IV

The Winners

Chapter 8

Life after America's Economic War

"… freedom is never more than one generation away from extinction."
Ronald Reagan[208]

America's Economic War is raging at this very moment. In 47 major battles and three special battles against the institutions of American Capitalism, socialists are waging war against American Culture, American Government, and the American Economy. The Christian Church, the Family, the Constitution, Freedom, the Free Market, and Free Enterprise are all under relentless assault. Religious freedom, political freedom, and economic freedom are all under siege. You and your family's freedom, money and lives are in imminent and very real danger.

Indeed, America is at a very critical junction today. America will live with American Capitalism in Freedom, or it will live under socialism and government-dictated centralized planning, control, coercion, compulsion and violence.

Which side will prevail? Which side will win? Will it be American Capitalism or will it be socialism? Remember from Chapter 5 that all those "third ways," all those attempts at hybrid systems (combining some elements of American Capitalism and some elements of socialism) are not sustainable in the long run. So, the choice is clear. Will it be American Capitalism or will it be socialism?

Of course, forecasting the future is a tough job. But, this chapter will attempt to do just that. This chapter presents two distinct visions for America. One vision assumes American Capitalism wins America's Economic War; it's upbeat, positive, and optimistic. The other vision is pessimistic. It describes what America might be like if American Capitalism loses to socialism.

This chapter also discusses some political and economic consequences of America's Economic War. Of particular importance to many people is the likely outcome of America's current financial crises. Will the American economy turn-around quickly, or get bogged down in a bad recession, or worse, collapse into a ten-year depression? This chapter addresses that question.

In addition, some profound changes will probably take place within the Republican and Democratic Parties. This chapter anticipates and explains these changes. As will be seen, even the red and blue colors on our electoral maps (corresponding to red states and blue states), will likely change as a result of America's Economic War. Plus, the nature of political campaigns will change as well.

Finally, this chapter predicts when America's Economic War will probably end and which side will likely win.

Let's start by looking at life in America if American Capitalism is victorious over socialism in America's Economic War.

If American Capitalism Wins the War ...

Appendix B presents a detailed and optimistic 21st century vision for America that assumes that American Capitalism wins America's Economic War. The essence of this vision is simple. America will *preserve, protect and defend*[209] the institutions of American Capitalism. America will live in peace and prosperity through Freedom. Let's summarize that optimistic vision here.

Christian Church, Family, and Religious Freedom

If American Capitalism wins America's Economic War, American Culture will be based on its Christian heritage, but it will not be a Christian theocracy.

Americans will have religious freedom. Americans will have the freedom to express their religious beliefs in the public square without restrictions. Americans will affirm America's Christian heritage and American Culture. American Government (elected leaders and employees) will have the freedom to make references to our religious heritage without restrictions.

Americans will promote a *culture of life* and will reject a *culture of death*. Americans will promote and nurture all life, at all stages, as a gift from God.

Americans will reject abortion (at all stages), infanticide, euthanasia, suicide and the death penalty.

Americans will have renewed moral strength and morality. Americans will have stronger and more vibrant personal, professional, and business relationships. Americans will have stronger, more peaceful, and more prosperous relationships with other nations.

Americans will have stronger and more vibrant marriages and families. America will affirm marriage between a man and woman for the purpose of love and procreating children as the model for marriage that is consistent with America's Christian heritage and with American Civilization.

America will affirm family values, such as abstinence until marriage. America will reject violence, brutality, prostitution, and pornography in education and in the entertainment industry as inconsistent with America's Christian heritage and with American Civilization. Censorship is not required. Within the Free Market, everyone votes with their buying decisions.

Constitution, Religious Freedom, Political Freedom, and Economic Freedom

If American Capitalism wins America's Economic War, American Government will be based on the Constitution, preserving and protecting our Freedom.

The Constitution will be restored, interpreted, and followed as it was originally written. Justices and judges will restore, interpret, and follow the Constitution as it was originally written. Justices and judges will not function in a legislative or political role. Americans will live under the *Rule of Law*. Americans will have *Due Process*. Americans will have *Equal Protection*.

America will not recognize the power of any global organization or treaty to supersede the Constitution of the United States of America. American sovereignty will not be abridged by the United Nations or other global organizations. Americans will not pay taxes imposed by global organizations on America. America will create a new global organization, the *Free Nations,* comprised of free nations that seek to protect and promote Freedom, Free Markets and Free Trade.

America will maintain strong Armed Forces, ready to protect and defend America. American Government will never launch an offensive war. American Government will never lose a defensive war. America will safeguard and protect its borders from unlimited and illegal immigration. America will enforce its immigration laws.

Americans will have political freedom. Americans will have freedom of speech. Americans will have religious freedom of speech without "hate speech" and "offensive speech" restrictions. Americans will have political freedom of speech without "campaign finance reform," "Fairness Doctrine," "Web Fairness Doctrine" and other restrictions.

Americans will not be forced to accept the beliefs of others. For example, Christians will not be forced to accept non-Christian beliefs and values. Christians will not be forced to perform actions that they believe are morally wrong. Americans will have the freedom to follow their own consciences (the *Right of Conscience),* subject to the Rule of Law.

Americans will have the right to keep and bear arms. Americans will have the right to be secure in their persons, homes, and businesses. Americans will not be subject to unreasonable strip searches. Americans will not be subject to warrantless searches of homes and businesses.

Americans will have economic freedom. Americans will support the Free Market and Free Enterprise. Americans will support Free Trade with other nations. America will not permit discrimination for the purpose of eliminating (alleged or real) past discrimination. Affirmative action will be eliminated. Quotas will be eliminated. Reverse discrimination will be eliminated. The only way to eliminate discrimination is to eliminate discrimination.

Americans will have intellectual freedom. Faculty and students in colleges and universities will have true academic freedom and the intellectual freedom to question, debate, discuss, and explore the issues of the day (without threat to their academic positions, class grades, or other intimidation). Faculty hiring decisions will be based on teaching, research, and service capabilities, not on the political positions potential professors might or might not hold.

America will maintain adequate police capabilities to protect and defend

Americans from domestic violence, crime and fraud.

America will have positive and honest elections with debate on substantive issues, not personal attacks. America will have efficient, reliable, and honest elections using common sense voter ID rules and innovative technologies.

Free Market, Free Enterprise, and Economic Freedom

If American Capitalism wins America's Economic War, the American Economy will be based on economic freedom, creating economic growth, peace and prosperity.

Americans will have economic freedom. Americans will support the Free Market and Free Enterprise. Americans will support Free Trade with other nations.

Americans will experience unprecedented economic growth at the rate of 4% – 8% GDP per year, with economic freedom, the Free Market and Free Enterprise, by cutting the tax and regulatory burden on individuals, small businesses, and corporations, and by promoting and developing Free Trade between America and other nations.

America's charitable giving and compassion will likewise increase substantially. This is true because of America's increasing economic growth and wealth creation and long-standing tradition of generosity and compassion. America will care for its poor and downtrodden individuals and families with generosity and compassion. America will aid the poor of the world with generosity and compassion.

America will place the dollar back on the gold standard. *The dollar will be as good as gold.* Americans will experience price stability. The insidious tax of inflation will be eliminated. The dollar will stay strong against other currencies. A stable dollar means international trade and economic growth will be promoted.

America will promote and exercise Free Trade with all nations of the world. There will be <u>no</u> tariffs or duties imposed. Many economic incentives for war will be removed. An unprecedented era of peace among nations will emerge.

Government's tax and regulatory burden will be limited to 17% of America's

GDP. Federal taxes will be limited to 10% of GDP. State tax will be limited to 3% of GDP. Local (city and/or county) taxes will be limited to 2% of GDP. The Federal regulatory burden will be limited to 1.5% of GDP. The State regulatory burden will be limited to 0.3% of GDP. The local (city and/or county) regulatory burden will be limited to 0.2% of GDP.

All taxes on income, savings, investment, capital formation, property, gift, and estates (death) will be eliminated. This means that economic growth and wealth creation will not be taxed. This is a major incentive to encourage and promote economic growth. Income taxes will be eliminated. Capital gains taxes will be eliminated. Interest and dividend taxes will be eliminated. Property taxes will be eliminated. Estate (death) taxes will be eliminated. Income tax returns will be eliminated.

Tax revenues will come from sales (consumption) taxes on both *Internet* and traditional *Bricks and Mortar* transactions. This is an incentive to save and invest. This is a major incentive to encourage and promote economic growth.

American Government at the Federal, State and Local levels will be scaled back slowly as the tax and regulatory burden decreases. The primary purpose of the American Government is to protect America from external threats such as wars and terrorism, and from internal violence, crime and fraud. It also has additional roles that support its primary purpose, such as public safety and enforcing voluntary contracts. But, the Constitution was not put in place to control every aspect of American life. Government taxing and the subsequent funding of government programs is a process that involves controlling individuals and families. It is also a means for limiting or eliminating religious freedom, political freedom, and economic freedom.

Americans will have the freedom to buy, own, use, and sell private property, without burdensome government regulations, except for limited regulations related to public safety and the prevention of fraud.

Americans will not have their private property taken away by the government, except under these limited circumstances: if it's for a *public use* (in the narrowest sense), there is *due process* (in the broadest sense), and there is *just compensation* (in the broadest sense).

Americans will not have their private property taken by excessive and unfair legal judgments. Losing parties in trivial lawsuits will be required to pay for legal costs on both sides.

Americans will not have their private property taken by excessive and unfair environmental regulations. American environmental regulations will promote the environment and conservation. At the same time, those benefits will be balanced with the needs of individuals, small businesses, corporations, and America. Human needs will <u>not</u> be subordinated to the needs of every animal and insect in nature. Individuals and families will have the freedom to live in cities, suburbs, and in rural America.

America will have a strong and innovative Free Market in energy. Americans will have abundant energy at reasonable market prices. America will be energy independent to the extent it chooses based on the global market. America will develop its own energy resources within the Free Market. America will drill for oil, build new oil refineries, and will have adequate supplies of gasoline at reasonable prices. America will rely on other conventional energy sources such as coal and nuclear. America will innovate and rapidly develop new alternative sources of energy such as solar, wind, and geothermal through the power of the Free Market and its profit incentives.

America will have a strong and innovative Free Market in health care. Americans will have outstanding health care at reasonable market prices. Medicare and Medicaid will be privatized with premiums for the poor covered by the government.

America will have a strong and innovative Free Market in health care insurance. Americans will have excellent health care insurance at reasonable market prices. Employers will provide direct compensation to employees (in the form of higher wages, salaries, commissions, bonuses, stock options, etc.). Employers will <u>not</u> provide indirect compensation (in the form of health insurance and other indirect benefits).

America's education system will be the best in the world. Indoctrination will give way to education. School choice will encourage positive competition and will give parents control of their children's education. Homeschooling will be fully supported. Faculty and students in colleges and universities will have true academic freedom and the intellectual freedom to question, debate, discuss, and explore the issues of the day (without threat to their academic positions, class grades, or other intimidation). Faculty hiring decisions will be based on teaching, research, and service capabilities, not on the political positions potential professors might or might not hold.

If American Capitalism Loses the War ...

Appendix C presents a totally different vision. It summarizes a pessimistic vision for America, if American Capitalism loses America's Economic War.

The essence of this vision is simple as well. The institutions of American Capitalism will be significantly damaged or will be destroyed completely. Americans will lose their religious freedom, political freedom, and economic freedom. Americans will lose their economic prosperity. Americans will lose their lifestyles. America will drift toward moral and economic bankruptcy. Hopefully, America will never have to live through this awful scenario.

Christian Church, Family, and Religious Freedom

If American Capitalism loses America's Economic War, America's Socialist Culture will be atheistic and secular, with little (or no) value for human life and love, with value placed instead on power and pleasure. Moral bankruptcy will result.

Americans will <u>not</u> have religious freedom. Americans will <u>not</u> have the freedom to express their religious beliefs in the public square. American Government (elected leaders and employees) will <u>not</u> have the freedom to make references to our religious heritage.

Americans will reject America's Christian heritage and American Culture. Americans will promote a *culture of death* and will reject a *culture of life*. Americans will <u>not</u> promote and nurture all life, at all stages, as a gift from God. Americans will accept abortion (at all stages), infanticide, euthanasia, suicide and the death penalty.

Americans will have little (or no) moral strength and morality. Americans will have more untrusting personal, professional, and business relationships. Americans will have more strained and belligerent relationships with other nations.

Americans will have weaker marriages and families. Marriages and families will be seen as a relic of the past. Love will be seen as a foolish idea for unrealistic people. America will reject marriage between a man and woman for the purpose of love and procreating children. America will see marriage as an inconvenience without value. America will reject family values, such as abstinence until marriage, as old-fashioned. America will accept violence, brutality, prostitution, and pornography in education and in the entertainment industry as normal and commonplace.

Constitution, Religious Freedom, Political Freedom, and Economic Freedom

If American Capitalism loses America's Economic War, America's Socialist Government will be based on ignoring (or circumventing) the Constitution, Americans having little (or no) freedom, and socialist elites controlling you and your family's lives. Psychological depression and suicide will be commonplace.

The Constitution will be ignored or circumvented. Justices and judges will ignore and circumvent the Constitution as it was originally written. Justices and judges will function in a legislative and political role to advance the socialist agenda. Americans will not live under the *Rule of Law*. Americans will not have *Due Process*. Americans will not have *Equal Protection*.

America will recognize the power of global organizations and treaties to supersede the Constitution of the United States of America. American sovereignty will be abridged by the United Nations and other global organizations. Americans will pay taxes imposed by global organizations on America.

America will not maintain strong Armed Forces, ready to protect and defend America. American Government will launch offensive wars as necessary to advance the socialist agenda. America will not safeguard and protect its borders from unlimited and illegal immigration. America will not enforce its immigration laws.

Americans will not have political freedom. Americans will not have freedom of speech. Americans will not have religious freedom of speech. "Hate speech" and "offensive speech" restrictions will expand until Americans are afraid to speak in public or private. Americans will not have political freedom of speech because of "campaign finance reform," "Fairness Doctrine," "Web Fairness Doctrine" and other restrictions.

Americans will be forced to accept the beliefs of others. For example, Christians will be forced to accept non-Christian beliefs and values. Christians will be forced to perform actions that they believe are morally wrong. Americans will <u>not</u> have the freedom to follow their own consciences (the *Right of Conscience),* subject to the Rule of Law.

Americans will not have the right to keep and bear arms. Strict gun control laws will be imposed on Americans. Americans will not have the right to be secure in their persons, homes, and businesses. Americans will be subject to unreasonable strip searches. Americans will be subject to warrantless searches of homes and businesses.

Americans will <u>not</u> have economic freedom. American Government will <u>not</u> permit the Free Market and Free Enterprise. American Government will <u>not</u> permit Free Trade with other nations. American Government will permit discrimination to advance the socialist agenda. Affirmative action will be expanded. Quotas will be expanded. Reverse discrimination will be expanded. Major financial reparations will be paid to relatives of former slaves, even when the evidence is uncertain. Major financial reparations will be paid to other nations for alleged damages caused by America, even when the evidence of any damages is tenuous.

Americans will <u>not</u> have intellectual freedom. Faculty and students in colleges and universities will <u>not</u> have true academic freedom and will <u>not</u> have the intellectual freedom to question, debate, discuss, and explore the issues of the day (without threat to their academic positions, class grades, or other intimidation). Faculty hiring decisions will <u>not</u> be based on teaching, research, and service capabilities. Instead, such decisions will be based on the political positions potential professors hold.

America will live in a police state.

America will have sham elections without debate on substantive issues, but with personal attacks and negative campaigning. America will have dishonest elections with voter fraud seen as normal.

Free Market, Free Enterprise, and Economic Freedom

If American Capitalism loses America's Economic War, America's Socialist Economy will be based on little (or no) economic freedom. There will be little, no, or negative economic growth initially. Shortages and rationing will be widespread. Poverty and destitution will be widespread. Economic bankruptcy will result inevitably.

Americans will _not_ have economic freedom. American Government will _not_ permit the Free Market and Free Enterprise. American Government will _not_ permit Free Trade with other nations.

Americans will experience little, no, or negative economic growth at the rate of -4% to 1% GDP per year, without economic freedom, the Free Market and Free Enterprise; by substantially increasing the tax and regulatory burden on individuals, small businesses, and corporations; and by preventing Free Trade between America and other nations.

America's charitable giving and compassion will decrease substantially. This is true because of America's declining economic growth and capital consumption under socialist policies and programs. America will _not_ be able to afford compassion and generosity. The socialist culture will _not_ value compassion and generosity.

America will _not_ place the dollar back on the gold standard. _The dollar will not be as good as gold. The dollar will not be worth the paper it's printed on._ Americans will experience price instability. Americans will experience inflation, and possibly hyperinflation. The dollar will _not_ stay strong against other currencies. International trade and economic growth will _not_ be promoted.

America will _not_ promote and exercise Free Trade with all nations of the world. There will be many tariffs and duties imposed. Many economic incentives for war will be created. An unprecedented era of conflict and belligerence among nations will emerge.

Government's tax and regulatory burden will be very high. It will exceed 60% of America's GDP. It will stifle innovation, incentive, capital creation, economic growth, and wealth creation.

All taxes on income, savings, investment, capital formation, property, gift, and estates (death) will be increased. This means that economic growth and wealth creation will be taxed at high rates. This is a major disincentive to encourage and promote economic growth. Income taxes will be increased. Capital gains taxes will be increased. Interest and dividend taxes will be increased. Property taxes will be increased. Gift taxes will be increased. Estate (death) taxes will be increased. Income tax returns will be more complicated.

Tax revenues from sales (consumption) taxes on *Internet* and traditional *Bricks and Mortar* transactions will be increased. Sales taxes on Internet transactions will be increased (if already in existence) and will be added (if not already in existence). Sales taxes on services will be added to the already excessive tax burden of the American people.

American Government at the Federal, State and Local levels will grow in size and complexity dramatically. The tax and regulatory burden on Americans will be enormous. The primary purpose of the American Government will be to control the lives and lifestyles of all Americans. Government will limit or eliminate religious freedom, political freedom, and economic freedom.

Americans will not have the freedom to buy, own, use, and sell private property without burdensome government regulations, and without the permission of the government.

Americans will have their private property taken away by the government for *public or private use,* without *due process,* and without *just compensation.* For all practical purposes, private property will no longer exist. Private property will effectively be public property, since private property will be controlled by government.

Americans will have their private property taken by excessive and unfair legal judgments. Trivial lawsuits will be a means to steal private property from its rightful owner.

Americans will have their private property taken by excessive and unfair environmental regulations. American environmental regulations will trump the private property rights of Americans. Human needs will be subordinated to the needs of every animal and insect in nature. Individuals and families will not have the freedom to live in cities, suburbs, and in rural America at their own discretion. Government permission will be required.

America will not have a strong and innovative free market in energy. Americans will not have abundant energy at reasonable market prices.

America will <u>not</u> be energy independent to the extent it chooses based on the global market. America will <u>not</u> develop its own energy resources within the Free Market. America will <u>not</u> drill for oil, will <u>not</u> build new oil refineries, and will <u>not</u> have adequate supplies of gasoline at reasonable prices. America will <u>not</u> rely on other conventional energy sources such as coal and nuclear. America will <u>not</u> innovate and rapidly develop new alternative sources of energy such as solar, wind, and geothermal through the power of the Free Market and its profit incentives. America will have energy shortages and government rationing. Americans will pay new Carbon Taxes and Energy Taxes. Americans will have to cut back on their energy usage and their lifestyles. American businesses will <u>not</u> have adequate energy supplies to meet consumer needs for products and services.

America will not have a strong and innovative free market in health care. Americans will <u>not</u> have outstanding health care at reasonable market prices. Americans will have inferior health care. Medicare and Medicaid will be extended to include all Americans at all ages. Shortages and government rationing of health care services will be commonplace. Americans will suffer and die waiting for urgent services. Americans will be denied medical care and drugs that are deemed by government to be too expensive. New drugs and innovative therapies will <u>not</u> be developed without economic freedom and Free Market incentives.

America will not have a strong and innovative free market in health care insurance. Americans will be forced to enroll in a socialist universal, health care system run inefficiently by the government.

America's education system will not be the best in the world. Indoctrination will grow. Education will be eliminated. School choice will <u>not</u> be permitted. Homeschooling will <u>not</u> be permitted. Faculty and students in colleges and universities will <u>not</u> have true academic freedom and will <u>not</u> have the intellectual freedom to question, debate, discuss, and explore the issues of the day (without threat to their academic positions, class grades, or other intimidation). Faculty hiring decisions will <u>not</u> be based on teaching, research, and service capabilities. They will be based on the political positions potential professors hold.

With that look at the two visions for life in America after America's Economic War, let's consider some other consequences of America's Economic War on America.

It's No Longer ...

America's Economic War will have a number of other political and economic consequences on America. These consequences include various political changes we can expect to see in America as a result of America's Economic War. In addition, America's Economic War continues to impact the American economy. We will attempt to answer the very important question that was posed at the beginning of Chapter 1, namely, will the American economy turn-around quickly, or get bogged down in a bad recession, or worse, collapse into a ten-year depression?

But, first, let's predict some of the political changes we can expect to see on the American Political Landscape in the next few years.

It's No Longer Republicans vs. Democrats – It's American Capitalists vs. Socialists

The Republican Party and the Democratic Party as we have known them are both collapsing as this book is being written. They are casualties of America's Economic War.

Clearly, both the Republican Party and the Democratic Party have evolved over the years since their respective beginnings. Today, both parties are struggling to define themselves. Both parties are straining to create and maintain a fragile (and probably temporary) sense of unity. Within both parties, there are major power struggles for control of policies and platforms. Within both parties, there is widespread confusion and dissatisfaction among constituencies. Why is this happening now? What can we expect in the future?

Without question, the defining conflict of our times is America's Economic War, the war between American Capitalism and socialism. America's cultural battles, political battles, and economic battles all radiate from the hub of America's Economic War.

Politics always reflects the major and minor conflicts of a nation. However, as this book is being written, neither the Republican Party nor the Democratic Party has dealt clearly and concisely with America's Economic War. Neither party has taken a definitive stand. Neither party has taken a clear-cut position. There are American Capitalists in both parties and there are socialists in both parties. This has caused undo confusion for Americans in general and voters in particular. Some individuals say that there are no differences between the two parties. To some extent, these individuals have a valid point and are right.

There are three potential outcomes that can resolve the current dilemma of political parties that lack a clear vision and focus:

- Outcome #1 – The Republican Party and the Democratic Party can morph into the American Capitalist Party and the Socialist Party.
- Outcome #2 – The Republican Party and the Democratic Party can cease to exist entirely. In their place, two new parties can emerge: the American Capitalist Party and the Socialist Party.
- Outcome #3 – One of the two parties will morph into a new party, one will cease to exist, and a new party will come into existence. After those changes, there can be two parties: the American Capitalist Party and the Socialist Party.

By having two parties that more precisely reflect the defining conflict of our times, America's Economic War, Americans will know who they support, why they support them, what they can expect if someone is elected to office from one party or the other. It will also help Americans to know who to vote for in any given election. In fact, it makes things easier for everyone concerned: the parties, the candidates, the constituencies, the media, and of course, the voters. Widespread confusion will be eliminated. Communication will be enhanced.

Some other names for the new (or morphed) parties come to mind as well. Instead of the American Capitalist Party, there can be a Freedom Lover's Party, or a Constitutional Freedom Party. In place of the Socialist Party, there might be a Progressive Socialist Party or an Environmental Socialist Party. Obviously, the party members can choose the names of their respective parties.

Most likely, we will see one of the three outcomes listed above take place in the next few years. Since national party infrastructure is a challenge to build from scratch, the highest probability outcome above is Outcome #1. We can expect the two parties to morph into new parties with clear platforms representing the two major religious/cultural, political, and economic systems, American Capitalism and socialism.

With the new parties, we can also expect many politicians and individuals to switch their party loyalties and affiliations.

Indeed, we can say with a fair degree of certainty that it's no longer Republicans vs. Democrats. It will probably be American Capitalists vs. Socialists or something comparable.

It's No Longer Red States vs. Blue States –
Red is the Color of Socialism, Blue is the Color of Freedom

When the parties change, so will the colors on electoral maps for a very simple and historical reason.

The color red has long been associated with socialism.[210] Recall the Red Star. Or, remember Mao Tse-tung's *Little Red Book*.[211] In contrast, blue is the color of freedom and wide open skies[212]. It is the color associated with the heavens and heavenly thoughts. It's the color we see *when we look up* during daylight. It's the color of optimism.

In the media and on their electoral maps (as this book is being written), Red States are states that vote for Republicans, while Blue States are states that vote for Democrats.

It's no longer Red States (for Republicans) vs. Blue States (for Democrats). It will probably be Blue States (for American Capitalists) vs. Red States (for socialists).

It's No Longer Negative Campaigns that Win Elections –
It's Positive Campaigns that Win Mandates

With America's Economic War coming into sharper focus now and new or morphed political parties coming into existence that reflect the true conflict fault lines in America, we can expect a tectonic change in election dynamics. No longer will Americans need to vote against a candidate for negative reasons. Instead, Americans will be able to vote for a candidate for positive reasons. They can vote for American Capitalists if they prefer American Capitalism. They can vote for socialists if they prefer socialism.

When political parties and their respective candidates stand for something concrete, Americans have a substantive reason to vote for a candidate (as opposed to voting against a candidate by casting a vote for the other candidate). Convoluted and confused political parties, candidates, policies and programs leave voters little alternative but to consider other factors such as negative campaign ads that attack an opponent's character.

It's probably true that negative campaigns win elections when political parties and candidates offer confusing policies and programs. However, when political parties and candidates offer clear and concise policies and programs that align with the nation's conflicts, we can expect that positive campaigns will result in mandates for candidates and their platforms.

While negative political campaigns typically focus on personal attacks, positive campaigns focus on policies and programs that deal with the nation's challenges. We can expect to see more positive political campaigns in the future that result in decisive electoral mandates. This, too, is a change we will see as a consequence of America's Economic War.

So, it's no longer negative campaigns that win elections, it's positive campaigns that probably will win mandates.

Let's now turn our attention to the question we posed at the beginning in Chapter 1, will the American economy turn-around quickly, or get bogged down in a bad recession, or worse, collapse into a ten-year depression? Put slightly differently, what is the impact of America's Economic War on the American Economy for the near future?

The American Economy – A Quick Turn-Around, a Bad Recession, or a Ten-Year Depression?

By now, you can see why American Capitalism generates the most economic growth and prosperity of any economic system ever developed. In stark contrast, you can also understand why socialism always leads to moral and economic bankruptcy. Over recent years, as socialist ideas have become more in vogue in America, we can see socialist thinking taking root in our schools and on our campuses, in our politics and in our government, in our culture and somewhat surprisingly, even in our churches.

The results are becoming obvious to even the casual observer. Americans are experiencing a significant decline in American Culture, American Government, and the American Economy. Immorality is on the ascent, corruption in government is becoming more obvious, election recounts and results are sometimes suspect, and the economy is experiencing greater inflation, more layoffs, more foreclosures, and more bankruptcies. Capital investment and economic growth have been stifled by attacks on the Free Market by onerous and numerous government regulations and restrictions as well as by very high taxes. All of this is precisely what we should expect from the influence of socialism on our nation.

The fate of the American Economy and you and your family's finances are clear to see and easy to predict. To the extent that America adopts socialism as its guiding philosophy and its preferred religious/cultural, political, and economic system, America will move toward moral and economic bankruptcy. The velocity that propels America toward moral and economic bankruptcy depends only upon the degree to which socialist thinking is adopted by the nation. America's Economic War is precisely about the battle over which economic system will ultimately prevail in America.

This author believes that because socialist thinking is widespread and pervasive today and because it enjoys broad acceptance within the media, the "education" establishment, and the entertainment industry, all powerful vehicles for influencing citizens, the American Economy will continue to languish and decline further.

In this author's view, at the time this book is being written, America is on a fast track to a ten-year depression. The choice for the length of the potential depression, ten years, is not arbitrary. Given the current popularity of socialism and its seductive arguments, it will likely take at least eight years for Americans to see the devastating effects of socialism first hand, to become better educated on Free Market economics, and to understand what policies and programs are needed to once again rev up the engine of American Capitalism. It will then take another two years to have the economy attain significant economic growth once again. That means we face a potential economic depression lasting ten years. But, it need not be so.

Seven Free Market Principles that Can Generate Economic Prosperity Soon

While America is on a trajectory toward depression as this book is being written, the American Economy can turn around quickly, at any time, by following some basic Free Market principles:

- Eliminate (or at least cut) taxes on income, savings, capital formation, and investment

- Eliminate (or at least cut) taxes on private property, gifts, and estate (death) taxes
- Eliminate (or at least cut) government regulations and restrictions that inhibit economic growth
- Eliminate (or at least cut) government regulations and restrictions on the Free Market
- Eliminate (or at least cut) government regulations and restrictions on Free Trade
- Limit government spending + government regulatory impact to 17% of GDP
- Place the dollar back on the gold standard (or at least, establish a monetary policy that limits inflation to less than 1% per year)

The author predicts that following these seven Free Market principles will result in sustained economic growth in the range of 4% to 8% per year, generating enormous economic growth, wealth, and prosperity.

Finally, let's answer the two remaining questions. When will America's Economic War end? Who will win the war?

When Will the War End?

While forecasting is an extremely difficult process, it is the author's best estimate that America's Economic War will finally come to an end in the next 20 years. In the next four to eight years, we should all have a strong indication of the results of socialist policies in America. Americans will determine if they like what they see, or if they prefer the America our Founding Fathers envisioned as well as American Capitalism.

Assuming Americans choose Faith, Freedom and the Free Market, it will then take another 12 years to solidify the decision, undo the damage to the Constitution, to re-assert our freedoms, and apply the seven Free Market principles listed above. Thus, over the next generation, America will decide if it will live with American Capitalism in freedom, or it will live under socialism and government-dictated centralized planning, control, coercion, compulsion and violence.

The final big question, the bottom line as they say in business, is who will win the war?

Who Will Win the War?

America and American Capitalism have long relied on individual Americans and American families for survival and growth. Individual Americans wrote the Declaration of Independence and the Constitution. Individual Americans and American families fought and won the Revolutionary War. They fought and won the Civil War. Individual Americans and American families fought and won World War I and fought and won World War II.

Individual Americans and American families have explored the American wilderness and settled the American West. They have built the factories and the offices, and started the businesses that made America the richest nation in the world. They have built the apartments and the condos and all the homes across America. Individual Americans and American families have planted the seeds and harvested the crops, and filled our supermarkets with an abundance of goods.

Individual Americans and American families have fed the poor, healed the sick, and come to the rescue of thousands or even millions of people around the world when our neighbors called out to us for help.

Individual Americans have built the space program and explored the moon. They have solved problem after problem, designed solution after solution, and innovated in education, medicine, business, and technology.

Individual Americans have made innumerable scientific discoveries and innovations and have created countless technological inventions. Individual Americans' discoveries and innovations include anesthesia (ether), the atomic time clock, blood plasma storage (blood banks), the Laser, the polio vaccine, and xerography. American individuals have invented the incandescent lamp and the fluorescent lamp, the electric washer and the dishwasher, the bifocal lens and the corneal contact lens, the microprocessor and the electronic computer, the cell phone and the cordless phone, as well as frozen foods and the microwave oven, to name just a few of America's incredible inventions. [213]

Individual Americans and American families have done all these wonderful things and a whole lot more, living under Freedom.

Individual Americans and American families, living with faith in God, living under Freedom, living with an inextinguishable hope for life itself, and an unconquerable optimism for even a better life, are the true strength of America.

While Americans are even now toying with socialist policies and many are falling prey to its clever seductions, I have no doubt that Americans and America will choose American Capitalism in the long run.

America is all about Freedom. Americans will not give up their freedom to pursue happiness and fulfillment for the false promises and foolish prescriptions of socialism. Americans will reject the phony freedom from insecurity promised by socialists, a freedom socialists can never deliver.

America is all about Freedom. The freedom to live, to act, to do, to move, to travel, to create, to enjoy, to risk, to pursue happiness and fulfillment in whatever manner they choose (subject only to the limitation of not hurting others).

America is all about Freedom. God is the author of that freedom.

With faith in God and God's help, American Capitalism will win America's Economic War!

Part V
The Appendices

Appendix A

The War Room – Battle Summaries for All 47 Major Battles and 3 Special Battles

Major Battles against the Christian Church and Religious Freedom

Note that this section includes battlefront examples and references for each battle to indicate the scope and extent of America's Economic War.

Battle against Faith in God
- Attacking the Christian Church's faith in God.[214]
- Attacking the Christian Church's faith in reason.[215]
- Attacking the fact that faith and reason are both means to seeking the truth (and that both are compatible with each other).[216]
- Attacking the truth.[217]
- Attacking the existence of truth.[218]
- Promoting postmodernism and its socialist philosophy of atheism, nothingness, rage, and power.[219]

Battle against the Bible
- Attacking the Bible as "hate speech."[220]
- Banning the distribution of Bibles.[221]
- Banning the Bible in schools[222] and at work.[223]
- Banning Bible Study groups on campus.[224]
- Prohibiting children from discussing Bible stories in public schools.[225]
- Attacking Scripture verse citations (such as Isaiah 40:31) on clothing,[226] art,[227] and memorials.[228]

Battle against Christian Symbols
- Attacking the display of the Christian Cross.[229]
- Attacking the display of the Ten Commandments.[230]
- Attacking the display of Christmas Trees.[231]
- Attacking the display of Nativity Scenes.[232]
- Prohibiting U.S. Military personnel from displaying Christian symbols while fighting in certain areas of the world.[233]

Battle against the Free Expression of Christianity
- Attacking Christian art.[234]
- Banning Christian books in schools.[235]
- Prohibiting Christians from speaking about their moral values or beliefs in schools,[236] on campus,[237] and on state property.[238]
- Prohibiting children from wearing clothing that has Christian words on it in public schools.[239]
- Prohibiting Christian materials from being distributed in public[240].

- Prohibiting school choir members from voluntarily singing in an after-school, Church program.[241]
- Discriminating against Christians for their religious beliefs in hiring decisions[242] and for promotions.[243]
- Discriminating against Christian groups for equal access to public facilities[244] and funding.[245]
- Discriminating against Christian students for scholarship awards.[246]

Battle against Prayer
- Banning prayer in schools[247] and at school graduations.[248]
- Banning references to God[249] and Jesus[250] in graduation speeches.
- Banning praying in public parks.[251]
- Attacking a child from bowing and praying individually during lunch in a public school.[252]
- Attacking the distribution of the President's National Day of Prayer Proclamation using public school email.[253]

Battle against Christmas and Easter
- Attacking the use of the word Christmas.[254]
- Replacing the word Christmas with the word "Holiday."[255]
- Attacking the display of Christmas Trees.[256]
- Attacking the display of Nativity scenes in public places.[257]
- Attacking the use of Christmas jewelry.[258]
- Attacking the singing of Christmas songs.[259]
- Replacing the words in Christmas songs to eliminate Christian
- references.[260]
- Attacking the use of the word Easter.[261]
- Attacking Good Friday as a holiday.[262]

Battle against Christian Churches
- Using zoning laws to limit the size and location of Christian Churches.[263]
- Using zoning laws to prohibit holding a Christian small group meeting at someone's home.[264]

Battle against Other Traces of Christianity
- Eliminating the words "under God" from the Pledge of Allegiance.[265]
- Eliminating the recitation of the Pledge of Allegiance.[266]
- Trying to eliminate the words "In God We Trust" from display in schools.[267]
- Banning a Christian charity from giving shoes to needy children.[268]

- Attacking a prison ministry program.[269]

Battle against Tolerance for Christianity
- Lack of tolerance for (and open hostility toward) Christianity.[270]
- Tolerance for (and sometimes promotion of) atheism.[271]
- Tolerance for (and sometimes promotion of) non-Christian religions, including Islam and Hinduism.[272]
- Tolerance for (and sometimes promotion of) spiritual, religious, and other practices, rituals, and beliefs including New Age, Mother Earth, Native American, Human Sacrifice, and Death Education.[273]

Major Battles against the Family and Religious Freedom
Note that this section includes battlefront examples and references for each battle to indicate the scope and extent of America's Economic War.

Battle against Traditional Marriage
- Attacking traditional marriage between a man and a woman.[274]
- Attacking marriage with "no fault" divorces.[275]
- Promoting the *Unmarriage Revolution* (separating marriage from child-rearing).[276]
- Promoting same-sex "marriages."[277]
- Promoting domestic partnerships.[278]
- Promoting open same-sex "marriages" (where same-sex partners are not faithful to their partner).[279]
- Promoting marriage benefits for non-traditional "marriages" and domestic partnerships.[280]
- Promoting polygamy.[281]

Battle against Family Life
- Attacking pro-life free speech.[282]
- Attacking the culture of life.[283]
- Attacking the *Right of Conscience*.[284]
- Attacking meaningful death.[285]
- Promoting fatherless children through artificial insemination.[286]
- Promoting the culture of death.[287]
- Promoting abortion.[288]
- Permitting newborn death by intentional neglect.[289]
- Promoting infanticide.[290]
- Promoting physician-assisted suicide.[291]
- Promoting euthanasia.[292]

- Promoting "anonymous death."[293]
- Promoting the pagan custom of cremation.[294]

Battle against Family Values
- Attacking abstinence until marriage.[295]
- Promoting sexual education and on-demand contraception, despite research data that indicates it's not effective in teens under age 16.[296]
- Promoting "Anonymous Sex."[297]
- Promoting pornography in the entertainment industry and on the Internet.[298]
- Promoting violence and brutality in the entertainment industry and on the Internet.[299]
- Promoting sexually-oriented businesses.[300]
- Promoting dehumanization of men and women,[301] and the objectification of individuals.[302]
- Promoting "diversity training" that seeks to replace Christian values with secular values and that seeks to teach tolerance for many things, but not for Christianity.[303]

Battle against Parenting
- Attacking the role of women in child-rearing.[304]
- Attacking parental notification and approval for a child's abortion.[305]
- Attacking parental notification and approval for condoms and birth control pills for pre-teens and teens.[306]
- Attacking a parent's authority to be with their children in a doctor's office during a physical exam.[307]
- Attacking the parent's authority to make medical decisions for a child.[308]

Battle against Children
- Attacking larger families (more than two children).[309]
- Attacking children as the cause of pollution and the so-called problem of overpopulation.[310]
- Attacking the health and financial security of children with "no fault" divorces.[311]
- Attacking the Boy Scouts.[312]
- Promoting childhood androgyny(making boys and girls alike).[313.]
- Promoting violence in entertainment that can negatively impact children.[314]

Battle against Homeschooling

- Attacking homeschooling.[315]
- Attacking funding for charter schools that support homeschooling.[316]
- Attacking school choice and school vouchers.[317]

Major Battles against the Constitution and Religious Freedom, Political Freedom, and Economic Freedom

Note that this section includes battlefront examples and references for each battle to indicate the scope and extent of America's Economic War.

Battle against the Constitution as Originally Written

We the People of the United States, in Order to form a more perfect Union ... and secure the Blessings of Liberty to ourselves and our Posterity, do ordain and establish this Constitution for the United States of America. '

- Attacking the original meaning of the Constitution (as written and explained by our Founding Fathers).[318]
- Attacking the concept of limited and democratic, self-government.[319]
- Attacking the Rule of Law.[320]
- Promoting judicial activism with justices and judges –
  o Giving new and unintended meaning to some parts of the Constitution,[321]
  o Ignoring other parts of the Constitution,[322] and
  o Legislating from the bench.[323]
  o Promoting unlimited and elite, centralized government. [324]
  o Denying the exceptionality of our Constitution and promoting the use of foreign constitutional law to interpret our Constitution.[325]

Battle against the First Amendment and Religious Freedom

Congress shall make no law respecting an establishment of religion, or prohibiting the free exercise thereof ...

- Attacking Christian free speech.[326]
- Attacking free speech that references God[327] or Jesus.[328]
- Attacking Christian symbols that are displayed in public.[329]
- Attacking the free exercise of Christianity.[330]
- Attacking the free expression of Christianity in public.[331]
- Attacking the free expression of Christianity at school,[332] on

campus[333], and at work.[334]

- Attacking the free expression of Christianity in art.[335]
- Attacking the free expression of Christianity on clothing,[336] with jewelry,[337] and on memorials.[338]
- Attempting to force Christians to violate their religious beliefs (such as trying to force a pharmacist to dispense a "morning after" pill).[339]
- Attempting to force Christians to accept non-Christian values and beliefs.[340]
- Attacking a Christian charity.[341]
- Banning Christian books in schools.[342]
- Banning prayer in schools[343] and public places.[344]
- Discriminating against Christians on campus,[345] and at work.[346]
- Discriminating against Christians for the right to distribute Christian materials in public.[347]
- Discriminating against Christians for equal access to public facilities.[348]
- For additional examples, please see the section in this appendix on the Major Battles against the Christian Church and Religious Freedom as well as the section in this appendix on the Major Battles against the Family and Religious Freedom.

Battle against the First Amendment and Free Speech – Religious Freedom, Political Freedom, Economic Freedom

Congress shall make no law ... abridging the freedom of speech ...

- Attacking Christian free speech.[349]
- Attacking free speech that references God[350] or Jesus.[351]
- Attacking Freedom of Expressive Association.[352]
- Attacking free speech on talk radio with the so-called "Fairness Doctrine."[353]
- Attacking free speech on the Internet with the so-called "Web Fairness Doctrine."[354]
- Attacking free speech during political campaigns with "campaign finance reform."[355]
- Attacking free speech over ballot questions with State campaign finance laws.[356]
- Attacking free speech on campus with "political correctness."[357]
- Attacking free speech on the Internet as political, requiring groups to become "political committees."[358]
- Attacking free speech as "hate speech."[359]

- Attacking free speech as "offensive speech."[360]
- Attacking free speech by government-compelled speech (that is contrary to an individual's own views).[361]
- Attacking free speech of businesses by banning the sale of books in public without a license and then, not issuing this type of license.[362]
- Attacking free speech of businesses by banning small micro-radio stations without a license and then, not issuing this type of license.[363]
- Attacking free speech of businesses by banning portable signs.[364]
- Attacking free speech of businesses by licensing information provided by certain Internet websites.[365]
- Attacking free speech of businesses by government-forced (vs. business-chosen) advertising.[366]

Battle against the Second Amendment and Guns

... the right of the people to keep and bear Arms, shall not be infringed

- Attacking the right of citizens to have guns in their homes for self-defense and protection.[367]

Battle against the Fourth Amendment and Warrantless Searches

The right of the people to be secure in their persons, houses, papers, and effects, against unreasonable searches and seizures, shall not be violated ...

- Permitting unreasonable strip searches of children.[368]
- Promoting warrantless searches of homes and businesses[369].

Battle against the Fifth Amendment and Private Property

No person shall ... be deprived of life, liberty, or property, without due process of law; nor shall private property be taken for public use, without just compensation.

- Taking private property away from a private owner and <u>not</u> providing just compensation.
  - o This is an issue of *eminent domain*.[370]
- Taking private property (away from a private owner) for *private use* (by a different private party) as a means of government-controlled economic development.
  - o This is an issue of the proper use of *eminent domain*.[371]
- Designating private property as "blighted" and taking the "blighted"

private property away as a means of government-controlled economic development.

- o   This is also an issue of the proper use of *eminent domain.*[372]
- Defining the term "blighted" to include a broad range of private property that might not be hazardous, dangerous, or in bad condition.
  - o   This is a third related issue to the proper use of *eminent domain.*[373]
- Taking some portion of private property away from a private owner and <u>not</u> providing any compensation, since some private property and some value remain.
  - o   This is the issue of *relevant parcel.*[374]
- Taking private property without due process and without just compensation under the authority of the government's police power.
  - o   This is the issue of *civil asset forfeiture.*[375]
- Regulating <u>if and how</u> private property can be used (and thereby limiting or lowering the value of the private property) without just compensation.
  - o   This is the issue of *regulatory takings.*[376]

Battle against the Ninth Amendment and Freedom

The enumeration in the Constitution, of certain rights, shall not be construed to deny or disparage others retained by the people.

- Attacking the concept of democratic self-governance.[377]
- Attacking rights not enumerated in the Constitution.
  - o   These attacks go against the *Presumption of Liberty* which assumes rights not enumerated in the Constitution are retained by the people (unless government can prove a law that limits or eliminates a right is *necessary and proper*).[378]
- Promoting and upholding laws that limit or eliminate rights not enumerated in the Constitution.
  - o   This approach relies on a legal construction known as *presumption of constitutionality* which assumes that laws are presumed to be constitutional (unless specifically found to be in error).[379]

Battle against the Tenth Amendment and Freedom

The powers not delegated to the United States by the Constitution, nor prohibited by it to the States, are reserved to the States respectively, or to the people.

- Attacking the concept of Federalism, with a limited Federal Government and separate sovereign States.[380]
- Attacking the rights of States to conduct their own operations independently of the Federal Government.[381]
- Promoting laws that limit or eliminate the rights of States not enumerated in the Constitution.[382]

Battle against the Fourteenth Amendment and Freedom

... nor shall any State deprive any person of life, liberty, or property, without due process of law; nor deny to any person within its jurisdiction the equal protection of the laws.

- Attacking the right of due process with regard to economic regulations.[383]
- Attacking the right of equal protection with affirmative action laws.[384]
- Attacking the Rule of Law.[385]
- Promoting and upholding the criminalization of social and economic conduct.[386]
- Promoting and upholding very high damage awards.[387]
- Promoting and upholding frivolous lawsuits.[388]

Battle against Article 1 Section 8 (Clauses 1, 3, 18) and Economic Freedom

The Congress shall have Power To ... provide for the common Defence and general Welfare ...

To regulate Commerce with foreign Nations, and among the several States ...

To make all Laws which shall be necessary and proper for carrying into Execution the foregoing Powers, and all other Powers vested by this Constitution in the Government of the United States ...

- Attacking private property rights with environmental laws such as the Endangered Species Act.[389]
- Attacking private property rights with scenic regulations.[390]
- Attacking private property rights with architectural design regulations.[391]
- Attacking private property rights with building permit regulations and regulatory delays.[392]

- Attacking economic freedom using eminent domain. For many examples, please see the Battle against the Fifth Amendment and
- Private Property in this appendix.
- Attacking the Free Market, Free Enterprise, and economic freedom. For many examples, please see the economic battles in this appendix.

Battle against Article 1 Section 8 (Clauses 11, 12) and the Military

To raise and support Armies ...

To provide and maintain a Navy ...

- Attacking religious freedom in the military.[393]
- Attacking American military training by saying it promotes torture and murder in Latin America.[394]
- Attacking the American military's right to recruit on campus[395] and in public.[396]
- Promoting the American military's purpose as "humanitarian warriors" who are "social engineers" of the world.[397]

Battle against Article 1 Section 10, Contract Law, and Economic Freedom

No State shall ... pass any ... Law impairing the Obligation of Contracts ...

- Attacking voluntary private contracts.[398]
- Attacking voluntary private labor contracts.[399]
- Attacking the Free Market, Free Enterprise, and economic freedom. For many examples, please see the economic battles in this appendix.

Battle against Article 2 and the President

The executive Power shall be vested in a President of the United States of America ...

Each State shall appoint, in such Manner as the Legislature thereof may direct, a Number of Electors ...

The President shall be Commander in Chief of the Army and Navy of the United States ...

- Attacking the integrity of the President.[400]
- Attacking the Electoral College system for the election of the President and Vice President.[401]
- Attacking the President as commander-in-chief.[402]

A Special Battle against The Declaration of Independence and America's Sovereignty

Note that this section includes battlefront examples and references to indicate the scope and extent of America's Economic War.

Battle against The Declaration of Independence and America's Sovereignty

When in the Course of human events, it becomes necessary for one people ... to assume among the powers of the earth, the separate and equal station to which the Laws of Nature and of Nature's God entitle them, a decent respect to the opinions of mankind ...

We hold these truths to be self-evident, that all men are created equal, that they are endowed by their Creator with certain unalienable Rights, that among these are Life, Liberty and the pursuit of Happiness ...

- Attacking America's sovereignty using the "norming" argument.[403]
- Attacking America using a *moral equivalency* argument.[404]
- Attacking America's moral standing in the world.[405]
- Attacking America's President.[406]
- Attacking America's military.[407]
- Attacking the American Flag.[408]
- Failing to enforce America's immigration laws.[409]
- Promoting open borders and unlimited immigration.[410]
- Permitting illegal aliens who reside in California to pay in-state tuition at California public colleges and universities.
  - At the same time, requiring out-of-state American citizens to pay out-of-state tuition at California public colleges and universities.[411]
- Promoting new United Nations Taxes on nations.[412]
  - Promoting United Nations Global Carbon Taxes.[413]
  - Promoting United Nations Global Poverty Taxes.[414]
  - Promoting United Nations Emigrant Taxes.[415]
  - Promoting United Nations Currency Transaction Taxes.[416]

- Promoting new regulatory powers for the United Nations in the area of national tax policies.
  - o For example, nations with free markets might be forced to raise taxes to avoid *tax competition* with socialist countries.[417]
  - o *"Unfair Tax Competition"* refers to some nations choosing to charge lower taxes and hence, having market advantages over other countries that choose higher taxes.[418]

Major Battles against the Free Market, Free Enterprise, and Economic Freedom

Note that this section includes battlefront examples and references for each battle to indicate the scope and extent of America's Economic War.

Battle against Private Property – Personal Taxes

All personal taxes transfer private property (in the form of money) from individuals to government.

The number and types of taxes and the amount of taxes paid by Americans are too high.

Note that Dividend Taxes and Estate (Death) Taxes are both forms of double taxation.

- Attacking attempts to lower taxes.
- Supporting and maintaining America's current high tax burden on individuals and in some cases promoting even higher taxes.[419]
  - o Federal Income Taxes.
  - o State Income Taxes.
  - o Local Income Taxes.
  - o Social Security (FICA) Taxes.
  - o Medicare Taxes.
  - o Self-Employment Taxes.
  - o Capital Gains Taxes.
  - o Dividend Taxes.
  - o Alternative Minimum Taxes (AMT).
  - o State Sales Taxes.
  - o State Use Taxes.
  - o County Sales Taxes.

o   City Sales Taxes.
o   Property Taxes.
o   Car Ownership Taxes.
o   Phone Taxes.
o   Cell Phone Taxes.
o   Cable TV Taxes.
o   State Gasoline Taxes.
o   Spirits (Alcohol) Taxes.
o   Table Wine Taxes.
o   Beer Taxes.
o   Cigarette Taxes.
o   School Taxes.
o   Library Taxes.
o   Health District Taxes.
o   Conservation Taxes.
o   Pest Control Taxes.
o   Natural Gas Taxes.
o   Electric Energy Taxes.
o   Water Usage Taxes.
o   Stormwater Taxes.
o   Wastewater Taxes.
o   City Occupation Taxes.
o   Airline Ticket Taxes.
o   Hotel Room Taxes.
o   Car Rental Taxes.
o   Gift Taxes.
o   Estate (Death) Taxes.[420]
o   Jewelry Taxes.
o   Fur Taxes.
o   Gasohol Taxes.
o   Diesel Fuels Taxes.
o   Noncommercial Aviation Fuels Taxes.
o   Inlands Waterway Users' Fuel Taxes.
o   Federal Gasoline Taxes.
o   Highway Tire Taxes.
o   Truck Sales Taxes.
o   Firearms, Shells and Cartridges Taxes.
o   Pistol and Revolver Taxes.
o   Bow and Arrow Taxes.
o   Fishing Equipment Taxes.

o   Amusement Taxes.[421]

o   Litigation Taxes.[422]

Battle against Private Property –
Personal Taxes (Newer Taxes and Proposed New Taxes)

All personal taxes transfer private property (in the form of money) from individuals to government.

The number of taxes and the amount of taxes paid by Americans are both too high.

- Promoting Jock Taxes.
  - o   *Jock Taxes* are "state and local income taxes on traveling business professionals, particularly visiting professional athletes."[423]
- Promoting new Internet Taxes.[424]
- Promoting new Carbon Taxes.[425]
- Promoting new "Cap and Trade" Taxes.[426]
- Promoting new Service Taxes.[427]
  - o   *Service Taxes* might be levied on such things as car repairs, health club memberships, tickets to movies, golf courses, accountants and lawyers.[428]
  - o   *Service Taxes* might also be levied on such things as ski tickets, consultants, commercial landscaping and janitorial services.[429]
- Promoting new United Nations Taxes on nations.[430]
  - o   Promoting United Nations Global Carbon Taxes.[431]
  - o   Promoting United Nations Global Poverty Taxes.[432]
  - o   Promoting United Nations Emigrant Taxes.[433]
  - o   Promoting United Nations Currency Transaction Taxes.[434]
- Promoting new regulatory powers for the United Nations in the area of national tax policies.
  - o   For example, nations with free markets might be forced to raise taxes to avoid *tax competition* with socialist countries.[435]
  - o   *"Unfair Tax Competition"* refers to some nations choosing to charge lower taxes and hence, having market advantages over other countries that choose higher taxes.[436]

Battle against Private Property –
Personal Taxes (by Other Names)

All personal taxes (regardless of the name given to them) transfer private property (in the form of money) from individuals to government.

Some Fees, Special Benefit Assessments, and Surcharges might better be called Taxes because the proposed benefits go to the general public rather than to the individuals who pay them.

- Promoting high (or even higher) Income Taxes by raising your taxable "income" with *Imputed Income*.
  - o *Imputed Income* is a method to selectively tax some employee benefits.
  - o It treats benefits as if they were actual cash income to an employee.
  - o For example, the value of some life insurance and child care benefits can be taxed as imputed income.[437]
- Promoting high (or even higher) "Trade Tariffs" and "Duties."[438]
  - o *Trade Tariffs* are lists of duties (or actual duties) placed on products coming into (or leaving) a country.
  - o *Duties* are Taxes.
  - o *Free Trade* among nations is the absence of tariffs and duties.[439]
- Promoting high (or even higher) "Fees."[440]
  - o Some *Fees* might better be called Taxes.[441]
- Promoting high (or even higher) "Special Benefit Assessments."[442]
  - o Some *Special Benefit Assessments* might better be called Taxes.[443]
- Promoting high (or even higher) Federal and State Universal Service Fund "Surcharges."[444]
  - o Some *Surcharges* might better be called Taxes.[445]
- Promoting Homeowner's Insurance "Surcharge."[446]
  - o Promoting taxes on insurance policies.[447]
- Promoting State Lotteries.[448]
  - o *State Lotteries* might better be called *Implicit Taxes*.[449]
  - o *Implicit Taxes* have the tax built into the price of the product (as opposed to being charged explicitly, that is, separately from the product as with a regular Sales Tax).[450]
  - o It's interesting to note that "… the average American spends more money on lotteries than on reading materials or movie

theatres."[451]

Battle against Private Property – Inflation

Inflation is an insidious, hidden, and very immoral tax.

- Promoting inflation with monetary policy.[452]
- Promoting inflation by weakening the American dollar.[453]
- Promoting inflation with ethanol mandates.[454]
- For more information on inflation, please see Chapter 5.

Battle against Private Property –
Corporate and Business Taxes

All corporate and business taxes transfer private property (in the form of money) from corporations and businesses to government.

All corporate and business taxes are an expense of doing business and are passed along to customers (who are generally either other businesses or consumers).

All corporate and business taxes are ultimately paid by individuals.

- Supporting and maintaining America's current high tax burden on corporations and in some cases promoting even higher taxes.[455]
  - o Federal, State and Local Income Taxes.
  - o Social Security (FICA) and Medicare Taxes.
  - o Federal Unemployment (FUTA) Taxes.
  - o State and City Sales Taxes.
  - o Property Taxes.
  - o Accumulated Earnings Taxes.[456]
  - o Corporate Alternative Minimum Taxes (AMT).[457]
  - o Federal Coal Sales Excise Taxes.
  - o Federal Environmental "Superfund" Chemical Excise Taxes.
  - o Plus, other taxes individuals also pay.
- Promoting high "Windfall" Profit Taxes on selected industries that will restrict new investment.[458]
  - o These industries are precisely where consumers are demanding greater supplies and where new investments are needed most.

Battle against Private Property – Regulations and Mandates

Regulations and mandates are expenses to corporations, businesses, and individuals and generally restrict economic growth and wealth creation.

Regulations and mandates act as a tax on the economy.

- Regulating the manufacture of cars with the Corporate Average Fuel Economy (CAFÉ) standards.
  - One study estimates an additional 46,000 people died as a result of driving lighter weight vehicles that were manufactured as a response to the CAFÉ program.[459]
- Regulating America cost the Federal government an estimated $41B in 2006.[460]
  - But, the actual regulations themselves cost the American Economy an estimated $1,142B in 2006, about 9% of America's GDP![461]
- Attacking the insurance industry with regulations that make it difficult to tie risk and premiums together, and to earn a profit on its insurance products.[462]
- Permitting inappropriate absenteeism and tardiness with the Family Medical Leave Act.[463]
  - Also, permitting disrupted business operations as well as bonus and reward program cuts.[464]
- Mandating that either "affordable" housing be built, or a $96,182 <u>per unit</u> in-lieu fee be paid instead.[465]
- Prohibiting a summer camp from continuing to use a river for whitewater rafting (that it has been using for 31 years).[466]
- Prohibiting a steakhouse that features country and western music from allowing its customers to dance outside.[467]

Battle against Private Property – Environmental Regulations

Environmental regulations are a special case of regulations that are also expenses to corporations, businesses, and individuals and generally restrict economic growth and wealth creation.

Environmental regulations act as a tax on the economy.

- Attacking the building of hydraulically-powered gates to prevent hurricane storm surges from causing flood damage (to protect shrimp and crab).

- o The *Lake Pontchartrain Hurricane Barrier Project* might have saved many lives during Hurricane Katrina.[468]
- Attacking the repair of a levee meant to protect against flooding (to protect Longhorn Elderberry Beetles).
  - o When the Feather River levee broke, 25 square miles of land were flooded, at least two people died, 32,000 people were forced from their homes, 600 cattle head of livestock were drowned, and the beetles were washed away anyway.[469]
- Attacking farmers, their family incomes, and the property values of their farms by cutting off irrigation water delivered under contract (to protect two species of sucker fish and coho salmon).
  - o *Rural cleansing* is the idea that individuals should not live or work in rural areas, and therefore, it's acceptable if they are forced out.[470]
- Attacking private property usage with a *critical habitat* designation under the Endangered Species Act (ESA).
  - o This is the issue of *environmental takings.*[471]
- Attacking private property usage with slow *land use proposal* reviews.[472]
- Attacking private property land use under the Clean Water Act when "… the alleged wetland was separated from the nearest navigable water by 3 nonnavigable streams and approximately 64 miles away!"[473]
- Attacking cattle grazing as pollution requiring Clean Water Act review and requiring permits in some cases.[474]
- Attacking urban sprawl.[475]
- Prohibiting a Fourth of July fireworks display as "development."[476]
- Promoting anti-conservation incentives and effects (in attempts to protect private property), an unintended consequence of the Endangered Species Act.[477]

Battle against Private Property – Environmental Regulations that Hurt America's Energy Supplies

Environmental regulations that hurt America's energy supplies are a special case of regulations that are also expenses to corporations, businesses, and individuals and generally restrict economic growth and wealth creation.

Environmental regulations that hurt America's energy supplies act as a very high tax on the economy.

These environmental regulations also tend to make America dependent on foreign countries for our energy needs.

- Promoting environmental energy policies in California that lead to electric shortages, rolling blackouts, high energy costs and dependence on other states for needed energy.[478]
  - California's use of energy generated in other states (and therefore the shift in associated pollution generation to other states) has been termed "a sort of energy colonialism."[479]
  - California's energy costs are nearly double the cost of the national average.[480]
- Attacking nuclear power as an energy source.[481]
  - Shutting down the Rancho Seco Nuclear Generating Station that had a capacity of 900 MegaWatts (MW), enough power for 900,000 homes.[482]
- Attacking uranium mining.[483]
  - Uranium is the fuel for nuclear power plants.[484]
  - Nuclear power plants provide energy without atmospheric emissions.[485]
- Attacking coal mining[486] and coal-fired power plants.[487]
- Attacking large-scale hydropower.[488]
  - Promoting the destruction of dams.[489]
- Attacking the construction of new power plants.[490]
- Attacking plans to construct liquefied natural gas (LNG) receiving terminals along the California coast.[491]
- Attacking a $1B wind power transmission line to San Diego.[492]
- Attacking oil-sands production.[493]
- Attacking oil shale development in the West with up to 2 trillion barrels of capacity.[494]
- Prohibiting nuclear power plants from being built.[495]
- Prohibiting new oil refineries from being built, making America more dependent on foreign oil refiners.[496]
- Prohibiting drilling for American oil, making America more dependent on foreign sources of oil.[497]
  - Alaska's Arctic National Wildlife Refuge (ANWR) includes an area with an estimated 10 billion barrels of oil. Only a few thousand acres of ANWR's 19.6 million acres contain this oil. But, oil drilling is not permitted.[498]

Battle against Private Property –
Eminent Domain (and Takings)

Takings generally transfer private property to the government (or another private party), with or without due process, and with or without just compensation.

In the case of regulatory takings, private property is not transferred to government, but the value of the private property is limited or lowered by government action.

- Taking private property away from a private owner and <u>not</u> providing just compensation.
  - o   This is an issue of *eminent domain.*[499]
- Taking private property (away from a private owner) for *private use* (by a different private party) as a means of government-controlled economic development.
  - o   This is an issue of the proper use of *eminent domain.*[500]
- Designating private property as "blighted" and taking the "blighted" private property away as a means of government-controlled economic development.
  - o   This is also an issue of the proper use of *eminent domain.*[501]
- Defining the term "blighted" to include a broad range of private property that might not be hazardous, dangerous, or in bad condition.
  - o   This is a third related issue to the proper use of *eminent domain.*[502]
- Taking some portion of private property away from a private owner and <u>not</u> providing any compensation, since some private property and some value remain.
  - o   This is the issue of *relevant parcel.*[503]
- Taking private property without due process and without just compensation under the authority of the government's police power.
  - o   This is the issue of *civil asset forfeiture.*[504]
- Regulating <u>if and how</u> private property can be used (and thereby limiting or lowering the value of the private property) without just compensation.
  - o   This is the issue of *regulatory takings.*[505]

Battle against Private Property –
Usage Controls and Lack of Protection

At Issue – The freedom to <u>use</u> your own private property

- Prohibiting an individual land-owner from sub-dividing their investment property, thereby reducing its value.[506]
- Permitting increased *identity theft* and loss of private property (including credit ratings) by not enforcing immigration laws.
  - "... immigrants' identity theft has become so pervasive ..."[507]

Battle against Private Property – Excessive Legal Judgments

At Issue – The freedom to keep your own private property.

- Promoting and upholding very high damage awards.[508]
- Promoting and upholding frivolous lawsuits.[509]

Battle against the Freedom to Set Prices – Wage and Price Controls

At Issue – The freedom to set wages and prices freely at their fair market values.

- Promoting minimum wages for employees.[510]
- Promoting "living wages" and hurting the poor.[511]
  - *Living wages* are a form of minimum wages that are set to a level of about 50% to 100% higher than the Federal minimum wage or even higher.[512]
- Promoting maximum compensation for executives.[513]
- Promoting rent control.[514]
- Promoting price controls.[515]
  - Requiring some homes to be sold at prices substantially below market value.[516]
  - Prohibiting a gas station from selling gasoline at a discounted price to senior citizens.[517]

Battle against the Free Market – Voiding Voluntary Private Contracts

At Issue – The freedom to enter into voluntary private contracts and to expect all parties to perform according to the terms of their contracts.

- Attacking voluntary private contracts.[518]
- Attacking voluntary private labor contracts.[519]
- Attacking mortgage contracts.[520]
- Applying Tort Law principles in Contract Law disputes.[521]

Battle against the Freedom to Choose Your Own Work

At Issue – The freedom to choose your own work <u>and</u> to earn a living from that work.

- Attacking the freedom to choose your own work with government-created business *cartels, protectionist licensing laws*, and *title laws*.[522]
    - o A *cartel* is a group of businesses that together control a market. In contrast, a *monopoly* is one business that controls a market.
    - o Note that the term *cartel* can also apply to a group of countries that together control a market, such as the oil cartel.
    - o *Protectionist licensing laws* make it more difficult for new businesses to enter existing markets, by restricting the issuance of required licenses.[523]
    - o *Title laws* regulate who can use certain titles in their line of work.[524]

Battle against Investors

At Issue – The freedom to be an investor in new or existing corporations or businesses <u>and</u> to earn a living from that work.

- Attacking investment in corporations with high corporate statutory tax rates, plus government tax rules that might lead to even higher effective tax rates.[525]
- Attacking investment in corporations with a high tax compliance burden.[526]
- Attacking investment profits with high capital gains taxes.[527]

Battle against Entrepreneurs

At Issue – The freedom to start (or exit) a new business or corporation <u>and</u> to earn a living from that work.

- Attacking the right of entrepreneurs from starting new businesses.[528]
- Attacking the right of entrepreneurs from exiting old businesses.
    - o Prohibiting rent-controlled units from being demolished or converted to condominiums.[529]
- Attacking entrepreneurs from growing new businesses with costly financial and burdensome regulations under the Sarbanes-Oxley Act

of 2002.[530]

- Attacking entrepreneurs from raising capital under the Sarbanes-Oxley Act of 2002.[531]
- Attacking entrepreneurs with the threat of litigation under the Sarbanes-Oxley Act of 2002.[532]
- Prohibiting a bed and breakfast business from continuing operation after a city changes its interpretation of its own law.[533]

Battle against Venture Capitalists and Capital Formation

At Issue – The freedom to bring together capital from investors and savers (capital formation) for the purpose of making investments and to earn a living from that work.

- Attacking venture capitalists from investing in new businesses and participating on independent audit committees (and thereby withholding their expertise) under the Sarbanes-Oxley Act of 2002.[534]
- Attacking *hedge funds* that help to lower risk during price declines and that offer other advantages to the economy.
   - o A *hedge fund* is a private investment vehicle that by Federal law is reserved for wealthy investors.[535]

Battle against Profits

At Issue – The freedom for corporations and businesses to earn profits from their products and services.

- Attacking profits as immoral.[536]
- Promoting high "Windfall" Profit Taxes on selected industries that will restrict new investment.[537]
   - o These industries are precisely where consumers are demanding greater supplies and where new investments are needed most.
- For more information on profits, please see Chapter 3.

Battle against Competition

At Issue – The freedom to compete and to earn profits by creating faster, better, and cheaper products and services.

- Attacking competition with litigation.[538]
   - o Company A's employees sue Company B because Company A took steps to be more competitive with Company B.[539]
- Attacking competition with anti-competitive government

regulations.[540]
- Attacking retail innovation by Wal-Mart.[541]
- Attacking pharmaceutical innovation by Merck with tort lawsuits after FDA approval of Vioxx.[542]
- Attacking competition with school choice, despite the evidence that it improves academic achievement.[543]
- For more information on competition, please see Chapter 3.

Two Special Battles against the Free Market, Free Enterprise, and Economic Freedom

Note that this section includes battlefront examples and references for each battle to indicate the scope and extent of America's Economic War.

Battle against a Free Market in the Energy Industry – The So-Called Global Warming "Crisis"

At Issue –

- *Will the energy industry be a Free Market?*
- *Will it be given the freedom it needs to supply all of America's energy needs?*
- *Will it be given the freedom it needs to make America energy independent?*
- *Or, will American Capitalism lose America's Economic War?*
- *Will America succumb to environmental socialism?*

The so-called global warming "crisis" (or climate change "crisis") is a myth used to create fear, and to gain control of the energy industry.

Since energy empowers and drives all economic activity, socialists want to control the energy industry.

By controlling the energy industry, socialists will effectively control the entire economy.

By controlling the entire economy, socialists will effectively control you and your family.

- Promoting the so-called global warming "crisis."

- o   For more information, please see Chapter 1.
- Attacking conventional energy development and use.
  - o   Attacking nuclear energy.[544]
  - o   Attacking nuclear power plants.[545]
  - o   Attacking uranium mining.[546]
  - o   Attacking coal mining.[547]
  - o   Attacking coal-fired power plants.[548]
  - o   Attacking large-scale hydropower.[549]
  - o   Attacking hydropower dams.[550]
  - o   Attacking liquefied natural gas.[551]
  - o   Attacking oil-sands.[552]
  - o   Attacking oil shale.[553]
  - o   Attacking oil refineries.[554]
  - o   Attacking oil drilling.[555]
  - o   Attacking power transmission lines.[556]
  - o   For more information, please see the economic battles in this appendix.
- Promoting environmental socialism by:
  - o   Promoting new "Cap and Trade" Programs.
  - o   Promoting new "Cap and Trade" Taxes.[557]
  - o   Promoting new Carbon Taxes.[558]
  - o   Promoting higher Energy Taxes.[559]
  - o   Promoting high "Windfall" Profit Taxes.[560]
- Promoting environmental socialism equates to:
  - o   Attacking your economic freedom.
  - o   Attacking your economic activities.
  - o   Attacking your lifestyle.
  - o   Attacking your standard of living.
  - o   Attacking corporations and small businesses.
  - o   Attacking commercial and business activities.
  - o   Attacking the Free Market and Free Enterprise.
  - o   Attacking Free Trade.
  - o   Attacking economic wealth creation.
  - o   Attacking economic growth.
  - o   Promoting energy shortages and rationing.
  - o   Promoting energy blackouts.
  - o   Promoting government control of the energy industry.
  - o   Promoting government control of all industries.
  - o   Promoting government control of all individuals.
  - o   Promoting economic wealth redistribution.

o   Promoting economic wealth consumption.
o   Promoting incentives for fraud.
o   Promoting incentives for corruption.
o   Promoting moral and economic bankruptcy.

Battle against a Free Market in the Health Care Industry – The So-Called Health Care "Crisis"

At Issue –

- *Will the health care industry be a Free Market?*
- *Will it be given the freedom it needs to supply America's health care needs?*
- *Will all the current burdensome tax policies, subsidies, and regulations on the health care industry be eliminated to give the Free Market the opportunity to work efficiently and effectively?*

The so-called health care "crisis" is also a myth designed to convince you that the government must take-over the health care industry.

Important Note. If the government can't manage the current financially unsustainable Medicare program for seniors, how can socialists expect it can manage the entire health care industry for everyone?

Socialists often make grandiose promises. Also, socialists often make grandiose plans. But, socialism always leads to moral and economic bankruptcy, not their promised utopia.

You and your family can expect a government-controlled health care system to negatively impact the quality of you and your family's health care.

You and your family can expect very low quality of health care, long waits for health care, rationing of some health care and drugs, denial of some health care and drugs, as well as few (if any) new health care and drug innovations.

You can also expect to have much less freedom and much higher taxes.

- Attacking the current health care industry as not meeting current health care needs.[561]
  - o   The current health care industry is being dragged down by

burdensome tax policies, subsidies, and regulations.[562]
- o It is also being burdened by Medicare price controls, spending targets, and regulations.[563]
- Attacking Free Market solutions for providing better private health care insurance.[564]
  - o Attacking health care insurance *portability*.[565]
  - o Attacking the concept of a *health insurance exchange* similar to a stock market.[566]
  - o Attacking the elimination of expensive and outdated state health insurance mandates.[567]
- Attacking Free Market solutions for providing better health care.[568]
  - o Attacking the freedom of individuals to choose their own health care providers and services.[569]
  - o Attacking the freedom of individuals to choose if they want health care insurance, the type of plan, and the actual plan.[570]
  - o Attacking the freedom of individuals to choose their own health care plans in retirement, rather than be forced into Medicare.[571]
  - o Attacking the freedom of doctors to run their own practices as they deem best for themselves and their patients.[572]
  - o Attacking the freedom to choose how to mitigate the risk of malpractice. Insurance can replace litigation at a much lower cost.[573]
- Promoting the current financially unsustainable Medicare program.
  - o "The 2008 Medicare Trustees Report notes that Medicare expenditures in 2007 were $432 billion, or 3.2 percent of gross domestic product (GDP)."[574]
  - o "The trustees … estimate that Medicare's long-term unfunded obligation – the benefits promised but unpaid for – will amount to more than $36 trillion …" [575]
- Promoting a new government-controlled, national health care system.
  - o "… s*ingle-payer, universal coverage, national health insurance,* or *national health care"* are all names for such a system.[576]
  - o All refer to socialist programs for a government take-over of the health care industry.
- Promoting a new government-controlled, national health care system, while ignoring how other socialist health care programs have failed to provide quality health care for all citizens.[577]

Examples include –

- o   In Britain, Elizabeth Jones was twice turned away from a hospital on the date of birth of her baby because the hospital was full.[578]
- o   In Britain, when a person can't find a dentist, some people resort to pulling out their own teeth.[579]
- o   In Canada, wait times for medical care can be staggering. Wait times for <u>emergency</u> heart surgeries range from five to six weeks, while wait times for <u>emergency</u> neurosurgeries are 10.7 weeks.[580]

- Promoting a new government-controlled, national health care system equates to –
  - o   Attacking the availability of critical health care.
    - -   You and your family's lives might be in jeopardy.
  - o   Attacking your economic freedom.
  - o   Attacking the quality of your health care.
  - o   Attacking the quality of your health.
  - o   Attacking innovation in health care services.
  - o   Attacking innovation in pharmaceuticals.
    - ■   Potential, new life-saving drugs and medical therapies might never be discovered.
  - o   Promoting delays in receiving critical health care.
  - o   Promoting rationing of health care.
    - ■   In the absence of a Free Market, rationing can be expected.
  - o   Promoting shortages of doctors and dentists.
    - ■   In the absence of a Free Market, doctors and dentists have little incentive to study, sacrifice, and work as hard as needed to deliver quality health care.
  - o   Promoting shortages in health care services.
  - o   Promoting higher costs for health care.
  - o   Promoting higher taxes.
  - o   Promoting more burdensome regulations.
  - o   Promoting incentives for waste.
  - o   Promoting incentives for fraud.
  - o   Promoting incentives for corruption.
  - o   Promoting moral and economic bankruptcy.

An Optimistic 21st Century Vision for America
(if American Capitalism Wins the War)

An Optimistic 21st Century Vision for America (if American Capitalism Wins the War)

Note that this appendix provides a vision for life in America with American Capitalism. The vision is organized by the institutions of American Capitalism.

Christian Church, Family, and Religious Freedom

American Culture – Christian Heritage, But <u>Not</u> a Christian Theocracy

- <u>Americans will have religious freedom.</u>
    - o Americans will have the freedom to express their religious beliefs in the public square without restrictions.
    - o American Government (elected leaders and employees) will have the freedom to make references to our religious heritage without restrictions.
- <u>Americans will affirm America's Christian heritage and American Culture.</u>
    - o Americans will promote a *culture of life* and will reject a *culture of death.*
        - Americans will promote and nurture all life, at all stages, as a gift from God.
        - Americans will reject abortion (at all stages), infanticide, euthanasia, suicide and the death penalty.
    - o Americans will have renewed moral strength and morality.
    - o Americans will have stronger and more vibrant personal, professional, and business relationships.
    - o Americans will have stronger, more peaceful, and more prosperous relationships with other nations.
- <u>Americans will have stronger and more vibrant marriages and families.</u>
    - o America will affirm marriage between a man and woman for the purpose of love and procreating children as the model for marriage that is consistent with America's Christian heritage and with American Civilization.
    - o America will affirm family values, such as abstinence until marriage.
    - o America will reject violence, brutality, prostitution, and pornography in education and in the entertainment industry as inconsistent with America's Christian heritage and with

American Civilization.

- ■ Censorship is <u>not</u> required. Within the Free Market, everyone votes with their buying decisions.

Constitution, Religious Freedom, Political Freedom, and Economic Freedom

American Government – The Constitution Preserving and Protecting Our Freedom

- <u>The Constitution will be restored, interpreted, and followed as it was originally written.</u>
    - o Justices and judges will restore, interpret, and follow the Constitution as it was originally written.
    - o Justices and judges will <u>not</u> function in a legislative or political role.
    - o Americans will live under the *Rule of Law.*
    - o Americans will have *Due Process.*
    - o Americans will have *Equal Protection.*
- <u>America will not recognize the power of any global organization or treaty to supersede the Constitution of the United States of America.</u>
    - o American sovereignty will <u>not</u> be abridged by the United Nations or other global organizations.
    - o Americans will <u>not</u> pay taxes imposed by global organizations on America.
    - o America will create a new global organization, the *Free Nations.*
        - ■ It will be comprised of free nations that seek to protect and promote Freedom, Free Markets and Free Trade.
- <u>America will maintain strong Armed Forces, ready to protect and defend America.</u>
    - o American Government will <u>never</u> launch an offensive war.
    - o American Government will <u>never</u> lose a defensive war.
    - o America will safeguard and protect its borders from unlimited and illegal immigration.
    - o America will enforce its immigration laws.
- <u>Americans will have political freedom.</u>
- <u>Americans will have freedom of speech.</u>
    - o Americans will have religious freedom of speech without "hate speech" and "offensive speech" restrictions.

- o Americans will have political freedom of speech without "campaign finance reform," "Fairness Doctrine," "Web Fairness Doctrine" and other restrictions.
- o Americans will not be forced to accept the beliefs of others. For example,
  - Christians will <u>not</u> be forced to accept non-Christian beliefs and values.
  - Christians will <u>not</u> be forced to perform actions that they believe are morally wrong.
- o Americans will have the freedom to follow their own consciences (the *Right of Conscience),* subject to the Rule of Law.
- <u>Americans will have the right to keep and bear arms.</u>
- <u>Americans will have the right to be secure in their persons, homes, and businesses.</u>
  - o Americans will <u>not</u> be subject to unreasonable strip searches.
  - o Americans will <u>not</u> be subject to warrantless searches of homes and businesses.
- <u>Americans will have economic freedom.</u>
  - o Americans will support the Free Market and Free Enterprise.
  - o Americans will support Free Trade with other nations.
  - o America will not permit discrimination for the purpose of eliminating (alleged or real) past discrimination.
    - Affirmative action will be eliminated.
    - Quotas will be eliminated.
    - Reverse discrimination will be eliminated.
    - The <u>only</u> way to eliminate discrimination is to eliminate discrimination.
- <u>Americans will have intellectual freedom.</u>
  - o Faculty and students in colleges and universities will have true academic freedom and the intellectual freedom to question, debate, discuss, and explore the issues of the day (without threat to their academic positions, class grades, or other intimidation).
  - o Faculty hiring decisions will be based on teaching, research, and service capabilities, not on the political positions potential professors might or might not hold.
- <u>America will maintain adequate police capabilities to protect and defend Americans from domestic violence, crime and fraud.</u>
- <u>America will have positive and honest elections with debate on</u>

substantive issues, not personal attacks.
- o America will have efficient, reliable, and honest elections using common sense voter ID rules and innovative technologies.

Free Market, Free Enterprise, and Economic Freedom
American Economy – Peace, Prosperity, and Economic Growth through Economic Freedom

- Americans will have economic freedom.
  - o Americans will support the Free Market and Free Enterprise.
  - o Americans will support Free Trade with other nations.
- Americans will experience unprecedented economic growth at the rate of 4% – 8% GDP per year –
  - o With economic freedom, the Free Market and Free Enterprise,
  - o By cutting the tax and regulatory burden on individuals, small businesses, and corporations, and
  - o By promoting and developing Free Trade between America and other nations.
- America's charitable giving and compassion will likewise increase substantially.
  - o This is true because of America's increasing economic growth and wealth creation and long-standing tradition of generosity and compassion.
  - o America will care for its poor and downtrodden individuals and families with generosity and compassion.
  - o America will aid the poor of the world with generosity and compassion.
- America will place the dollar back on the gold standard.
  - o *The dollar will be as good as gold.*
  - o Americans will experience price stability.
  - o The insidious tax of inflation will be eliminated.
  - o The dollar will stay strong against other currencies.
  - o A stable dollar means international trade and economic growth will be promoted.
- America will promote and exercise Free Trade with all nations of the world.
  - o There will be no tariffs or duties imposed.
  - o Many economic incentives for war will be removed.

- o An unprecedented era of peace among nations will emerge.
- Government's tax and regulatory burden will be limited to 17% of America's GDP.
  - o Federal Tax Limit = 10% GDP
  - o State Tax Limit = 3% GDP
  - o Local (City and/or County) Tax Limit = 2% GDP
  - o Federal Regulatory Burden Limit = 1.5% GDP
  - o State Regulatory Burden Limit = 0.3% GDP
  - o Local (City and/or County) Regulatory Burden Limit = 0.2% GDP
- All taxes on income, savings, investment, capital formation, property, gift, and estates (death) will be eliminated.
  - o This means that economic growth and wealth creation will not be taxed.
  - o This is a major incentive to encourage and promote economic growth.
  - o Income Taxes will be eliminated.
  - o Capital Gains Taxes will be eliminated.
  - o Interest and Dividend Taxes will be eliminated.
  - o Property Taxes will be eliminated.
  - o Estate (Death) Taxes will be eliminated.
  - o Income Tax Returns will be eliminated.
- Tax revenues will come from Sales (Consumption) Taxes on both *Internet* and traditional *Bricks and Mortar* transactions.
  - o This is an incentive to save and invest.
  - o This is a major incentive to encourage and promote economic growth.
- American Government at the Federal, State and Local levels will be scaled back slowly as the tax and regulatory burden decreases.
  - o The primary purpose of the American Government is to protect America from external threats such as wars and terrorism, and from internal violence, crime and fraud.
  - o It also has additional roles that support its primary purpose, such as public safety and enforcing voluntary contracts.
  - o But, the Constitution was not put in place to control every aspect of American life.
  - o Government taxing and the subsequent funding of government programs is a process that involves controlling individuals and families.
  - o It is also a means for limiting or eliminating religious

freedom, political freedom, and economic freedom.
- <u>Americans will have the freedom to buy, own, use, and sell private property</u> –
  - o Without burdensome government regulations,
  - o Except for limited regulations related to public safety and the prevention of fraud.
- <u>Americans will not have their private property taken away by the government, except under these limited circumstances</u> –
  - o If it's for a *public use* (in the narrowest sense),
  - o There is *due process* (in the broadest sense), and
  - o There is *just compensation* (in the broadest sense).
- <u>Americans will not have their private property taken by excessive and unfair legal judgments.</u>
  - o Losing parties in trivial lawsuits will be required to pay for legal costs on both sides.
- <u>Americans will not have their private property taken by excessive and unfair environmental regulations.</u>
  - o American environmental regulations will promote the environment and conservation.
  - o At the same time, those benefits will be balanced with the needs of individuals, small businesses, corporations, and America.
  - o Human needs will <u>not</u> be subordinated to the needs of every animal and insect in nature.
  - o Individuals and families will have the freedom to live in cities, suburbs, and in rural America.
- <u>America will have a strong and innovative Free Market in energy.</u>
  - o Americans will have abundant energy at reasonable market prices.
  - o America will be energy independent to the extent it chooses based on the global market.
  - o America will develop its own energy resources within the Free Market.
  - o America will drill for oil, build new oil refineries, and will have adequate supplies of gasoline at reasonable prices.
  - o America will rely on other conventional energy sources such as coal and nuclear.
  - o America will innovate and rapidly develop new alternative sources of energy such as solar, wind, and geothermal through the power of the Free Market and its profit

incentives.

- America will have a strong and innovative Free Market in health care.
    - o Americans will have outstanding health care at reasonable market prices.
    - o Medicare and Medicaid will be privatized with premiums for the poor covered by the government.
- America will have a strong and innovative Free Market in health care insurance.
    - o Americans will have excellent health care insurance at reasonable market prices.
    - o Employers will provide direct compensation to employees (in the form of higher wages, salaries, commissions, bonuses, stock options, etc.)
    - o Employers will not provide indirect compensation (in the form of health insurance and other indirect benefits).
- America's education system will be the best in the world.
    - o Indoctrination will give way to education.
    - o School choice will encourage positive competition and will give parents control of their children's education.
    - o Homeschooling will be fully supported.
    - o Faculty and students in colleges and universities will have true academic freedom and the intellectual freedom to question, debate, discuss, and explore the issues of the day (without threat to their academic positions, class grades, or other intimidation).
    - o Faculty hiring decisions will be based on teaching, research, and service capabilities, not on the political positions potential professors might or might not hold.

A Pessimistic 21st Century Vision for America
(if American Capitalism Loses the War)

A Pessimistic 21st Century Vision for America (if American Capitalism Loses the War)

Note that this appendix provides a vision for life in America under socialism. The vision is organized by the institutions of American Capitalism.

Christian Church, Family, and Religious Freedom

Socialist Culture –

- *Atheistic and Secular*
- *With Little (or No) Value for Human Life and Love*
- *With Value Placed Instead on Power and Pleasure*
- *Moral bankruptcy will result*

- Americans will not have religious freedom.
    - o Americans will <u>not</u> have the freedom to express their religious beliefs in the public square.
    - o American Government (elected leaders and employees) will <u>not</u> have the freedom to make references to our religious heritage.
- Americans will reject America's Christian heritage and American Culture.
    - o Americans will promote a *culture of death* and will reject a *culture of life.*
        - ■ Americans will <u>not</u> promote and nurture all life, at all stages, as a gift from God.
        - ■ Americans will accept abortion (at all stages), infanticide, euthanasia, suicide and the death penalty.
    - o Americans will have little (or no) moral strength and morality.
    - o Americans will have more untrusting personal, professional, and business relationships.
    - o Americans will have more strained and belligerent relationships with other nations.
- Americans will have weaker marriages and families.
    - o Marriages and families will be seen as a relic of the past.
    - o Love will be seen as a foolish idea for unrealistic people.
    - o America will reject marriage between a man and woman for the purpose of love and procreating children.
    - o America will see marriage as an inconvenience without

value.

- o America will reject family values, such as abstinence until marriage, as old-fashioned.
- o America will accept violence, brutality, prostitution, and pornography in education and in the entertainment industry as normal and commonplace.

Constitution, Religious Freedom, Political Freedom, and Economic Freedom

Socialist Government –

- *The Constitution will be ignored (or circumvented)*
- *Americans will have little (or no) Freedom*
- *Socialist elites will control you and your family's lives*
- *Psychological depression and suicide will be commonplace*

- The Constitution will be ignored or circumvented.
    - o Justices and judges will ignore and circumvent the Constitution as it was originally written.
    - o Justices and judges will function in a legislative and political role to advance the socialist agenda.
    - o Americans will not live under the *Rule of Law.*
    - o Americans will not have *Due Process.*
    - o Americans will not have *Equal Protection.*
- America will recognize the power of global organizations and treaties to supersede the Constitution of the United States of America.
    - o American sovereignty will be abridged by the United Nations and other global organizations.
    - o Americans will pay taxes imposed by global organizations on America.
- America will not maintain strong Armed Forces, ready to protect and defend America.
    - o American Government will launch offensive wars as necessary to advance the socialist agenda.
    - o America will not safeguard and protect its borders from unlimited and illegal immigration.
    - o America will not enforce its immigration laws.
- Americans will not have political freedom.
- Americans will not have freedom of speech.

- o Americans will <u>not</u> have religious freedom of speech.
- o "Hate speech" and "offensive speech" restrictions will expand until Americans are afraid to speak in public or private.
- o Americans will <u>not</u> have political freedom of speech because of "campaign finance reform," "Fairness Doctrine," "Web Fairness Doctrine" and other restrictions.
- o Americans will be forced to accept the beliefs of others. For example,
  - ▪ Christians will be forced to accept non-Christian beliefs and values.
  - ▪ Christians will be forced to perform actions that they believe are morally wrong.
- o Americans will <u>not</u> have the freedom to follow their own consciences (the *Right of Conscience),* subject to the Rule of Law.
- • <u>Americans will not have the right to keep and bear arms.</u>
  - o Strict gun control laws will be imposed on Americans.
- • <u>Americans will not have the right to be secure in their persons, homes, and businesses.</u>
  - o Americans will be subject to unreasonable strip searches.
  - o Americans will be subject to warrantless searches of homes and businesses.
- • <u>Americans will not have economic freedom.</u>
  - o American Government will not permit the Free Market and Free Enterprise.
  - o American Government will not permit Free Trade with other nations.
  - o American Government will permit discrimination to advance the socialist agenda.
    - ▪ Affirmative action will be expanded.
    - ▪ Quotas will be expanded.
    - ▪ Reverse discrimination will be expanded.
    - ▪ Major financial reparations will be paid to relatives of former slaves, even when the evidence is uncertain.
    - ▪ Major financial reparations will be paid to other nations for alleged damages caused by America, even when the evidence of any damages is tenuous.
- • <u>Americans will not have intellectual freedom.</u>

- o Faculty and students in colleges and universities will <u>not</u> have true academic freedom and will <u>not</u> have the intellectual freedom to question, debate, discuss, and explore the issues of the day (without threat to their academic positions, class grades, or other intimidation).
  - o Faculty hiring decisions will <u>not</u> be based on teaching, research, and service capabilities. Instead, such decisions will be based on the political positions potential professors hold.
- <u>America will live in a police state.</u>
- <u>America will have sham elections without debate on substantive issues, but with personal attacks and negative campaigning.</u>
  - o America will have dishonest elections with voter fraud seen as normal.

Free Market, Free Enterprise, and Economic Freedom

Socialist Economy –

- *There will be little (or no) economic freedom*
- *There will be little, no, or negative economic growth initially*
- *Shortages and rationing will be widespread*
- *Poverty and destitution will be widespread*
- *Economic bankruptcy will result inevitably*

- <u>Americans will not have economic freedom.</u>
  - o American Government will not permit the Free Market and Free Enterprise.
  - o American Government will not permit Free Trade with other nations.
- <u>Americans will experience little, no, or negative economic growth at the rate of -4% to 1% GDP per year</u> –
  - o Without economic freedom, the Free Market and Free Enterprise,
  - o By substantially increasing the tax and regulatory burden on individuals, small businesses, and corporations, and
  - o By preventing Free Trade between America and other nations.
- <u>America's charitable giving and compassion will decrease substantially.</u>
  - o This is true because of America's declining economic growth

and capital consumption under socialist policies and programs.

- o America will <u>not</u> be able to afford compassion and generosity.
- o The socialist culture will <u>not</u> value compassion and generosity.

- <u>America will not place the dollar back on the gold standard.</u>
  - o *The dollar will <u>not</u> be as good as gold.*
  - o *The dollar will <u>not</u> be worth the paper it's printed on.*
  - o Americans will experience price instability.
  - o Americans will experience inflation, and possibly hyperinflation.
  - o The dollar will <u>not</u> stay strong against other currencies.
  - o International trade and economic growth will <u>not</u> be promoted.

- <u>America will not promote and exercise Free Trade with all nations of the world.</u>
  - o There will be many tariffs and duties imposed.
  - o Many economic incentives for war will be created.
  - o An unprecedented era of conflict and belligerence among nations will emerge.

- <u>Government's tax and regulatory burden will be very high.</u>
  - o It will exceed 60% of America's GDP.
  - o It will stifle innovation, incentive, capital creation, economic growth, and wealth creation.

- <u>All taxes on income, savings, investment, capital formation, property, gift, and estates (death) will be increased.</u>
  - o This means that economic growth and wealth creation will be taxed at high rates.
  - o This is a major disincentive to encourage and promote economic growth.
  - o Income Taxes will be increased.
  - o Capital Gains Taxes will be increased.
  - o Interest and Dividend Taxes will be increased.
  - o Property Taxes will be increased.
  - o Gift Taxes will be increased.
  - o Estate (Death) Taxes will be increased.
  - o Income Tax Returns will be more complicated.

- <u>Tax revenues from Sales (Consumption) Taxes on *Internet* and traditional *Bricks and Mortar* transactions will be increased.</u>

- Sales Taxes on Internet transactions will be increased (if already in existence) and will be added (if not already in existence).
- Sales Taxes on services will be added to the already excessive tax burden of the American people.

- <u>American Government at the Federal, State and Local levels will grow in size and complexity dramatically.</u>
  - The tax and regulatory burden on Americans will be enormous.
  - The primary purpose of the American Government will be to control the lives and lifestyles of all Americans.
  - Government will limit or eliminate religious freedom, political freedom, and economic freedom.

- <u>Americans will not have the freedom to buy, own, use, and sell private property</u> –
  - Without burdensome government regulations, and
  - Without the permission of the government.

- <u>Americans will have their private property taken away by the government</u> –
  - For *public or private use,*
  - Without *due process,* and
  - Without *just compensation.*
  - For all practical purposes, private property will no longer exist.
  - Private property will effectively be public property, since private property will be controlled by government.

- <u>Americans will have their private property taken by excessive and unfair legal judgments.</u>
  - Trivial lawsuits will be a means to steal private property from its rightful owner.

- <u>Americans will have their private property taken by excessive and unfair environmental regulations.</u>
  - American environmental regulations will trump the private property rights of Americans.
  - Human needs will be subordinated to the needs of every animal and insect in nature.
  - Individuals and families will <u>not</u> have the freedom to live in cities, suburbs, and in rural America at their own discretion. Government permission will be required.

- <u>America will not have a strong and innovative free market in energy.</u>

- o Americans will <u>not</u> have abundant energy at reasonable market prices.
- o America will <u>not</u> be energy independent to the extent it chooses based on the global market.
- o America will <u>not</u> develop its own energy resources within the Free Market.
- o America will <u>not</u> drill for oil, will <u>not</u> build new oil refineries, and will <u>not</u> have adequate supplies of gasoline at reasonable prices.
- o America will <u>not</u> rely on other conventional energy sources such as coal and nuclear.
- o America will <u>not</u> innovate and rapidly develop new alternative sources of energy such as solar, wind, and geothermal through the power of the Free Market and its profit incentives.
- o America will have energy shortages and government rationing.
- o Americans will pay new Carbon Taxes and Energy Taxes.
- o Americans will have to cut back on their energy usage and their lifestyles.
- o American businesses will <u>not</u> have adequate energy supplies to meet consumer needs for products and services.
- <u>America will not have a strong and innovative free market in health care</u>.
  - o Americans will <u>not</u> have outstanding health care at reasonable market prices.
  - o Americans will have inferior health care.
  - o Medicare and Medicaid will be extended to include all Americans at all ages.
  - o Shortages and government rationing of health care services will be commonplace.
  - o Americans will suffer and die waiting for urgent services.
  - o Americans will be denied medical care and drugs that are deemed by government to be too expensive.
  - o New drugs and innovative therapies will <u>not</u> be developed without economic freedom and Free Market incentives.
- <u>America will not have a strong and innovative free market in health care insurance</u>.
  - o Americans will be forced to enroll in a socialist universal, health care system run inefficiently by the government.

- America's education system will not be the best in the world.
    - Indoctrination will grow.
    - Education will be eliminated
    - School choice will <u>not</u> be permitted.
    - Homeschooling will <u>not</u> be permitted.
    - Faculty and students in colleges and universities will <u>not</u> have true academic freedom and will <u>not</u> have the intellectual freedom to question, debate, discuss, and explore the issues of the day (without threat to their academic positions, class grades, or other intimidation).
    - Faculty hiring decisions will <u>not</u> be based on teaching, research, and service capabilities. They will be based on the political positions potential professors hold.

About the Author

Gerard Francis Lameiro, *America's Citizen-Philosopher*, is a philosopher, economist, and engineer. Dr. Lameiro is Founder and CEO of Lameiro Economics LLC, a company focused on bringing practical economic knowledge about freedom, economic growth and prosperity to America and to the world.

Dr. Lameiro was previously a member of Hewlett-Packard's Strategy and Corporate Development team where he was Director of New Business Ventures for HP worldwide and managed HP's Technology Evaluation Process worldwide. He is the former President of the Association of Energy Engineers (AEE), Founder of AEE's National Energy Policy Council, and a National Science Foundation Post-Doctoral Energy-Related Fellow. Dr. Lameiro was also an Assistant Professor in Colorado State University's College of Business.

Dr. Lameiro, a popular platform speaker, is an expert in economic, business, and engineering models and in free market economics. For more information or to contact Dr. Lameiro, please visit: http://www.LameiroBooks.com .

Notes

Chapter 1

1. From the U. S. Census Bureau's website on December 3, 2007, webpage URL is: http://factfinder.census.gov/servlet/ACSSAFFFacts?_submenuId=factsheet_0&_sse =on .

2. From Google's website on December 3, 2007, webpage URL is: http://www.google.com/intl/en/corporate/history.html .

3. From Google's website on December 3, 2007, webpage URL is: http://finance.google.com/finance?q=GOOG .

4. Percentages computed from data obtained from the Central Intelligence Agency's publication: *The World Factbook 2007* on December 6, 2007; webpage URL is: https://www.cia.gov/library/publications/the-world-factbook/index.html . Specific webpage URLs are:
   (a) Rank Order - Population https://www.cia.gov/library/publications/the-world-factbook/rankorder/2119rank.html
   (b) Rank Order – GDP (purchasing power parity) https://www.cia.gov/library/publications/the-world-factbook/rankorder /2001rank.html
   (c) Rank Order – Electricity – production https://www.cia.gov/library/publications/the-world-factbook/rankorder /2038rank.html
   (d) Rank Order – Natural gas – production https://www.cia.gov/library /publications/the-world-factbook/rankorder/2180rank.html
   (e) Rank Order – Oil – production https://www.cia.gov/library/publications/ the-world-factbook/rankorder/2173rank.html .

5. From the Central Intelligence Agency's website on December 6, 2007, webpage URL is https://www.cia.gov/library/publications/the-world-factbook/rankorder/2173rank.html .

6. Karl Marx and Frederick Engels, *The Communist Manifesto* (London: Junius Publications Ltd., 1996), 17.

7. From the Heritage Foundation's website on January 23, 2009, webpage URL is: http://www.heritage.org/index/Ranking.aspx .

8. Please see the following references:
   (a) From the Heritage Foundation's website on January 23, 2009, webpage URL is: http://www.heritage.org/index/Country/Zimbabwe .
   (b) From the Heritage Foundation's website on December 7, 2007, webpage URL is: http://www.heritage.org/research/features/index/country.cfm?id=Zimbabwe.

9. From the Heritage Foundation's website on December 7, 2007, webpage URL is: http://www.heritage.org/research/features/index/country.cfm?id=Syria .

10. Charles Q. Choi, "Forecast: Sex and Marriage with Robots by 2050," FoxNews.com, October 15, 2007. From the Fox News website on October 15, 2007, webpage URL is: http://www.foxnews.com/printer_friendly_story/0,3566,301736,00.html .

11. Newt Gingrich, *Rediscovering God in America: Reflections on the Role of Faith in Our Nation's History and Future* (Franklin, TN: Integrity Publishers, 2006), 46.

12. Gerard Francis Lameiro, *Lameiro's First Law of Economics*. From the Architecture of American Capitalism website on June 18, 2009, webpage URL is: http://www.architectureofamericancapitalism.com/id65.html .

13. Ibid.

14. Associated Press, "Colorado Student Files Lawsuit Over Commencement Speech That Mentioned Jesus," FoxNews.com, August 31, 2007. From the Fox News website on August 31, 2007, webpage URL is: http://www.foxnews.com/printer_friendly_story/0,3566,295432,00.html .

15. Richard A. Viguerie, *Conservatives Betrayed: How George W. Bush and Other Big Government Republicans Hijacked the Conservative Cause* (Los Angeles: Bonus Books, 2006), 106.

16. Laura Ingraham, *Power to the People* (Washington, DC: Regnery Publishing Inc., 2007), 215-216.

17. David E. Bernstein, *You Can't Say That! The Growing Threat to Civil Liberties from Antidiscrimination Laws* (Washington, DC: Cato Institute, 2003), 61.

18. For more information, you can visit the Federal Election Commission website. Please see, for example, the following webpage (URL is current as of December 6, 2007): http://www.fec.gov/pages/brochures/fecfeca.shtml .

19. Adam D. Thierer, "A Fairness Doctrine for the Internet," *City Journal*, October 18, 2007, http://www.city-journal.org/html/eon2007-10-18at.html .

20. Michael F. Cannon and Michael D. Tanner, *Healthy Competition: What's Holding Back Health Care and How to Free It* (Washington, DC: Cato Institute, 2005), 10.

21. Ibid, 7-8.

22. "Socialized Medicine's Waiting Room," *The Limbaugh Letter*, November 2007, Vol. 16, No. 11, 12.

23. Ibid.

24. Please see the accompanying table for reference notes.

25. S. Fred Singer, "Global Warming: Man-Made or Natural?," *Imprimis*, August 2007, Vol. 36, No. 8, 2.

26. James Schlesinger, "The Theology of Global Warming," *The Wall Street Journal*, August 8, 2005, A10. From The Wall Street Journal's website on August 8, 2005, webpage URL is: http://online.wsj.com/article_print/0,,SB112346586472807229,00.html .

27. S. Fred Singer, "Global Warming: Man-Made or Natural?," *Imprimis*, August 2007, Vol. 36, No. 8, 2.

28. Ibid.

29. Ibid.

30. Ibid, 4.

31. William M. Gray, "Hurricanes and Hot Air," *The Wall Street Journal*, July 26, 2007, A12. From The Wall Street Journal's website on July 26, 2007, webpage URL is: http://online.wsj.com/article_print/SB118541193645178412.html .

32. Ibid.

33. Ibid.

34. Ibid.

35. Please see, for example, the following references:
   (a) Christopher C. Horner, *The Politically Incorrect Guide™ to Global Warming and Environmentalism* (Washington, DC: Regnery Publishing, Inc., 2007).
   (b) Patrick J. Michaels, Editor, *Shattered Consensus: The True State of Global*

Warming (Lanham, MD: Rowman & Littlefield Publishers, Inc., 2005).

(c) Patrick J. Michaels, *Meltdown: The Predictable Distortion of Global Warming by Scientists, Politicians, and the Media* (Washington, DC: Cato Institute, 2004).

(d) S. Fred Singer and Dennis T. Avery, *Unstoppable Global Warming: Every 1,500 Years Updated and Expanded Edition* (Lanham, MD: Rowman & Littlefield Publishers, Inc., 2008).

36. S. Fred Singer, "Global Warming: Man-Made or Natural?," *Imprimis*, August 2007, Vol. 36, No. 8, 5.

37. "Al-Gae Gore," *Investor's Business Daily*, July 31, 2007, A13.

38. James Schlesinger, "The Theology of Global Warming," *The Wall Street Journal*, August 8, 2005, A10. From The Wall Street Journal's website on August 8, 2005, webpage URL is:

http://online.wsj.com/article_print/0,,SB112346586472807229,00.html .

39. Christopher C. Horner, *The Politically Incorrect Guide™ to Global Warming and Environmentalism* (Washington, DC: Regnery Publishing, Inc., 2007), 69.

40. Brittany Sauser, "Ethanol Demand Threatens Food Prices," *Technology Review*, February 13, 2007,

http://www.technologyreview.com/printer_friendly_article.aspx?id=18173 .

41. From American Petroleum Institute's website on December 6, 2007, webpage URL is:

http://www.api.org/statistics/fueltaxes/upload/July_2007_gasoline_and_diesel_sum mary_pages.pdf .

42. Computed by the author as follows: (($0.628 / ($3.00 - $0.628)) * 100.00 = 26.5%.

43. "Carbon tax? City is first to try it: Boulder surcharge on coal aims to reduce emissions tied to global warming," MSNBC.com, November 10, 2006. From the MSNBC.com on May 27, 2008, website URL is:

http://www.msnbc.msn.com/id/15651688/print/1/displaymode/1098/ .

44. Steven Milloy, "Asbestos Could Have Saved WTC Lives," FoxNews.com, September 14, 2001. From the Fox News website on November 12, 2007, webpage URL is: http://www.foxnews.com/printer_friendly_story/0,3566,34342,00.html .

45. Ibid.

46. Ibid.

47. James M. Taylor, "Cost of Asbestos Junk Science Continues to Mount," *Environment News*, July 2002,

http://www.heartland.org/PrinterFriendly.cfm?theType=artId&theID=918 .

48. Steven Milloy, "Asbestos Could Have Saved WTC Lives," FoxNews.com, September 14, 2001. From the Fox News website on November 12, 2007, webpage URL is: http://www.foxnews.com/printer_friendly_story/0,3566,34342,00.html .

49. Charli E. Coon, "Why the Government's CAFE Standards for Fuel Efficiency Should Be Repealed, not Increased," Backgrounder #1458, *The Heritage Foundation*, July 11, 2001,

http://www.heritage.org/Research/EnergyandEnvironment/BG1458.cfm .

50. Ibid.

51. Please see the following references:

(a) "Judicial Overreach," *Investor's Business Daily*, November 19, 2007, A16.

(b) Reuters, "US Appeals Court Orders New Fuel Economy Standards," Reuters AlertNet, November 16, 2007,
http://www.alertnet.org/thenews/newsdesk/N15327695.htm .

52. F. A. Hayek, *The Fatal Conceit: The Errors of Socialism* (Chicago: The University of Chicago Press, 1988), 106.
53. F. A. Hayek, *The Road to Serfdom* (Chicago: The University of Chicago Press, 1972), 155.
54. F. A. Hayek, *The Fatal Conceit: The Errors of Socialism* (Chicago: The University of Chicago Press, 1988), 110.
55. Ludwig von Mises, *Human Action: A Treatise on Economics, Third Edition* (Chicago: Contemporary Books, Inc. and Henry Regnery Company, 1966), 152.
56. F. A. Hayek, *The Fatal Conceit: The Errors of Socialism* (Chicago: The University of Chicago Press, 1988), 114-117.
57. Ibid, 118.
58. For an in-depth study of "social justice," please see the following book. Friedrich A. Hayek, *Law Legislation and Liberty Volume 2: The Mirage of Social Justice* (Chicago: The University of Chicago Press, 1976).
59. Milton and Rose Friedman, *Free to Choose: A Personal Statement* (San Diego: Harcourt, Brace & Company, 1990), 134-135.
60. Lord Acton, *Letter to Bishop Mandell Creighton*, 1877. From the Quotations Page website on December 7, 2007, webpage URL is: http://www.quotationspage.com/quotes/Lord_Acton/ .
61. Alexis de Tocqueville, *Democracy in America*, Volume I (New York: Vintage Books Edition, 1990), 55-58.
62. "Another Ice Age?," *Time*, June 24, 1974. From the Time website on November 29, 2007, webpage URL is: http://www.time.com/time/printout/0,8816,944914,00.html .
63. Julian L. Simon, *The Ultimate Resource 2* (Princeton, NJ: Princeton University Press, 1996), 212-222.
64. Ibid, 84-126.
65. Ibid, 109.
66. Steven Malloy, "Top Ten Junk Science Stories of the Past Decade," FoxNews.com, April 6, 2006. From the Fox News website on November 29, 2007, webpage URL is: http://www.foxnews.com/printer_friendly_story/0,3566,189706,00.html .
67. Ibid.
68. Please see, for example, *"A Guide to Historical Holdings in the Eisenhower Library: CRANBERRY SCARE OF 1959,"* Compiled by Barbara Constable, Eisenhower Presidential Library and Museum, March 1994. From the Eisenhower Presidential Library and Museum website on November 29, 2007, webpage URL is: http://www.eisenhower.archives.gov/Research/GUIDES/1959_Cranberry_Scare.pdf
69. See, for example, *"The Plot Against Alar: an ACSH Interview with Robert Bidinotto, author of "The Great Apple Scare","* American Council on Science and Health, January 1, 1991. From the American Council on Science and Health's website on November 29, 2007, webpage URL is: http://www.acsh.org/healthissues/newsID.840/healthissue_detail.asp .
70. John R. Bolton, "Does the United Nations Advance the Cause of Freedom?," Heritage Lectures No. 1047, Delivered on September 6, 2007, *The Heritage Foundation*, October 23, 2007.
71. From the United Nations website on December 3, 2007, webpage URL is: http://www.un.org/aboutun/unhistory/ .

72. From the United Nations website on December 3, 2007, webpage URL is: http://www.un.org/aboutun/charter/ .

73. From the United Nations website on January 26, 2009, webpage URL is: http://www.un.org/members/list.shtml .

74. John R. Bolton, "Does the United Nations Advance the Cause of Freedom?," Heritage Lectures No. 1047, Delivered on September 6, 2007, *The Heritage Foundation*, October 23, 2007.

75. Ibid.

76. Steven Groves, "Why Reagan Would Still Reject the Law of the Sea Treaty," WebMemo No. 1676, *The Heritage Foundation*, October 24, 2007. From The Heritage Foundation website on May 19, 2008, webpage URL is: http://www.heritage.org/Research/InternationalOrganizations/upload/wm_1676.pdf .

77. John R. Bolton, "Does the United Nations Advance the Cause of Freedom?," Heritage Lectures No. 1047, Delivered on September 6, 2007, *The Heritage Foundation*, October 23, 2007.

78. Ibid.

79. Ibid.

80. From the Heritage Foundation's website on January 26, 2009, webpage URL is: http://www.heritage.org/index/Ranking.aspx .

81. From the United Nations website on January 26, 2009, webpage URL is: http://www.un.org/members/list.shtml .

82. John R. Bolton, "Does the United Nations Advance the Cause of Freedom?," Heritage Lectures No. 1047, Delivered on September 6, 2007, *The Heritage Foundation*, October 23, 2007.

Chapter 3

83. Rodney Stark, *The Victory of Reason: How Christianity Led to Freedom, Capitalism, and Western Success* (New York: Random House, 2005), x. Note that the emphasis placed on some words in the quote was from Professor Stark's book.

84. Both figures were created by this author from ideas adapted in part from Professor Stark's book referenced in the note above.

85. Rodney Stark, *The Victory of Reason: How Christianity Led to Freedom, Capitalism, and Western Success* (New York: Random House, 2005), 5-12.

86. Ibid, 5-68.

87. Pope Leo XIII, "Libertas Praestantissimum (Human Liberty)," June 20, 1888, *The Great Encyclical Letters of Pope Leo XIII* (Rockford, IL: Tan Books and Publishers, Inc., 1903), 137.

88. From the U.S. Supreme Court's website on December 17, 2007, webpage URL is: http://www.supremecourtus.gov/about/courtbuilding.pdf .

89. Alvin J. Schmidt, *How Christianity Changed the World* (Grand Rapids, MI: Zondervan, 2004), 248-250.

90. John W. Robbins, *"The Sine Qua Non of Enduring Freedom," A Man of Principle: Essays in Honor of Hans F. Sennholz,* Volume Editors, John W. Robbins, Mark Spangler (Grove City, PA: Grove City College Press, 1992), 395.

91. Pope Leo XIII, "Libertas Praestantissimum (Human Liberty)," June 20, 1888, *The Great Encyclical Letters of Pope Leo XIII* (Rockford, IL: Tan Books and Publishers, Inc., 1903), 144.

92. Rodney Stark, *The Victory of Reason: How Christianity Led to Freedom, Capitalism, and Western Success* (New York: Random House, 2005), 79.

93. Ibid.

94. Pope Leo XIII, "Rerum Novarum (The Condition of the Working Classes)," May 15, 1891, *The Great Encyclical Letters of Pope Leo XIII* (Rockford, IL: Tan Books and Publishers, Inc., 1903), 216.

95. Rodney Stark, *The Victory of Reason: How Christianity Led to Freedom, Capitalism, and Western Success* (New York: Random House, 2005), 57-67.

96. Ibid.

97. Ibid.

98. Ibid.

99. Ibid, xi.

100. Alvin J. Schmidt, *How Christianity Changed the World* (Grand Rapids, MI: Zondervan, 2004), 125-150.

101. Ibid.

102. Ibid, 129.

103. Ibid, 125-169.

104. From The White House website on December 19, 2007, webpage URL is: http://www.whitehouse.gov/news/releases/2007/05/print/20070530-5.html .

105. Alvin J. Schmidt, *How Christianity Changed the World* (Grand Rapids, MI: Zondervan, 2004), 185-186.

106. Rodney Stark, *The Victory of Reason: How Christianity Led to Freedom, Capitalism, and Western Success* (New York: Random House, 2005), 52-53.

107. Ibid, 227-228.

108. Alvin J. Schmidt, *How Christianity Changed the World* (Grand Rapids, MI: Zondervan, 2004), 190.

109. Thomas E. Woods, Jr., *How the Catholic Church Built Western Civilization* (Washington, DC: Regnery Publishing, Inc., 2005), 81. Note that the emphasis placed on some words in the quote was from Professor Woods' book.

110. Please see, for example, the following references:
   (a) Rodney Stark, *The Victory of Reason: How Christianity Led to Freedom, Capitalism, and Western Success* (New York: Random House, 2005).
   (b) Alvin J. Schmidt, *How Christianity Changed the World* (Grand Rapids, MI: Zondervan, 2004).
   (c) Thomas E. Woods, Jr., *How the Catholic Church Built Western Civilization* (Washington, DC: Regnery Publishing, Inc., 2005).

111. J. Budziszewski, *Written on the Heart: The Case for Natural Law* (Downers Grove, IL: InterVarsity Press, 1997), 65-69.

112. F. A. Hayek, *The Road to Serfdom* (Chicago: The University of Chicago Press, 1972), 103-104.

113. Charles J. Chaput, "Education and Our Witness to Christ," *First Things,* September 10, 2007. From First Things' website on September 20, 2007, webpage URL is: http://www.firstthings.com/onthesquare/?p=843 .

114. Brian C. Anderson, *Democratic Capitalism and Its Discontents* (Wilmington, DE: ISI Books, Intercollegiate Studies Institute, 2007), 3.

115. Edmund A. Opitz, *Religion: Foundation of the Free Society* (Irvington-on-Hudson, NY: The Foundation for Economic Education, Inc., 1996), 18.

116. George Gilder, *Wealth and Poverty* (San Francisco, CA: ICS Press, Institute for Contemporary Studies, 1993), 21.

117. Charles J. Chaput, "Education and Our Witness to Christ," *First Things,* September 10, 2007. From First Things' website on September 20, 2007, webpage URL is: http://www.firstthings.com/onthesquare/?p=843 .

118. Ludwig von Mises, *Human Action: A Treatise on Economics, Third Revised Edition* (Chicago, IL: Contemporary Books, Inc., 1966), 257-326.
119. Ibid, 257.
120. Ibid, 257-326.
121. Ibid, 327.
122. Bernard Wysocki Jr., "Lack of Vaccines Goes Beyond Flu Inoculations: Eight Shortages Have Occurred Since 2000; Fewer Shots From Tetanus to Chickenpox," *The Wall Street Journal,* December 8, 2003, http://online.wsj.com/article_print/0,,SB107083848883637900,00.html .
123. Ibid.
124. Henry Hazlitt, *Economics in One Lesson* (New York, NY: Crown Publishing, Inc., 1979), 134.
125. Ludwig von Mises, *Human Action: A Treatise on Economics, Third Revised Edition* (Chicago, IL: Contemporary Books, Inc., 1966), 598.
126. Ibid.
127. Maggie Gallagher, *The Abolition of Marriage: How We Destroy Lasting Love* (Washington, DC: Regnery Publishing, Inc., 1996), 143-152.
128. Ibid.
129. Robert L. Plunkett, "Vow for Now – Harmful Effects of No-Fault Divorce," *National Review,* May 29, 1995. From BNET's website on January 28, 2008, webpage URL is: http://findarticles.com/p/articles/mi_m1282/is_n10_v47/ai_16936591/print .
130. Linda J. Waite and Maggie Gallagher, *The Case for Marriage: Why Married People are Happier, Healthier, and Better Off Financially* (New York, NY: Doubleday, Random House, Inc., 2000), 112.
131. Ibid, 47.
132. Richard Pipes, *A Concise History of the Russian Revolution* (New York, NY: Vintage Books, Random House, Inc., 1996), 330.
133. Maggie Gallagher, *The Abolition of Marriage: How We Destroy Lasting Love* (Washington, DC: Regnery Publishing, Inc., 1996), 143.
134. Karl Marx and Frederick Engels, *The Communist Manifesto* (London: Junius Publications Ltd., 1996), 31.
135. Ibid, 31-33.
136. Frederick Engels, *The Origin of the Family Private Property and the State* (Honolulu, HI: University Press of the Pacific, 2001, Reprinted from the 1902 Edition), 96-100.
137. John Powell, *Fully Human, Fully Alive: A New Life Through a New Vision* (Niles, IL: Argus Communications, 1976).

Chapter 4

138. F. A. Hayek, *The Fatal Conceit: The Errors of Socialism* (Chicago: The University of Chicago Press, 1988), 7.
139. Ludwig von Mises, *Socialism: An Economic and Sociological Analysis* (Indianapolis, IN: Liberty Fund, Inc., 1981), 74.
140. Ludwig von Mises, *Human Action: A Treatise on Economics, Third Revised Edition* (Chicago, IL: Contemporary Books, Inc., 1966), 295.
141. Ibid, 238.
142. Karl Marx, *Das Kapital: A Critique of Political Economy*, Edited by Frederick Engels, Condensed by Serge L. Levitsky (Washington, DC: Regnery Publishing,

Inc., 2000), 174-179.

143. Ibid.

144. Karl Marx and Frederick Engels, *The Communist Manifesto* (London: Junius Publications Ltd., 1996), 28.

145. Ludwig von Mises, *Socialism: An Economic and Sociological Analysis* (Indianapolis, IN: Liberty Fund, Inc., 1981), 32-39.

146. Steve H. Hanke and Stephen J. K. Walters, "Economic Freedom, Prosperity, and Equality: A Survey," *The Cato Journal,* Volume 17, Number 2, Fall/Winter 1997. From the Cato Institute's website on February 13, 2008, webpage URL is: http://www.cato.org/pubs/journal/cj17n2-1.html .

147. F. A. Hayek, *The Fatal Conceit: The Errors of Socialism* (Chicago: The University of Chicago Press, 1988).

148. William J. O'Neil, *How to Make Money in Stocks: A Winning System in Good Times or Bad, Third Edition – Completely Updated* (New York, NY: McGraw-Hill, 2002), 181.

149. "IBD's 197 Industry Group Rankings," *Investor's Business Daily,* February 11, 2008, B8.

150. Karl Marx and Frederick Engels, *The Communist Manifesto* (London: Junius Publications Ltd., 1996), 13.

151. Ludwig von Mises, *Socialism: An Economic and Sociological Analysis* (Indianapolis, IN: Liberty Fund, Inc., 1981), 281-283.

152. James Lennox, "Darwinism," *Stanford Encyclopedia of Philosophy,* August 13, 2004. From the Stanford Encyclopedia of Philosophy website on February 19, 2008, webpage URL is: http://plato.stanford.edu/entries/darwinism/ .

153. David Weinstein, "Herbert Spencer," *Stanford Encyclopedia of Philosophy,* December, 15, 2002. From the Stanford Encyclopedia of Philosophy website on February 19, 2008, webpage URL is: http://plato.stanford.edu/entries/spencer/ .

154. Ludwig von Mises, *Socialism: An Economic and Sociological Analysis* (Indianapolis, IN: Liberty Fund, Inc., 1981), 281-283.

155. Francis Fukuyama, *Trust: The Social Virtues & the Creation of Prosperity* (New York, NY: The Free Press, 1995), 7.

Chapter 5

156. Ludwig von Mises, *Human Action: A Treatise on Economics, Third Revised Edition* (Chicago, IL: Contemporary Books, Inc., 1966), 740.

157. James C. Humes, *The Wit & Wisdom of Ronald Reagan* (Washington, DC: Regnery Publishing, Inc., 2007), 41.

158. From the Central Intelligence Agency's publication: *The 2008 World Factbook* on February 27, 2008; webpage URL is: https://www.cia.gov/library/publications/the-world-factbook/geos/us.html#Econ .

159. John Maynard Keynes, *The End of Laissez-Faire: The Economic Consequences of the Peace* (Amherst, NY: Prometheus Books, 2004), 246-247.

160. George Reisman, *Capitalism: A Treatise on Economics* (Ottawa, IL: Jameson Books, 1996), 922-923.

161. Milton and Rose Friedman, *Free to Choose: A Personal Statement* (San Diego: Harcourt, Brace & Company, 1990), 264.

162. Ibid, 264-265.

163. Ibid, 91-127.

164. Ludwig von Mises, *Human Action: A Treatise on Economics, Third Revised*

Edition (Chicago, IL: Contemporary Books, Inc., 1966), 833-854.

165. Brian M. Reidl, "Federal Spending by the Numbers 2008," *The Heritage Foundation,* February 25, 2008. From The Heritage Foundation's website on March 1, 2008, webpage URL is: http://www.heritage.org/Research/Taxes/upload/FederalSpendingByTheNumbers2008.pdf .

166. Ludwig von Mises, *Human Action: A Treatise on Economics, Third Revised Edition* (Chicago, IL: Contemporary Books, Inc., 1966), 851.

167. John Gray, *Men Are from Mars, Women Are from Venus: The Classic Guide to Understanding the Opposite Sex* (New York, NY: HarperCollins Publishers Inc., 2004).

168. Ludwig von Mises, *Human Action: A Treatise on Economics, Third Revised Edition* (Chicago, IL: Contemporary Books, Inc., 1966), 851.

169. Arthur C. Brooks, "What Really Buys Happiness? Not income equality, but mobility and opportunity," *City Journal,* Summer 2007. From the City Journal website on January 18, 2008, webpage is: http://www.city-journal.org/printable.php?id=2298 .

170. Joseph A. Schumpeter, *Capitalism, Socialism and Democracy* (New York, NY: Harper & Row Publishers, Inc., 1975), 82-83.

171. Ludwig von Mises, *Human Action: A Treatise on Economics, Third Revised Edition* (Chicago, IL: Contemporary Books, Inc., 1966), 845.

172. Mary Parker Follett, "Training Democratic Citizens," in *The Social and Political Thought of American Progressivism, Edited, with an Introduction, by Eldon J. Eisenach* (Indianapolis, IN: Hackett Publishing Company, Inc., 2006), 105.

173. Ibid, 105-106.

174. Richard A. Epstein, *How Progressives Rewrote the Constitution* (Washington, DC: Cato Institute, 2006).

175. The three reasons cited and their explanations have been strongly influenced by the thinking of Ludwig von Mises. For Ludwig von Mises' rationale for the impact of government intervention and why intervention must end, please see: Ludwig von Mises, *Human Action: A Treatise on Economics, Third Revised Edition* (Chicago, IL: Contemporary Books, Inc., 1966), 858-861.

176. Please see, for example, the following references:

   (a) Irving Kristol, *Neo-Conservatism: The Autobiography of an Idea* (New York, NY: The Free Press, A Division of Simon & Schuster Inc., 1995), ix-xi.

   (b) Irving Kristol, "The Neoconservative Persuasion: What it was, and what it is," *The Weekly Standard*, Volume 008, Issue 47, August 25, 2003. From The Weekly Standard's website on March 26, 2008, webpage URL is: http://www.weeklystandard.com/content/public/articles/000/000/003/000tzmlw.asp?pg=1 .

   (c) Bill Steigerwald, "So, what is a 'neocon'?, *Pittsburgh Tribune-Review,* May 29, 2004. From the PittsburghLIVE's website on March 26, 2008, webpage URL is: http://www.pittsburghlive.com/x/pittsburghtrib/s_196286.html .

Chapter 6

177. Rich Lowry, "Theo-Panic! Emotional, self-righteous, and close-minded politics," *National Review Online,* October 17, 2006. From National Review's website on June 11, 2008, webpage URL is:

http://article.nationalreview.com/print/?q=Njk1Y2RmN2E5NmRjMjVkN2RkZjQw
MTljMDQ0ZTgxN2U= .
178. Please see, for example, the following references:
   (a) Steven G. Calabresi, Editor, *Originalism: A Quarter-Century of Debate*
        (Washington, DC: Regnery Publishing, Inc., 2007).
   (b) *The Heritage Guide to the Constitution,* Edwin Meese III. Chairman of the
        Editorial Advisory
        Board (Washington, DC: The Heritage Foundation, 2005).
   (c) Richard A. Epstein, *How Progressives Rewrote the Constitution*
        (Washington, DC: Cato Institute, 2006).
179. Richard A. Epstein, *How Progressives Rewrote the Constitution* (Washington,
DC: Cato Institute, 2006).
180. Ronald Reagan, Speech at *The Investiture of Chief Justice William H.
Rehnquist and Associate Justice Antonin Scalia at The White House,* Washington,
D.C., September 26, 1986. From Steven G. Calabresi, Editor, *Originalism: A
Quarter-Century of Debate* (Washington, DC: Regnery Publishing, Inc., 2007), 95-
97.
181. Robert A. Levy and William Mellor, *The Dirty Dozen: How Twelve Supreme
Court Cases Radically Expanded Government and Eroded Freedom* (New York, NY:
Sentinel, Penguin Group (USA) Inc., 2008), 155-168.
182. Ibid.
183. Ibid.
184. *The Heritage Guide to the Constitution,* Edwin Meese III. Chairman of the
Editorial Advisory Board (Washington, DC: The Heritage Foundation, 2005), 341-
345.
185. Robert A. Levy and William Mellor, *The Dirty Dozen: How Twelve Supreme
Court Cases Radically Expanded Government and Eroded Freedom* (New York, NY:
Sentinel, Penguin Group (USA) Inc., 2008), 165.
186. *The Heritage Guide to the Constitution,* Edwin Meese III. Chairman of the
Editorial Advisory Board (Washington, DC: The Heritage Foundation, 2005), 341.
187. Robert A. Levy and William Mellor, *The Dirty Dozen: How Twelve Supreme
Court Cases Radically Expanded Government and Eroded Freedom* (New York, NY:
Sentinel, Penguin Group (USA) Inc., 2008), 165-168.
188. David E. Bernstein, *You Can't Say That! The Growing Threat to Civil Liberties
from Antidiscrimination Laws* (Washington, DC: Cato Institute, 2003), 47-57.
189. *The Jerusalem Bible: Readers' Edition* (Garden City, NY: Doubleday &
Company, Inc., 1968).
190. Ronald Reagan, Speech at *The Investiture of Chief Justice William H.
Rehnquist and Associate Justice Antonin Scalia at The White House,* Washington,
D.C., September 26, 1986. From Steven G. Calabresi, Editor, *Originalism: A
Quarter-Century of Debate* (Washington, DC: Regnery Publishing, Inc., 2007), 95-
97.
191. Ibid.
192. Richard A. Epstein, *How Progressives Rewrote the Constitution* (Washington,
DC: Cato Institute, 2006), 132.
193. Karl Marx and Frederick Engels, *The Communist Manifesto* (London: Junius
Publications Ltd., 1996), 28.
194. Catharine Paddock, "America Will Be Spending One Fifth Of GDP On
Healthcare By 2017," *Medical News Today,* February 27, 2008. From the Medical
News Today website on June 18, 2008, webpage URL is:

http://www.medicalnewstoday.com/printerfriendlynews.php?newsid=98711 .
195. Michael F. Cannon and Michael D. Tanner, *Healthy Competition: What's Holding Back Health Care and How to Free It* (Washington, DC: Cato Institute, 2005), 10.
196. "Socialized Medicine's Waiting Room," *The Limbaugh Letter*, November 2007, Vol. 16, No. 11, 12.
197. Michael Tanner, "The Grass Is Not Always Greener: A Look at National Health Care Systems Around the World," Policy Analysis No. 613, *Cato Institute*, March 18, 2008. From the Cato Institute website on August 6, 2009, webpage URL is: http://www.cato.org/pubs/pas/pa-613.pdf .
198. Ibid.
199. "Socialized Medicine's Waiting Room," *The Limbaugh Letter*, November 2007, Vol. 16, No. 11, 12.

Chapter 7

200. Hans A. von Spakovsky, "Stolen Identities, Stolen Votes: A Case Study in Voter Impersonation," Legal Memorandum No. 22, *The Heritage Foundation*, March 10, 2008. From The Heritage Foundation website on June 20, 2008, webpage URL is: http://www.heritage.org/Research/LegalIssues/upload/lm_22.pdf .
201. Hans A. von Spakovsky, "Where There's Smoke, There's Fire: 100,000 Stolen Votes in Chicago," Legal Memorandum No. 23, *The Heritage Foundation*, April 16, 2008. From The Heritage Foundation website on June 20, 2008, webpage URL is: http://www.heritage.org/Research/LegalIssues/upload/lm_23.pdf .
202. "A Desperate Man," *Investor's Business Daily,* June 24, 2008, A10.
203. John Fund, *Stealing Elections: How Voter Fraud Threatens Our Democracy* (New York, NY: Encounter Books, 2008), 2.
204. Hans A. von Spakovsky, "Stolen Identities, Stolen Votes: A Case Study in Voter Impersonation," Legal Memorandum No. 22, *The Heritage Foundation*, March 10, 2008. From The Heritage Foundation website on June 20, 2008, webpage URL is: http://www.heritage.org/Research/LegalIssues/upload/lm_22.pdf .
205. Hans A. von Spakovsky, "Where There's Smoke, There's Fire: 100,000 Stolen Votes in Chicago," Legal Memorandum No. 23, *The Heritage Foundation*, April 16, 2008. From The Heritage Foundation website on June 20, 2008, webpage URL is: http://www.heritage.org/Research/LegalIssues/upload/lm_23.pdf .
206. Hans A. von Spakovsky, "Stolen Identities, Stolen Votes: A Case Study in Voter Impersonation," Legal Memorandum No. 22, *The Heritage Foundation*, March 10, 2008. From The Heritage Foundation website on June 20, 2008, webpage URL is: http://www.heritage.org/Research/LegalIssues/upload/lm_22.pdf .
207. Ludwig von Mises, *Socialism: An Economic and Sociological Analysis* (Indianapolis, IN: Liberty Fund, Inc., 1981), 18-19.

Chapter 8

208. Ronald Reagan, Speech at *The Investiture of Chief Justice William H. Rehnquist and Associate Justice Antonin Scalia at The White House,* Washington, D.C., September 26, 1986. From Steven G. Calabresi, Editor, *Originalism: A Quarter-Century of Debate* (Washington, DC: Regnery Publishing, Inc., 2007), 95-97.
209. The words *preserve, protect and defend* were taken from the Oath or

Affirmation for the Office of President of the United States from Article 2, Section 1 of the Constitution.

210. Michael Novak, *The Universal Hunger for Liberty: Why the Clash of Civilizations Is Not Inevitable* (New York, NY: Basic Books, 2004), 81.

211. Ibid, 83.

212. Ibid, 115.

213. *The World Almanac® and Book of Facts 2008* (New York, NY: World Almanac Education Group, Inc., World Almanac Books, 2008), 272-275.

Appendix A

214. Dinesh D'Souza, *What's So Great About Christianity?* (Washington, DC: Regnery Publishing, Inc., 2007), 21-29.

215. Ibid, 83-89.

216. Please see, for example, the following references:
   (a) Rodney Stark, *The Victory of Reason: How Christianity Led to Freedom, Capitalism, and Western Success* (New York: Random House, 2005), ix-xvi and 5-12
   (b) Dinesh D'Souza, *What's So Great About Christianity?* (Washington, DC: Regnery Publishing, Inc., 2007), 83-89.

217. F. A. Hayek, *The Road to Serfdom* (Chicago: The University of Chicago Press, 1972), 153-166.

218. Gene Edward Veith, Jr., *Postmodern Times: A Christian Guide to Contemporary Thought and Culture* (Wheaton, IL: Crossway Books, Good News Publishers, 1994), 47-70.

219. Ibid, 157-174.

220. Lauren Green, "Is Homosexuality a Sin?" FoxNews.com, July 25, 2007. From the Fox News website on April 4, 2008, webpage URL is: http://www.foxnews.com/printer_friendly_story/0,3566,290776,00.html .

221. L.A. Williams, "Ban on Gideon Bible Distribution to Children Spreads to Columbus County: Churches join forces calling upon School Board to reverse its decision," January 11, 2008. From the Christian Action League's website on April 4, 2008, webpage URL is: http://www.christianactionleague.org/article/890 .

222. David Limbaugh, *Persecution: How Liberals Are Waging War Against Christianity* (Washington, DC: Regnery Publishing, Inc., 2003), 45-47.

223. "Settlement allows religious expression for Okla. City government employees: ADF attorneys defended religious liberty rights of city employees," AllianceDefenseFund.org, February 20, 2008. From the Alliance Defense Fund's website on April 7, 2008, webpage URL is: http://www.alliancedefensefund.org/main/general/print.aspx?cid=4403 .

224. Scott Norvell, "Banned Bible Study, Stifled Santa," FoxNews.com, November 7, 2005. From the Fox News website on April 5, 2008, webpage URL is: http://www.foxnews.com/printer_friendly_story/0,3566,174719,00.html .

225. David Limbaugh, *Persecution: How Liberals Are Waging War Against Christianity* (Washington, DC: Regnery Publishing, Inc., 2003), 45-47.

226. Ibid, 233.

227. "Student Sues Wisconsin School After Getting a Zero for Religious Drawing," FoxNews.com, April 1, 2008. From the Fox News website on April 1, 2008, webpage URL is: http://www.foxnews.com/printer_friendly_story/0,3566,344350,00.html .

228. "ADF attorney to address N.M. veterans regarding defense of memorials: Speech will focus on project with American Legion to defend veterans' memorials nationwide," AllianceDefenseFund.org, February 8, 2008. From the Alliance Defense Fund's website on April 7, 2008, webpage URL is: http://www.alliancedefensefund.org/main/general/print.aspx?cid=4387 .

229. "Families of the fallen maintain right to decide: Inside the Issues with Alan Sears," AllianceDefenseFund.org, December 4, 2007. From the Alliance Defense Fund's website on April 7, 2008, webpage URL is: http://www.alliancedefensefund.org/main/general/print.aspx?cid=4315 .

230. "9th Circuit upholds constitutionality of Wash. Ten Commandments display: Court holds that Everett monument is constitutional," AllianceDefenseFund.org, March 26, 2008. From the Alliance Defense Fund's website on April 7, 2008, webpage URL is: http://www.alliancedefensefund.org/main/general/print.aspx?cid=4441 .

231. John Gibson, *The War on Christmas: How the Liberal Plot to Ban the Sacred Christian Holiday Is Worse Than You Thought* (New York, NY: Penguin Group (USA) Inc., 2005), 97-112.

232. Richard Willing, "Christians protest actions that play down Christmas' religious nature," USATODAY.com, December 21, 2004. From USA TODAY's website on April 7, 2008, webpage URL is: http://usatoday.printthis.clickability.com/pt/cpt?action=cpt&title=USATODAY.com+-+Christians+protest+actions+that+play+down+Christmas%27+religious+nature&expire=&urlID=12666829&fb=Y&url=http%3A%2F%2Fwww.usatoday.com%2Fnews%2Fnation%2F2004-12-21-holidaysuit_x.htm&partnerID=1660 .

233. David Limbaugh, *Persecution: How Liberals Are Waging War Against Christianity* (Washington, DC: Regnery Publishing, Inc., 2003), 185.

234. "Court sides with 5-year-old after school censors Jesus: School's suppression of kindergartner's artwork may violate constitutional rights," WorldNetDaily, October 20, 2005. From WorldNetDaily's website on April 7, 2008, webpage URL is: http://www.worldnetdaily.com/index.php?fa=PAGE.printable&pageId=32931 .

235. Taylour Nelson, "Book is removed because of religious references," *Coloradoan,* March 13, 2008, A3.

236. "Crackdown on biblical speech challenged," WorldNetDaily, April 2, 2008. From WorldNetDaily's website on April 7, 2008, webpage URL is: http://www.wnd.com/index.php?fa=PAGE.printable&pageId=60543 .

237. "College bars Christian from sharing faith: Religious expression not 'cultural, educational, social or recreational'," WorldNetDaily, September 9, 2005. From WorldNetDaily's website on April 7, 2008, webpage URL is: http://www.wnd.com/index.php?fa=PAGE.printable&pageId=32249 .

238. "Rights finally vindicated for pastor arrested for religious speech in public: Court enters order reflecting violation of Christian's constitutional rights," AllianceDefenseFund.org, January 18, 2008. From the Alliance Defense Fund's website on April 7, 2008, webpage URL is: http://www.alliancedefensefund.org/main/general/print.aspx?cid=4360 .

239. David Limbaugh, *Persecution: How Liberals Are Waging War Against Christianity* (Washington, DC: Regnery Publishing, Inc., 2003), 49-50.

240. "Ga. town repeals ordinance requiring permit to distribute religious tracts: ADF attorneys secure settlement for man arrested, jailed for exercising free speech rights on public sidewalk," AllianceDefenseFund.org, February 27, 2008. From the Alliance Defense Fund's website on April 7, 2008, webpage URL is:

http://www.alliancedefensefund.org/main/general/print.aspx?cid=4407 .

241. David Limbaugh, *Persecution: How Liberals Are Waging War Against Christianity* (Washington, DC: Regnery Publishing, Inc., 2003), 33.

242. Ibid, 39-40.

243. "Court refuses to dismiss professor's discrimination suit against UNC-Wilmington: Suit filed by ADF attorneys argues university denied full professorship to conservative professor and columnist Mike Adams because of his beliefs," AllianceDefenseFund.org, April 4, 2008. From the Alliance Defense Fund's website on April 7, 2008, webpage URL is:
http://www.alliancedefensefund.org/main/general/print.aspx?cid=4463 .

244. "The Bronx Household of Faith v. Board of Education of the City of New York," Christian Legal Society, April 3, 2008. From the Christian Legal Society website on April 9, 2008, webpage URL is:
http://www.clsnet.org/clrfPages/amicus/2008/FaithHousevNY.php?mode=print&PHPSESSID=b4596319a8603fee155e2bdd0fb3db3b&PHPSESSID=b4596319a8603fee155e2bdd0fb3db3b .

245. "Court grants ADF motion to stop UW-Madison from discriminating against student religious club," AllianceDefenseFund.org, January 18, 2008. From the Alliance Defense Fund's website on April 7, 2008, webpage URL is:
http://www.alliancedefensefund.org/main/general/print.aspx?cid=4361 .

246. "Court Strikes Down Anti-Religious State Scholarship Program," The Becket Fund for Religious Liberty, July 23, 2008. From The Becket Fund for Religious Liberty's website on January 22, 2009, website URL is:
http://www.becketfund.org/index.php/article/803.html/print/ .

247. David Limbaugh, *Persecution: How Liberals Are Waging War Against Christianity* (Washington, DC: Regnery Publishing, Inc., 2003), 17-20.

248. Ibid, 27.

249. Ibid, 30-31.

250. Associated Press, "Colorado Student Files Lawsuit Over Commencement Speech That Mentioned Jesus," FoxNews.com, August 31, 2007. From the Fox News website on August 31, 2007, webpage URL is:
http://www.foxnews.com/printer_friendly_story/0,3566,295432,00.html .

251. "ADF files appeal after court finds Christians "guilty" of praying: Christians who engaged in free speech in New York public park convicted by judge," AllianceDefenseFund.org, March 14, 2008. From the Alliance Defense Fund's website on April 7, 2008, webpage URL is:
http://www.alliancedefensefund.org/main/general/print.aspx?cid=4427 .

252. David Limbaugh, *Persecution: How Liberals Are Waging War Against Christianity* (Washington, DC: Regnery Publishing, Inc., 2003), 21.

253. Ibid, 35.

254. John Gibson, *The War on Christmas: How the Liberal Plot to Ban the Sacred Christian Holiday Is Worse Than You Thought* (New York, NY: Penguin Group (USA) Inc., 2005), 1.

255. Ibid, 2.

256. Ibid, 97-112.

257. Richard Willing, "Christians protest actions that play down Christmas' religious nature," USATODAY.com, December 21, 2004. From USA TODAY's website on April 7, 2008, webpage URL is:
http://usatoday.printthis.clickability.com/pt/cpt?action=cpt&title=USATODAY.com+-+Christians+protest+actions+that+play+down+Christmas%27+religious+nature&ex

pire=&urlID=12666829&fb=Y&url=http%3A%2F%2Fwww.usatoday.com%2Fnew
s%2Fnation%2F2004-12-21-holidaysuit_x.htm&partnerID=1660 .
258. David Limbaugh, *Persecution: How Liberals Are Waging War Against Christianity* (Washington, DC: Regnery Publishing, Inc., 2003), 42.
259. "Christmas carols banned, but Hanukkah songs OK: District axes 'dogmatic religious statements,' yet suggesting Jewish themes more cultural," WorldNetDaily, December 6, 2005. From WorldNetDaily's website on April 5, 2008, webpage URL is: http://www.worldnetdaily.com/index.php?fa=PAGE.printable&pageId=33750 .
260. Teacher takes 'Christmas' out of carol: 2nd-graders will sing 'winter' instead at upcoming concert," WorldNetDaily, December 6, 2003. From WorldNetDaily's website on April 5, 2008, webpage URL is:
http://www.worldnetdaily.com/index.php?fa=PAGE.printable&pageId=22165 .
261. David Limbaugh, *Persecution: How Liberals Are Waging War Against Christianity* (Washington, DC: Regnery Publishing, Inc., 2003), 40.
262. Ibid, 163-166.
263. "Help stop religious persecution in America: Opponents of religious freedom are targeting churches … and yours could be next," AllianceDefenseFund.org, March 24, 2008. From the Alliance Defense Fund's website on April 7, 2008, webpage URL is:
http://www.alliancedefensefund.org/main/general/print.aspx?cid=4436 .
264. David Limbaugh, *Persecution: How Liberals Are Waging War Against Christianity* (Washington, DC: Regnery Publishing, Inc., 2003), 209.
265. "ADF: Court should not hear Pledge of Allegiance case: ADF attorneys, Cornerstone Policy Research submit friend-of-the-court brief opposing lawsuit filed to remove "under God" from Pledge," AllianceDefenseFund.org, February 8, 2008. From the Alliance Defense Fund's website on April 7, 2008, webpage URL is: http://www.alliancedefensefund.org/main/general/print.aspx?cid=4391 .
266. "ADF attorneys come to defense of students wishing to recite Pledge of Allegiance: School quickly changes course on prohibiting Pledge after receiving letter," AllianceDefenseFund.org, January 25, 2007. From the Alliance Defense Fund's website on April 7, 2008, webpage URL is:
http://www.alliancedefensefund.org/main/general/print.aspx?cid=3993 .
267. Please see, for example, the following references:
(a) "California School District to Vote Whether 'In God We Trust' Belongs in Classroom," FoxNews.com, November 5, 2007. From the Fox News website on November 5, 2007 webpage URL is:
http://www.foxnews.com/printer_friendly_story/0,3566,308317,00.html.
(b) "California School District Approves 'In God We Trust' Classroom Displays," FoxNews.com, November 6, 2007. From the Fox News website on November 6, 2007 webpage URL is:
http://www.foxnews.com/printer_friendly_story/0,3566,308405,00.html .
268. "If the shoe fits…don't wear it: Inside the Issues with Alan Sears," AllianceDefenseFund.org, January 1, 2007. From the Alliance Defense Fund's website on April 7, 2008, webpage URL is:
http://www.alliancedefensefund.org/main/general/print.aspx?cid=4345 .
269. "ACLJ Files Amicus Brief Asking Appeals Court to Overturn $1.5 Million Judgment Against Faith-Based Prison Program," ACLJ.org, September 22, 2006. From the American Center for Law & Justice website on April 8, 2008, webpage URL is: http://www.aclj.org/News/Read.aspx?ID=2401# .
270. This appendix provides numerous examples of a lack of tolerance for

Christianity. For an illustration of open hostility toward Christianity, please see for example: Anita Vogel, "Student Sues 'Anti-Christian' Teacher Over Remarks in Class," FoxNews.com, April 2, 2008. From the Fox News website on April 2, 2008, webpage URL is:
http://www.foxnews.com/printer_friendly_story/0,3566,345274,00.html .

271. David Limbaugh, *Persecution: How Liberals Are Waging War Against Christianity* (Washington, DC: Regnery Publishing, Inc., 2003), 112.

272. Please see, for example, the following references:

    (a) David Limbaugh, *Persecution: How Liberals Are Waging War Against Christianity* (Washington, DC: Regnery Publishing, Inc., 2003), 74-87

    (b) Richard A. Viguerie, *Conservatives Betrayed: How George W. Bush and Other Big Government Republicans Hijacked the Conservative Cause* (Los Angeles: Bonus Books, 2006), 106.

273. David Limbaugh, *Persecution: How Liberals Are Waging War Against Christianity* (Washington, DC: Regnery Publishing, Inc., 2003), 74-87.

274. David L. Tubbs and Robert P. George, "Redefining Marriage Away: What would be left of marriage if we adopt the gay advocates' proposals?," *City Journal,* Summer, 2004. From the City Journal website on April 14, 2008, webpage URL is: http://www.city-journal.org/printable.php?id=1502 .

275. Maggie Gallagher, *The Abolition of Marriage: How We Destroy Lasting Love* (Washington, DC: Regnery Publishing, Inc., 1996), 143-152.

276. Kay S. Hymowitz, "The Incredible Shrinking Father," *City Journal,* Spring, 2007. From the City Journal website on April 14, 2008, webpage URL is: http://www.city-journal.org/html/17_2_artificial_insemination.html .

277. Kay S. Hymowitz, "Gay Marriage vs. American Marriage: The gay advocates' civil rights argument forgets what the Founders thought marriage is for," *City Journal,* Spring, 2004. From the City Journal website on April 14, 2008, webpage URL is: http://www.city-journal.org/printable.php?id=1501 .

278. "ADF attorneys file appeal to restore voters' rights in Oregon: 9th Circuit to hear case of disenfranchised Oregonians," AllianceDefenseFund.org, March 6, 2008. From the Alliance Defense Fund's website on April 16, 2008, webpage URL is: http://www.alliancedefensefund.org/main/general/print.aspx?cid=4417 .

279. David L. Tubbs and Robert P. George, "Redefining Marriage Away: What would be left of marriage if we adopt the gay advocates' proposals?," *City Journal,* Summer, 2004. From the City Journal website on April 14, 2008, webpage URL is: http://www.city-journal.org/printable.php?id=1502 .

280. "ADF files appeal to protect, preserve marriage in New York: Appeal aims to stop state officials from recognizing foreign same-sex "marriages"," AllianceDefenseFund.org, April 14, 2008. From the Alliance Defense Fund's website on April 16, 2008, webpage URL is: http://www.alliancedefensefund.org/main/general/print.aspx?cid=4470 .

281. Kay S. Hymowitz, "I Wed Thee, and Thee, and Thee: If homosexual marriage, then polygamy?," *City Journal,* Autumn, 2004. http://www.city-journal.org/html/14_4_sndgs04.html .

282. "ADF attorneys appeal ASU pro-life speech case to 9th Circuit: Arizona State University officials demand that pro-life club members purchase insurance before exercising free speech rights on campus," AllianceDefenseFund.org, April 14, 2008. From the Alliance Defense Fund's website on April 16, 2008, webpage URL is: http://www.alliancedefensefund.org/main/general/print.aspx?cid=4468 .

283. Please see, for example, the following references:

(a) "Court rejects California's challenge to healthcare conscience rights: California can't take federal funds while prosecuting pro-life medical professionals; CLS, ADF attorneys represented pro-life doctors," AllianceDefenseFund.org, March 19, 2008. From the Alliance Defense Fund's website on April 16, 2008, webpage URL is: http://www.alliancedefensefund.org/main/general/print.aspx?cid=4432 .

(b) "ADF attorneys assist Montana pro-life pharmacist: Montana Board of Pharmacy dismisses frivolous complaints against pharmacist who declined to dispense so-called "morning after" pill," AllianceDefenseFund.org, March 10, 2008. From the Alliance Defense Fund's website on April 16, 2008, webpage URL is: http://www.alliancedefensefund.org/main/general/print.aspx?cid=4425 .

284. ""Right of Conscience" at risk in Washington state: Inside the Issues with Alan Sears," AllianceDefenseFund.org, August 14, 2007. From the Alliance Defense Fund's website on April 16, 2008, webpage URL is: http://www.alliancedefensefund.org/main/general/print.aspx?cid=4207 .

285. Joseph Bottum, "Death & Politics," *First Things: The Journal of Religion, Culture, and Public Life,* firstthings.com, June/July 2007. From the First Things' website on April 16, 2008, webpage URL is: http://www.firstthings.com/article.php3?id_article=5917 .

286. Kay S. Hymowitz, "The Incredible Shrinking Father: Artificial insemination begets children without paternity, with troubling cultural and legal consequences," *City Journal,* Spring, 2007. From the City Journal website on April 14, 2008, webpage URL is: http://www.city-journal.org/html/17_2_artificial_insemination.html .

287. "The gift of life: Inside the Issues with Alan Sears," AllianceDefenseFund.org, October 30, 2007. From the Alliance Defense Fund's website on April 16, 2008, webpage URL is: http://www.alliancedefensefund.org/main/general/print.aspx?cid=4290 .

288. "ADF-allied attorney files suit against Planned Parenthood in Nebraska," AllianceDefenseFund.org, September 6, 2007. From the Alliance Defense Fund's website on April 16, 2008, webpage URL is: http://www.alliancedefensefund.org/main/general/print.aspx?cid=4233 .

289. "Hospitals cannot intentionally allow newborns to die, court rules in ADF-supported case: Wisconsin Supreme Court rules that hospital was legally obligated to stabilize baby boy born prematurely," AllianceDefenseFund.org, July 13, 2005. From the Alliance Defense Fund's website on April 18, 2008, webpage URL is: http://www.alliancedefensefund.org/main/general/print.aspx?cid=3487 .

290. "Princeton Bioethicist says only "Know-Nothing Religious Fundamentalists" will Value Human Life by 2040," LifeSiteNews.com, December 2, 2005. From the LifeSiteNews.com website on April 18, 2008, webpage URL is: http://www.lifesitenews.com/ldn/printerfriendly.html?articleid=05120205 .

291. Timothy E. Quill, MD; Diane E. Meier, MD; Susan D. Block, MD; and J. Andrew Billings, MD, "The Debate over Physician-Assisted Suicide: Empirical Data and Convergent Views," *Annals of Internal Medicine,* Volume 128, Issue 7, April 1, 1998, 552- 558. From the Annals of Internal Medicine website on April 18, 2008, webpage URL is: http://www.annals.org/cgi/content/full/128/7/552 .

292. "A Victory for Life: Family's determination in "end of life" case brings the chance of new beginning for Jesse Ramirez," AllianceDefenseFund.org, no date listed. From the Alliance Defense Fund's website on April 16, 2008, webpage URL

is: http://www.alliancedefensefund.org/main/general/print.aspx?cid=4283 .

293. Joseph Bottum, "Death & Politics," *First Things: The Journal of Religion, Culture, and Public Life,* firstthings.com, June/July 2007. From the First Things' website on April 16, 2008, webpage URL is: http://www.firstthings.com/article.php3?id_article=5917 .

294. Please see, for example, the following references:

    (a) Alvin J. Schmidt, *How Christianity Changed the World* (Grand Rapids, MI: Zondervan, 2004), 70-74.

    (b) Lou Jacquet, "Cremation Ashes to Ashes," *Catholic Heritage,* Our Sunday Visitor, Inc., March/April 1997, 22-23. From the Catholic Culture website on April 18, 2008, webpage URL is: http://www.catholicculture.org/library/view.cfm?recnum=645 .

295. David Limbaugh, *Persecution: How Liberals Are Waging War Against Christianity* (Washington, DC: Regnery Publishing, Inc., 2003), 90-94 and 255-256.

296. Kay S. Hymowitz, "Maybe It's Time for Abstinence: Study shows sex ed and contraception-on-demand make kids less sexually responsible," City Journal website, April 8, 2002. From the City Journal website on April 14, 2008, webpage URL is: http://www.city-journal.org/html/eon_4_8_02kh.html .

297. David L. Tubbs and Robert P. George, "Redefining Marriage Away: What would be left of marriage if we adopt the gay advocates' proposals?," *City Journal,* Summer, 2004. From the City Journal website on April 14, 2008, webpage URL is: http://www.city-journal.org/printable.php?id=1502 .

298. Laura Ingraham, *Power to the People* (Washington, DC: Regnery Publishing Inc., 2007), 157-194.

299. Michael Crowley, "Horror Show: The Internet has spawned a sick new craze: violence porn," *Reader's Digest,* August, 2004. From the Reader's Digest website on April 18, 2008, webpage URL is: http://www.rd.com/content/printContent.do?contentId=27399 .

300. "HOA supports neighborhood improvement: Inside the Issues with Alan Sears," AllianceDefenseFund.org, March 4, 2008. From the Alliance Defense Fund's website on April 16, 2008, webpage URL is: http://www.alliancedefensefund.org/main/general/print.aspx?cid=4415 .

301. Charles Q. Choi, "Forecast: Sex and Marriage with Robots by 2050," FoxNews.com, October 15, 2007. From the Fox News website on October 15, 2007, webpage URL is: http://www.foxnews.com/printer_friendly_story/0,3566,301736,00.html .

302. Pamela Paul, "The Porn Factor," *Time,* January 19, 2004. From the Time website on April 18, 2008, webpage URL is: http://www.time.com/time/printout/0,8816,993158,00.html .

303. David Limbaugh, *Persecution: How Liberals Are Waging War Against Christianity* (Washington, DC: Regnery Publishing, Inc., 2003), 229-230 and 235-237.

304. Stanley Kurtz, "Can We Make Boys and Girls Alike?: Even if the differences are cultural, rather than biological, they are ineradicable," *City Journal,* Spring, 2005. From the City Journal website on April 14, 2008, webpage URL is: http://www.city-journal.org/printable.php?id=1789 .

305. Pam Belluck, "New Hampshire to Repeal Parental Notification Law," *The New York Times,* June 8, 2007. From The New York Times website on April 18, 2008, webpage URL is: http://www.nytimes.com/2007/06/08/us/08parental.html?_r=1&pagewanted=print&o

ref=slogin .

306. "School Board Approves Birth Control Prescriptions at Maine Middle School," FoxNews.com, October 18, 2007. From the Fox News website on October 18, 2007, webpage URL is:
http://www.foxnews.com/printer_friendly_story/0,3566,303058,00.html .

307. Laura Ingraham, *Power to the People* (Washington, DC: Regnery Publishing Inc., 2007), 37-39.

308. Anna Jo Bratton, "Lawsuit says seizure of baby for test violated rights," JournalStar.com, October 25, 2007. From the JournalStar.com website on April 14, 2008, webpage URL is:
http://www.journalstar.com/articles/2007/10/26/news/nebraska/doc47214e6a400d48 88452933.prt .

309. Please see, for example, the following references:
  (a) Shmuley Boteach, "The contempt shown to parents of large families," WorldNetDaily, March 2, 2006. From WorldNetDaily's website on April 15, 2008, webpage URL is:
  http://www.worldnetdaily.com/news/article.asp?ARTICLE_ID=49074 .
  (b) Dalton Conley, "Two Is Enough: Why Large Families Don't Deserve Tax Breaks," *Slate,* March 29, 2004. From the Slate website on April 15, 2008, webpage URL is: http://www.slate.com/id/2097913/ .

310. Robert J. Hutchinson, *The Politically Incorrect Guide™ to the Bible* (Washington, DC: Regnery Publishing, Inc., 2007), 77-79.

311. Robert L. Plunkett, "Vow for Now – Harmful Effects of No-Fault Divorce," *National Review,* May 29, 1995. From BNET's website on January 28, 2008, webpage URL is:
http://findarticles.com/p/articles/mi_m1282/is_n10_v47/ai_16936591/print .

312. Stefan Kanfer, "Why the Scouts Ban Homosexuals: A New York scoutmaster's indictment explains everything," *City Journal,* Winter, 2002. From the City Journal website on April 14, 2008, webpage URL is: http://www.city-journal.org/html/12_1_sndgs12.html .

313. Stanley Kurtz, "Can We Make Boys and Girls Alike?: Even if the differences are cultural, rather than biological, they are ineradicable," *City Journal,* Spring, 2005. From the City Journal website on April 14, 2008, webpage URL is:
http://www.city-journal.org/printable.php?id=1789 .

314. "Joint Statement on the Impact of Entertainment Violence on Children: Congressional Public Health Summit," *American Academy of Pediatrics,* July 26, 2000. From the American Academy of Pediatrics' website on April 18, 2008, webpage URL is: http://www.aap.org/advocacy/releases/jstmtevc.htm .

315. Please see, for example, the following references:
  (a) "Court: Credential Needed to Home School," FoxNews.com, March 7, 2008. From the Fox News website on April 18, 2008, webpage URL is: http://www.foxnews.com/printer_friendly_wires/2008Mar07/0, 4675,HomeSchooling,00.html.
  (b) Tara Ross and Joseph C. Smith, Jr., "Tara Ross & Joseph C. Smith Jr.: Tough Lesson," FoxNews.com, March 28, 2008. From the Fox News website on April 18, 2008, webpage URL is:
  http://www.foxnews.com/printer_friendly_story/0,3566,342869,00.html .

316. "Parents Fight Governments to Homeschool," FoxNews.com, May 20, 2003. From the Fox News website on April 18, 2008, webpage URL is:
http://www.foxnews.com/printer_friendly_story/0,3566,87384,00.html .

317. Please see, for example, the following references:
- (a) Matthew Ladner, "Jeb Bush's Reforms Improved Public Schools," TownHall.com, April 17, 2008. From the TownHall.com website on April 18, 2008, website URL is: http://www.townhall.com/columnists/DrMatthewLadner/2008/04/17/ jeb_bushs_reforms_improved_public_schools .
- (b) Matthew Ladner, "School Choice in Arizona: A Review of Existing Programs and a Road Map for Future Reforms," Goldwater Institute Policy Report, *Goldwater Institute,* March 4, 2008. From the Goldwater Institute website on April 18, 2008, webpage URL is: http://www.goldwaterinstitute.org/AboutUs/Print.aspx?page= http://www.goldwaterinstitute.org/AboutUs/ArticleView.aspx?id=2067 .

318. Please see, for example, the following references:
- (a) *The Heritage Guide to the Constitution,* Edwin Meese III. Chairman of the Editorial Advisory Board (Washington, DC: The Heritage Foundation, 2005), 1-17.
- (b) Steven G. Calabresi, Editor, *Originalism: A Quarter-Century of Debate* (Washington, DC: Regnery Publishing, Inc., 2007), 1-40.

319. Steven G. Calabresi, Editor, *Originalism: A Quarter-Century of Debate* (Washington, DC: Regnery Publishing, Inc., 2007), 1-40.

320. *The Heritage Guide to the Constitution,* Edwin Meese III. Chairman of the Editorial Advisory Board (Washington, DC: The Heritage Foundation, 2005), 16.

321. Steven G. Calabresi, Editor, *Originalism: A Quarter-Century of Debate* (Washington, DC: Regnery Publishing, Inc., 2007), 14-17.

322. Ibid.

323. Ibid.

324. Ibid, 1-40.

325. Ibid, 18.

326. "Rights finally vindicated for pastor arrested for religious speech in public: Court enters order reflecting violation of Christian's constitutional rights," AllianceDefenseFund.org, January 18, 2008. From the Alliance Defense Fund's website on April 7, 2008, webpage URL is: http://www.alliancedefensefund.org/main/general/print.aspx?cid=4360 .

327. David Limbaugh, *Persecution: How Liberals Are Waging War Against Christianity* (Washington, DC: Regnery Publishing, Inc., 2003), 30-31.

328. Associated Press, "Colorado Student Files Lawsuit Over Commencement Speech That Mentioned Jesus," FoxNews.com, August 31, 2007. From the Fox News website on August 31, 2007, webpage URL is: http://www.foxnews.com/printer_friendly_story/0,3566,295432,00.html .

329. "Families of the fallen maintain right to decide: Inside the Issues with Alan Sears," AllianceDefenseFund.org, December 4, 2007. From the Alliance Defense Fund's website on April 7, 2008, webpage URL is: http://www.alliancedefensefund.org/main/general/print.aspx?cid=4315 .

330. "Fisher v. South Bend School District," The Becket Fund for Religious Liberty. From The Becket Fund for Religious Liberty's website on January 22, 2009, website URL is: http://www.becketfund.org/index.php/case/5.html/print/ .

331. "ADF files appeal after court finds Christians "guilty" of praying: Christians who engaged in free speech in New York public park convicted by judge," AllianceDefenseFund.org, March 14, 2008. From the Alliance Defense Fund's website on April 7, 2008, webpage URL is:

http://www.alliancedefensefund.org/main/general/print.aspx?cid=4427 .

332. "ADF asks Supreme Court to hear Mich. student religious speech case: Petition requests review of lower court decision regarding censorship of message attached to candy canes by fifth-grade student," AllianceDefenseFund.org, August 11, 2008. From the Alliance Defense Fund's website on January 21, 2009, webpage URL is: http://www.alliancedefensefund.org/main/general/print.aspx?cid=4642 .

333. "College bars Christian from sharing faith: Religious expression not 'cultural, educational, social or recreational'," WorldNetDaily, September 9, 2005. From WorldNetDaily's website on April 7, 2008, webpage URL is: http://www.wnd.com/index.php?fa=PAGE.printable&pageId=32249 .

334. "Settlement allows religious expression for Okla. City government employees: ADF attorneys defended religious liberty rights of city employees," AllianceDefenseFund.org, February 20, 2008. From the Alliance Defense Fund's website on April 7, 2008, webpage URL is: http://www.alliancedefensefund.org/main/general/print.aspx?cid=4403 .

335. "Court sides with 5-year-old after school censors Jesus: School's suppression of kindergartner's artwork may violate constitutional rights," WorldNetDaily, October 20, 2005. From WorldNetDaily's website on April 7, 2008, webpage URL is: http://www.worldnetdaily.com/index.php?fa=PAGE.printable&pageId=32931 .

336. David Limbaugh, *Persecution: How Liberals Are Waging War Against Christianity* (Washington, DC: Regnery Publishing, Inc., 2003), 233.

337. Ibid, 42.

338. "ADF attorney to address N.M. veterans regarding defense of memorials: Speech will focus on project with American Legion to defend veterans' memorials nationwide," AllianceDefenseFund.org, February 8, 2008. From the Alliance Defense Fund's website on April 7, 2008, webpage URL is: http://www.alliancedefensefund.org/main/general/print.aspx?cid=4387 .

339. "ADF defends right of conscience for pharmacists: ADF attorney submits letter to defend pharmacists opposed to dispensing contraceptives, including "morning-after" abortion pill," AllianceDefenseFund.org, March 14, 2006. From the Alliance Defense Fund's website on May 5, 2008, webpage URL is: http://www.alliancedefensefund.org/main/general/print.aspx?cid=3706 .

340. David Limbaugh, *Persecution: How Liberals Are Waging War Against Christianity* (Washington, DC: Regnery Publishing, Inc., 2003), 229-230 and 235-237.

341. "If the shoe fits...don't wear it: Inside the Issues with Alan Sears," AllianceDefenseFund.org, January 1, 2007. From the Alliance Defense Fund's website on April 7, 2008, webpage URL is: http://www.alliancedefensefund.org/main/general/print.aspx?cid=4345 .

342. Taylour Nelson, "Book is removed because of religious references," *Coloradoan,* March 13, 2008, A3.

343. David Limbaugh, *Persecution: How Liberals Are Waging War Against Christianity* (Washington, DC: Regnery Publishing, Inc., 2003), 17-20.

344. "ADF files appeal after court finds Christians "guilty" of praying: Christians who engaged in free speech in New York public park convicted by judge," AllianceDefenseFund.org, March 14, 2008. From the Alliance Defense Fund's website on April 7, 2008, webpage URL is: http://www.alliancedefensefund.org/main/general/print.aspx?cid=4427 .

345. "Southeastern Louisiana University: Christian speaker needs permit to share faith: ADF attorneys file suit after Christian man told to get permit for two hours of

free speech per week," AllianceDefenseFund.org, November 5, 2008. From the Alliance Defense Fund's website on January 21, 2009, webpage URL is: http://www.alliancedefensefund.org/main/general/print.aspx?cid=4739 .

346. "Court refuses to dismiss professor's discrimination suit against UNC-Wilmington: Suit filed by ADF attorneys argues university denied full professorship to conservative professor and columnist Mike Adams because of his beliefs," AllianceDefenseFund.org, April 4, 2008. From the Alliance Defense Fund's website on April 7, 2008, webpage URL is: http://www.alliancedefensefund.org/main/general/print.aspx?cid=4463 .

347. "Ga. town repeals ordinance requiring permit to distribute religious tracts: ADF attorneys secure settlement for man arrested, jailed for exercising free speech rights on public sidewalk," AllianceDefenseFund.org, February 27, 2008. From the Alliance Defense Fund's website on April 7, 2008, webpage URL is: http://www.alliancedefensefund.org/main/general/print.aspx?cid=4407 .

348. "The Bronx Household of Faith v. Board of Education of the City of New York," Christian Legal Society, April 3, 2008. From the Christian Legal Society website on April 9, 2008, webpage URL is: http://www.clsnet.org/clrfPages/amicus/2008/FaithHousevNY.php?mode=print&PHPSESSID=b4596319a8603fee155e2bdd0fb3db3b&PHPSESSID=b4596319a8603fee155e2bdd0fb3db3b .

349. "Rights finally vindicated for pastor arrested for religious speech in public: Court enters order reflecting violation of Christian's constitutional rights," AllianceDefenseFund.org, January 18, 2008. From the Alliance Defense Fund's website on April 7, 2008, webpage URL is: http://www.alliancedefensefund.org/main/general/print.aspx?cid=4360 .

350. David Limbaugh, *Persecution: How Liberals Are Waging War Against Christianity* (Washington, DC: Regnery Publishing, Inc., 2003), 30-31.

351. Associated Press, "Colorado Student Files Lawsuit Over Commencement Speech That Mentioned Jesus," FoxNews.com, August 31, 2007. From the Fox News website on August 31, 2007, webpage URL is: http://www.foxnews.com/printer_friendly_story/0,3566,295432,00.html .

352. "Federal Judge Halts Support of National Scout Jamboree at Fort A. P. Hill: *Winkler v. Chicago School Reform Board of Trustees,"* Pacific Legal Foundation's website. From Pacific Legal Foundation's website on May 8, 2008, webpage URL is: http://community.pacificlegal.org/NETCOMMUNITY/Page.aspx?pid=354&srcid=273 .

353. Rebecca Hagelin, "The (Un)fairness Doctrine," *The Heritage Foundation,* November 28, 2007. From the Heritage Foundation's website on May 5, 2008, webpage URL is: http://www.heritage.org/Press/Commentary/ed112807b.cfm?RenderforPrint=1 .

354. Adam D. Thierer, "A Fairness Doctrine for the Internet," *City Journal*, October 18, 2007, http://www.city-journal.org/html/eon2007-10-18at.html .

355. John Samples, *The Fallacy of Campaign Finance Reform* (Chicago, IL: The University of Chicago Press, 2006).

356. "Sued for Free Speech: Neighbors Go to Federal Court to Fight Colorado's Campaign Finance Laws That Chill Grassroots Advocacy," *Institute for Justice*, April 15, 2008. From the Institute for Justice's website on May 5, 2008, webpage URL is: http://www.ij.org/include/media_functions.asp?path=/first_amendment/parkernorth_

free_speech/4_15_08pr.html&cmd=print_out .

357. Laura Ingraham, *Power to the People* (Washington, DC: Regnery Publishing Inc., 2007), 215-216.

358. "Split FEC Vote Leaves SpeechNow.org Silenced: Chairman's Opinion Says Limits on Independent Citizen Groups Unconstitutional," *Institute for Justice*, January 24, 2008. From the Institute for Justice's website on May 5, 2008, webpage URL is:
http://www.ij.org/include/media_functions.asp?path=/first_amendment/speech_now/1_24_08pr.html&cmd=print_out .

359. Lauren Green, "Is Homosexuality a Sin?" FoxNews.com, July 25, 2007. From the Fox News website on April 4, 2008, webpage URL is:
http://www.foxnews.com/printer_friendly_story/0,3566,290776,00.html .

360. David E. Bernstein, *You Can't Say That! The Growing Threat to Civil Liberties from Antidiscrimination Laws* (Washington, DC: Cato Institute, 2003), 155-156.

361. Ibid, 73-83.

362. "Court Restrains City of New Orleans From Enforcing Book Ban: Book Venders On The Street Today!," *Institute for Justice*, April 15, 2003. From the Institute for Justice's website on May 5, 2008, webpage URL is:
http://www.ij.org/include/media_functions.asp?path=/first_amendment/new_orleans_book_ban/4_15_03pr.html&cmd=print_out .

363. "Micro-Broadcaster Seeks Vindication of Free Speech Rights In The First Micro-Radio Case To Reach the U.S. Supreme Court," *Institute for Justice*, October 4, 2000. From the Institute for Justice's website on May 5, 2008, webpage URL is:
http://www.ij.org/include/media_functions.asp?path=/first_amendment/microradio/10_4_00pr.html&cmd=print_out .

364. "Bagel Entrepreneur & IJ Punch a Hole in City of Redmond's Sign Ban With 9th Circuit First Amendment Victory," *Institute for Justice*, September 15, 2006. From the Institute for Justice's website on May 5, 2008, webpage URL is:
http://www.ij.org/include/media_functions.asp?path=/first_amendment/wa_redmond_bagel/9_15_06pr.html&cmd=print_out .

365. "Arizona Bureaucrats Launch Attack on Free Speech: Government Seeks to Restrict Your Ability to Research Home Prices," *Institute for Justice*, April 19, 2007. From the Institute for Justice's website on May 5, 2008, webpage URL is:
http://www.ij.org/include/media_functions.asp?path=/first_amendment/other/zillow_4_19_07pr.html&cmd=print_out .

366. "U.S. Supreme Court Vacates "Got Milk?" Decision; Remands to 3rd U.S. Circuit for Further Proceedings," *Institute for Justice*, May 31, 2005. From the Institute for Justice's website on May 5, 2008, webpage URL is:
http://www.ij.org/include/media_functions.asp?path=/first_amendment/got_milk/5_31_05pr.html&cmd=print_out .

367. "District of Columbia v. Heller," Mountain States Legal Foundation. From the Mountain States Legal Foundation's website on May 5, 2008, webpage URL is:
http://www.mountainstateslegal.org/legal_cases.cfm?legalcaseid=174 .

368. "Appeals Court Considers State Responsible for Illegally Strip-Searching Children," Liberty Counsel's website, May 20, 2008. From Liberty Counsel's website on May 20, 2008, webpage URL is:
http://www.lc.org/index.cfm?PID=14102&AlertID=839&printpage=y .

369. "Institute for Justice Minnesota Chapter Challenges Red Wing's Unconstitutional Rental Home Searches," *Institute for Justice*, November 15, 2006. From the Institute for Justice's website on May 5, 2008, webpage URL is:

http://www.ij.org/include/media_functions.asp?path=/private_property/redwing_insp
ections/11_15_06pr.html&cmd=print_out .

370. Timothy Sandefur, *Cornerstone of Liberty: Property Rights in 21ˢᵗ –Century
America* (Washington, DC: Cato Institute, 2006), 5-10.

371. Ibid, 90-106.

372. Ibid, 120-122.

373. Ibid.

374. Ibid, 123-124.

375. Ibid, 109-112.

376. Ibid, 79-90.

377. Steven G. Calabresi, Editor, *Originalism: A Quarter-Century of Debate*
(Washington, DC: Regnery Publishing, Inc., 2007), 1-40.

378. Randy E. Barnett, *Restoring the Lost Constitution: The Presumption of Liberty*
(Princeton, NJ: Princeton University Press, 2004), 253-269.

379. Ibid, 151-152.

380. *The Heritage Guide to the Constitution,* Edwin Meese III. Chairman of the
Editorial Advisory Board (Washington, DC: The Heritage Foundation, 2005), 371-
375.

381. Ibid.

382. Ibid.

383. Ibid, 394-404.

384. Ibid.

385. Ibid, 16.

386. Paul Rosenzweig, "The Over-Criminalization of Social and Economic
Conduct," Legal Memorandum No. 7, *The Heritage Foundation,* April 17, 2003.
From The Heritage Foundation website on May 8, 2008, webpage URL is:
http://overcriminalized.com/pdfs/lm_07.pdf .

387. Greg Stohr, "Exxon Valdez Award Questioned at U.S. Supreme Court
(Update3)," Bloomberg.com, February 27, 2008. From the Bloomberg.com website
on May 8, 2008, webpage URL is:
http://www.bloomberg.com/apps/news?pid=20670001&refer=news&sid=ajFkglZna
8uo .

388. Jackie Crosby, "Lost laptop? Sue for millions!," StarTribune.com, February 13,
2008. From the StarTribue.com website on May 8, 2008, webpage URL is:
http://www.startribune.com/templates/Print_This_Story?sid=15571092 .

389. Timothy Sandefur, *Cornerstone of Liberty: Property Rights in 21ˢᵗ –Century
America* (Washington, DC: Cato Institute, 2006), 79-90.

390. Ibid.

391. Ibid.

392. Ibid.

393. David Limbaugh, *Persecution: How Liberals Are Waging War Against
Christianity* (Washington, DC: Regnery Publishing, Inc., 2003), 185.

394. Matthew Bigg, "Thousands protest U.S. Army training program," *Reuters,*
November 18, 2007. From the Reuters website on May 8, 2008, webpage URL is:
http://www.reuters.com/articlePrint?articleId=USN18411507 .

395. Tiffany Hsu, "Military Recruiting Sparks a Protest at Career Fair," The Daily
Californian website, February 24, 2005. From The Daily Californian's website on
May 7, 2008, webpage URL is: http://www.dailycal.org/printable.php?id=17744 .

396. Melissa Underwood, "Report Cites Increase in Attacks on Military Recruiting

Centers," FoxNews.com, March 26, 2008. From the Fox News website on May 7,2008, webpage URL is:
http://www.foxnews.com/printer_friendly_story/0,3566,341695,00.html .
397. Kim R. Holmes, "Humanitarian Warriors: The Moral Folly of the Clinton Doctrine," Heritage Lecture #671, *The Heritage Foundation,* July 11, 2000. From The Heritage Foundation's website on May 12, 2008, webpage URL is:
http://www.heritage.org/Research/WorldwideFreedom/hl671.cfm .
398. "Contract Provisions on Liability Should Be Respected: *Lanier at McEver, L.P. v. Planners & Engineers Collaborative, Inc.*," Pacific Legal Foundation's website. From Pacific Legal Foundation's website on May 8, 2008, webpage URL is:
http://community.pacificlegal.org/NETCOMMUNITY/Page.aspx?pid=349&srcid=2 73 .
399. "Supporting the Integrity of Contract Provisions: *Circuit City Stores, Inc. v. Gentry,*" Pacific Legal Foundation's website. From Pacific Legal Foundation's website on May 8, 2008, webpage URL is:
http://community.pacificlegal.org/NETCOMMUNITY/Page.aspx?pid=474&srcid=2 73 .
400. Over the last several decades, some American Presidents appear to have been attacked relentlessly. It is one thing for opponents of a President to attack their policies because they are in disagreement. It is quite another thing to attack the President's integrity, intentions, and intelligence. *Ad hominem* (personal) attacks against the President hurt and weaken America because the President is a symbol for all of America.
401. Peter Hecht, "Race for '08: Presidential selection process is under siege," sacbee.com, September 3, 2007. From the Sacramento Bee's website on May 9, 2008, webpage URL is: http://www.sacbee.com/111/v-print/story/358041.html .
402. When America is involved in a declared or undeclared war or other military operations, and when American military personnel are in harm's way, it is important to support a President. Those that disagree can make their views known in ways that do not threaten American lives or that do not threaten the outcome of the war or military operations.
403. John R. Bolton, "Does the United Nations Advance the Cause of Freedom?," Heritage Lectures No. 1047, Delivered on September 6, 2007, *The Heritage Foundation*, October 23, 2007.
404. For an explanation of *moral equivalency,* please see:
> John R. Bolton, *Surrender is not an Option: Defending America at the United Nations and Abroad* (New York, NY: Threshold Editions, Simon & Schuster, Inc., 2007), 450-455.

For an example of *moral equivalency,* please see:
> Baker Spring, "Satellite Shootdown Was a Necessary Operation," WebMemo No. 1823, *The Heritage Foundation,* February 22, 2008. From The Heritage Foundation's website on May 12, 2008, webpage URL is:
> http://www.heritage.org/Research/NationalSecurity/upload/wm_1823.pdf .
405. Larry Diamond, "International Relations: Patching Things Up," *Hoover Digest: Research and Opinion on Public Policy,* No. 3, 2003. From the Hoover Institution's website on May 12, 2008, webpage URL is:
http://www.printthis.clickability.com/pt/cpt?action=cpt&title=Patching+Things+Up &expire=&urlID=21149230&fb=Y&url=http%3A%2F%2Fwww.hoover.org%2Fpub lications%2Fdigest%2F3057496.html&partnerID=109806 .
406. Over the last several decades, some American Presidents appear to have been

attacked relentlessly. It is one thing for opponents of a President to attack their policies because they are in disagreement. It is quite another thing to attack the President's integrity, intentions, and intelligence. *Ad hominem* (personal) attacks against the President hurt and weaken America because the President is a symbol for all of America.

407. As the defender of America, the American military is often a target of attack by those who oppose American Capitalism.

408. As a symbol of America, the American Flag is often a target of attack by those who oppose American Capitalism.

409. Heather Mac Donald, "The Illegal-Alien Crime Wave: Why can't our immigration authorities deport the hordes of illegal felons in our cities?," *City Journal,* Winter 2004. From the City Journal's website on May 12, 2008, webpage URL is: http://www.city-journal.org/printable.php?id=1204 .

410. Heather Mac Donald, "*Time* to Take Illegal Immigration Seriously: The newsweekly dramatically breaks with elite orthodoxy.," City Journal's website, September 16, 2004. From the City Journal's website on May 12, 2008, webpage URL is: http://www.city-journal.org/printable.php?id=1691 .

411. "Cut-Rate Tuition for Illegal Aliens Violates Common Sense – and Federal Law: *Martinez v. Regents of the University of California,*" Pacific Legal Foundation's website. From Pacific Legal Foundation's website on May 20, 2008, webpage URL is: http://community.pacificlegal.org/NETCOMMUNITY/Page.aspx?pid=509&srcid=2 72 ,

412. Daniel J. Mitchell, "Radical U.N. Tax Plans Threaten America," *The Heritage Foundation,* December 18, 2003. From The Heritage Foundation's website on May 27, 2008, webpage URL is: http://www.heritage.org/Press/Commentary/ed121803b.cfm?RenderforPrint=1 .

413. Melinda Selmys, "An Inconvenient Global Carbon Tax," *National Catholic Register,* December 9-15, 2007. From the National Catholic Register's website on May 28, 2008, webpage URL is: http://ncregister.com//site/print_article/7465/ .

414. "Proposals by Zedillo panel to fight poverty would alter international financial skyline," Press Release, *Report of the High-Level Panel on Financing for Development* (New York, NY: United Nations, June 28, 2001). From the United Nations' website on August 9, 2008, webpage URL is: http://www.un.org/reports/financing/press_release.htm .

415. Daniel J. Mitchell, "Radical U.N. Tax Plans Threaten America," *The Heritage Foundation,* December 18, 2003. From The Heritage Foundation's website on May 27, 2008, webpage URL is: http://www.heritage.org/Press/Commentary/ed121803b.cfm?RenderforPrint=1 .

416. Ted Galen Carpenter, "Putting the United Nations on Notice," *Cato Institute,* February 10, 2001. From the Cato Institute's website on May 28, 2008, webpage URL is: http://www.cato.org/pub_display.php?pub_id=4375 .

417. Please see, for example, the following references:
    (a) Daniel J. Mitchell, "Radical U.N. Tax Plans Threaten America," *The Heritage Foundation,* December 18, 2003. From The Heritage Foundation's website on May 27, 2008, webpage URL is: http://www.heritage.org/Press/Commentary/ed121803b.cfm? RenderforPrint=1 .
    (b) Richard W. Rahn, "Global Greed Screed," *Cato Institute,* July 12, 2003. From the Cato Institute's website on May 28, 2008, webpage URL is:

http://www.cato.org/pub_display.php?pub_id=3165 .
418. Ibid.
419. Despite America's high tax burden, there seems to be a relentless battle to increase our current taxes by socialists and other proponents of higher taxation. Sometimes, completely new taxes are proposed as well. For considerable data on taxes, please see the Tax Foundation's website. From the Tax Foundation's website on May 29, 2008, webpage URL is: http://www.taxfoundation.org/taxdata/ .
420. Chris Edwards, "Repealing the Federal Estate Tax," *Cato Institute,* Tax and Budget Bulletin No. 36, June 2006. From the Cato Institute's website on June 2, 2008, webpage URL is: http://www.cato.org/pubs/tbb/tbb-0606-36.pdf .
421. Jeanne Sahadi and Les Christie, "America's wackiest taxes: You might pay taxes on illegal drugs, Pepsi, playing cards, and being a star, and that's not all.," CNNMoney.com, February 22, 2005. From the CNNMoney.com website on May 22, 2008, webpage URL is:
http://cnnmoney.printthis.clickability.com/pt/cpt?action=cpt&title=Strangest+taxes+-+Feb.+22%2C+2005&expire=&urlID=13314946&fb=Y&url=http%3A%2F%2Fmoney.cnn.com%2F2005%2F02%2F18%2Fpf%2Ftaxes%2Fstrangetaxesupdate%2Findex.htm&partnerID=2200 .
422. Ibid.
423. "Jock Taxes," Tax Foundation's website. From the Tax Foundation's website on May 23, 2008, webpage URL is: http://www.taxfoundation.org/taxdata/topic/1.html .
424. Tony Aiello, "N.Y. Orders Large Web Retailers To Charge Tax: State Estimates New Rule Will Bring In $50 Million In 2008," wcbstv.com, April 25, 2008. From the wcbstv.com website on May 23, 2008, webpage URL is:
http://wcbstv.com/technology/ny.internet.tax.2.707820.html .
425. "Carbon tax? City is first to try it: Boulder surcharge on coal aims to reduce emissions tied to global warming," MSNBC.com, November 10, 2006. From the MSNBC.com on May 27, 2008, website URL is:
http://www.msnbc.msn.com/id/15651688/print/1/displaymode/1098/ .
426. Ben Lieberman, "Beware of Cap and Trade Climate Bills," WebMemo No. 1723, *The Heritage Foundation*, December 6, 2007. From The Heritage Foundation website on August 9, 2008, webpage URL is:
http://www.heritage.org/Research/Economy/upload/wm_1723.pdf .
427. "Service taxes just might work: The second in an editorial series on California's tax system.," *Los Angeles Times,* May 6, 2008. From the Los Angeles Times' website on May 27, 2008, webpage URL is:
http://www.latimes.com/news/opinion/la-ed-tax6-2008may06,0,6803250,print.story .
428. Ibid.
429. "Michigan Lawmakers Reach Budget Deal Hours After Government Shutdown," FoxNews.com, October 1, 2007. From the FoxNews.com website on May 30, 2008, webpage URL is:
http://www.foxnews.com/printer_friendly_story/0,3566,298723,00.html .
430. Daniel J. Mitchell, "Radical U.N. Tax Plans Threaten America," *The Heritage Foundation,* December 18, 2003. From The Heritage Foundation's website on May 27, 2008, webpage URL is:
http://www.heritage.org/Press/Commentary/ed121803b.cfm?RenderforPrint=1 .
431. `Melinda Selmys, "An Inconvenient Global Carbon Tax," *National Catholic Register,* December 9-15, 2007. From the National Catholic Register's website on May 28, 2008, webpage URL is: http://ncregister.com//site/print_article/7465/ .
432. "Proposals by Zedillo panel to fight poverty would alter international financial

skyline," Press Release, *Report of the High-Level Panel on Financing for Development* (New York, NY: United Nations, June 28, 2001). From the United Nations' website on August 9, 2008, webpage URL is: http://www.un.org/reports/financing/press_release.htm .

433. Daniel J. Mitchell, "Radical U.N. Tax Plans Threaten America," *The Heritage Foundation,* December 18, 2003. From The Heritage Foundation's website on May 27, 2008, webpage URL is: http://www.heritage.org/Press/Commentary/ed121803b.cfm?RenderforPrint=1 .

434. Ted Galen Carpenter, "Putting the United Nations on Notice," *Cato Institute,* February 10, 2001. From the Cato Institute's website on May 28, 2008, webpage URL is: http://www.cato.org/pub_display.php?pub_id=4375 .

435. Please see, for example, the following references:

   (c) Daniel J. Mitchell, "Radical U.N. Tax Plans Threaten America," *The Heritage Foundation,* December 18, 2003. From The Heritage Foundation's website on May 27, 2008, webpage URL is: http://www.heritage.org/Press/Commentary/ed121803b.cfm?RenderforPrint=1 .

   (d) Richard W. Rahn, "Global Greed Screed," *Cato Institute,* July 12, 2003. From the Cato Institute's website on May 28, 2008, webpage URL is: http://www.cato.org/pub_display.php?pub_id=3165 .

436. Ibid.

437. "Imputed Income Law & Legal Definition," USLegal's website. From USLegal's website on May 28, 2008, website URL is: http://definitions.uslegal.com/i/imputed-income/ .

438. Douglas A. Irwin, "International Trade Agreements," *The Concise Encyclopedia of Economics*, Edited by David R. Henderson (Indianapolis, IN: Liberty Fund, Inc., 2008), 298-301.

439. Ibid.

440. "Cotati Can't Force a Homebuilder To Provide Low Income Housing: *Mead v. City of Cotati,*" Pacific Legal Foundation's website. From Pacific Legal Foundation's website on May 20, 2008, webpage URL is: http://community.pacificlegal.org/NETCOMMUNITY/Page.aspx?pid=331&srcid=269 .

441. Ibid.

442. "Property Owners Singled Out To Pay Illegal Tax Disguised as "Special Benefit" Assessment: *Silicon Valley Taxpayers Association v. Santa Clara County Open Space Authority,*" Pacific Legal Foundation's website. From Pacific Legal Foundation's website on May 20, 2008, webpage URL is: http://community.pacificlegal.org/NETCOMMUNITY/Page.aspx?pid=398&srcid=269 .

443. Ibid.

444. Randolph J. May, "Universal Service Fund Needs FCC Attention this Year, Policy Analysts Say: Skyrocketing costs are entirely unjustified by meager benefits," *The Heartland Institute, Info Tech & Telecom News,* April 2008. From the Heartland Institute's website on May 28, 2008, webpage URL is: http://www.heartland.org/PrinterFriendly.cfm?theType=artId&theID=23014 .

445. "Federal Universal Service Fund," AT&T's website. From AT&T's website on May 28, 2008, webpage URL is: http://www.att.com/gen/corporate-citizenship?pid=2768 .

446. Michael C. Bender, "Florida homeowners will pay insurance surcharge until

2014," PalmBeachPost.com, June 10, 2008. From the PalmBeachPost.com website on August 9, 2008, webpage URL is: http://palmbeachpost.printthis.clickability.com/pt/cpt?action=cpt&title=Florida+hom eowners+will+pay+insurance+surcharge+until+2014&expire=&urlID=29069462&f b=Y&url=http%3A%2F%2Fwww.palmbeachpost.com%2Fstorm%2Fcontent%2Ftco ast%2Fepaper%2F2008%2F06%2F10%2F0610wilma.html&partnerID=491 .

447. Ibid.

448. Alicia Hansen, "Lotteries and State Fiscal Policy," Background Paper No. 46, Tax Foundation, October 1, 2004. From the Tax Foundation's website on August 9, 2008, webpage URL is: http://www.taxfoundation.org/news/printer/65.html .

449. "Lottery and Gambling Taxes," Tax Foundation's website. From the Tax Foundation's website on May 28, 2008, webpage URL is: http://www.taxfoundation.org/taxdata/topic/95.html .

450. Alicia Hansen, "State-Run Lotteries as a Form of Taxation," Speech given at the National Coalition Against Legalized Gambling's 12th Annual Conference, Tax Foundation's website. From the Tax Foundation's website on May 28, 2008, webpage URL is: http://www.taxfoundation.org/news/printer/1126.html .

451. "Lottery and Gambling Taxes," Tax Foundation's website. From the Tax Foundation's website on May 28, 2008, webpage URL is: http://www.taxfoundation.org/taxdata/topic/95.html .

452. Brian Wesbury, "Déjà Vu: The Fed's Interest Rate Dilemma," *The Wall Street Journal,* April 30, 2008. From The Wall Street Journal's website on April 30, 2008, webpage URL is: http://online.wsj.com/article_print/SB120951671713654689.html .

453. Please see, for example, the following references:
    (a) "Dollar Alarm," *The Wall Street Journal,* April 14, 2008. From The Wall Street Journal's website on April 14, 2008, webpage URL is: http://online.wsj.com/article_print/SB120812890806011487.html .
    (b) Ronald McKinnon, "The Dollar and the Credit Crunch," *The Wall Street Journal,* March 31, 2008. From The Wall Street Journal's website on April 14, 2008, webpage URL is: http://online.wsj.com/article_print/SB120692677175575901.html .

454. Brittany Sauser, "Ethanol Demand Threatens Food Prices," *Technology Review,* February 13, 2007, http://www.technologyreview.com/printer_friendly_article.aspx?id=18173 .

455. Despite America's high tax burden, there seems to be a relentless battle to increase our current taxes by socialists and other proponents of higher taxation. Sometimes, completely new taxes are proposed as well. For more information on corporate taxes and the corporate tax burden please see, for example, the following references:
    (a) The Tax Foundation's website. From the Tax Foundation's website on May 29, 2008, webpage URL is: http://www.taxfoundation.org/taxdata/ .
    (b) Daniel J. Mitchell, "Corporate Taxes: America is Falling Behind," *Cato Institute,* Tax and Budget Bulletin No. 48, July 2007. From the Cato Institute's website on June 2, 2008, webpage URL is: http://www.cato.org/pubs/tbb/tbb_0707_48.pdf .

456. "C Corporation Taxes," Business Owner's Toolkit website. From the Business Owner's Toolkit website on May 29, 2008, webpage URL is: http://www.toolkit.com/small_business_guide/sbg.aspx?nid=P07_2026 .

457. Ibid.

458. Jonathan Williams and Scott A. Hodge, "Oil Company Profits and Tax

Collections: Does the U.S. Need a New Windfall Profits Tax?," *Tax Foundation,* Fiscal Fact No. 41, November 9, 2005. From the Tax Foundation's website on June 2, 2008, webpage URL is: http://www.taxfoundation.org/news/printer/1168.html .
459. Charli E. Coon, "Why the Government's CAFÉ Standards for Fuel Efficiency Should Be Repealed, not Increased," Backgrounder #1458, *The Heritage Foundation,* July 11, 2001, http://www.heritage.org/Research/EnergyandEnvironment/BG1458.cfm .
460. Clyde Wayne Crews, Jr., "Ten Thousand Commandments 2007: An Annual Snapshot of the Federal Regulatory State," *Competitive Enterprise Institute,* July 3, 2007, 1. From the Competitive Enterprise Institute's website on May 20, 2008, webpage URL is: http://cei.org/pdf/6018.pdf .
461. Ibid.
462. Martin F. Grace and Robert W. Klein, "Facing Mother Nature: New laws and policies in the wake of Hurricane Katrina seem intended to scapegoat insurance companies rather than protect the public.," *Regulation,* Fall 2007, 28-34. From the Cato Institute website on May 16, 2008, webpage URL is: http://www.cato.org/pubs/regulation/regv30n3/v30n3-5.pdf .
463. James Sherk, "Use & Abuse of the Family and Medical Leave Act: What Workers and Employers Say," *The Heritage Foundation,* SR-16, August 28, 2007. From The Heritage Foundation's website on May 30, 2008, webpage URL is: http://www.heritage.org/Research/Labor/upload/SR_16.pdf .
464. Ibid.
465. ""Affordable Housing" Mandates Violate the Constitution: *Palmer/Sixth Street Properties, LP & Geoffrey Palmer v. City of Los Angeles,"* Pacific Legal Foundation's website. From Pacific Legal Foundation's website on May 20, 2008, webpage URL is: http://community.pacificlegal.org/NETCOMMUNITY/Page.aspx?pid=340&srcid=2 69 .
466. "Summer Camp In Court To Defend Its Right to Raft," *Institute for Justice,* April 7, 2008. From the Institute for Justice's website on May 15, 2008, webpage URL is: http://www.ij.org/include/media_functions.asp?path=/economic_liberty/pa_riverrafti ng/4_7_08pr.html&cmd=print_out .
467. "Institute for Justice Defeats AZ Dance Ban," *Institute for Justice,* May 1, 2008. From the Institute for Justice's website on May 15, 2008, webpage URL is: http://www.ij.org/include/media_functions.asp?path=/economic_liberty/az_santanfla t/5_1_08pr.html&cmd=print_out .
468. M. David Stirling, *Green Gone Wild: Elevating Nature Above Human Rights* (Bellevue, WA: Merril Press, 2008), 183-186.
469. Ibid, 186-189.
470. Ibid, 203-209.
471. Ibid, 98-102.
472. Ibid.
473. "Challenging Federal Government's Unlawful Wetlands Grab in Wisconsin: *Gerke v. United States,* Pacific Legal Foundation's website. From Pacific Legal Foundation's website on May 19, 2008, webpage URL is: http://community.pacificlegal.org/NETCOMMUNITY/Page.aspx?pid=477&srcid=2 70 .
474. "Cattle Grazing Isn't "Pollution": *Oregon Natural Desert Association v. United States Forest service,"* Pacific Legal Foundation's website. From Pacific Legal

Foundation's website on May 19, 2008, webpage URL is: http://community.pacificlegal.org/NETCOMMUNITY/Page.aspx?pid=479&srcid=2 70 .

475. "The Truth about Urban Sprawl," National Center for Policy Analysis' website, March 24, 1999. From the National Center for Policy Analysis' website on May 30, 2008, webpage URL is: http://www.ncpa.org/ba/ba287.html .

476. "PLF Defends July 4ᵗʰ Celebration From Coastal Commission Bullying: *Gualala Festivals Committee v. California Coastal Commission,*" Pacific Legal Foundation's website. From Pacific Legal Foundation's website on May 20, 2008, webpage URL is: http://community.pacificlegal.org/NETCOMMUNITY/Page.aspx?pid=492&srcid=2 69 .

477. Jonathan H. Adler, "Anti-Conservation Incentives: The Endangered Species Act is endangering species," *Regulation,* Winter 2008, 54-57. From the Cato Institute website on May 16, 2008, webpage URL is: http://www.cato.org/pubs/regulation/regv30n4/v30n4-6.pdf .

478. Max Schulz, "California's Potemkin Environmentalism: A celebrated green economy produces pollution elsewhere, ongoing power shortages, and business-crippling costs," City Journal's website, Spring 2008. From the City Journal's website on May 16, 2008, webpage URL is: http://www.city-journal.org/printable.php?id=2564 .

479. Ibid.

480. Ibid.

481. Ibid.

482. Ibid.

483. Jack Spencer and Nick Loris, "Uranium Mining Is Important for Securing America's Energy Future," *The Heritage Foundation,* WebMemo No. 1866, March 25, 2008. From The Heritage Foundation website on May 19, 2008, webpage URL is: http://www.heritage.org/Research/EnergyandEnvironment/upload/wm_1866.pdf .

484. Ibid.

485. Ibid.

486. Please see, for example, the following references:
  (a) Paul Giannamore, "Local Mines Could Close: Murray fights EPA over refuse site and salamanders," *The Intelligencer, Wheeling News-Register,* May 3, 2008. From The Intelligencer, Wheeling News-Register's website on June 3, 2008, webpage URL is: http://theintelligencer.net/page/content.detail/id/509009.html?showlayout=0
  (b) Sarah Hurst, "Petition calls for Cook Inlet coal mining ban: Alaska DNR commissioner to decide if reclamation is possible in salmon-rich region; developer continuing with baseline studies," *Mining News,* Volume 12, No. 25, June 24, 2007. From the Petroleum News' website on June 3, 2008, webpage URL is: http://www.petroleumnews.com/pnarchpop/070624-22.html .

487. Max Schulz, "California's Potemkin Environmentalism: A celebrated green economy produces pollution elsewhere, ongoing power shortages, and business-crippling costs," City Journal's website, Spring 2008. From the City Journal's website on May 16, 2008, webpage URL is: http://www.city-journal.org/printable.php?id=2564 .

488. Ibid.

489. Ibid.

490. Ibid.

491. Ibid.

492. Ibid.

493. Robert Fink, "Not-in-my-backyard feelings stop needed oil refineries," *JSOnline: Milwaukee Journal Sentinel,* March 22, 2008. From JSOnline: Milwaukee Journal Sentinel's website on May 19, 2008, webpage URL is: http://www.jsonline.com/story/index.aspx?id=730865&format=print .

494. Nick Loris, "Omnibus Prohibits Oil Shale Development," *The Heritage Foundation,* WebMemo No. 1754, December 18, 2007. From The Heritage Foundation website on August 11, 2008, webpage URL is: http://www.heritage.org/Research/EnergyandEnvironment/upload/wm_1754.pdf .

495. Max Schulz, "California's Potemkin Environmentalism: A celebrated green economy produces pollution elsewhere, ongoing power shortages, and business-crippling costs," City Journal's website, Spring 2008. From the City Journal's website on May 16, 2008, webpage URL is: http://www.city-journal.org/printable.php?id=2564 .

496. Robert Fink, "Not-in-my-backyard feelings stop needed oil refineries," *JSOnline: Milwaukee Journal Sentinel,* March 22, 2008. From JSOnline: Milwaukee Journal Sentinel's website on May 19, 2008, webpage URL is: http://www.jsonline.com/story/index.aspx?id=730865&format=print .

497. Ben Lieberman, "The Good and Bad Approaches to Affordable Energy Policy," *The Heritage Foundation,* WebMemo No. 1927, May 19, 2008. From The Heritage Foundation website on May 19, 2008, webpage URL is: http://www.heritage.org/Research/EnergyandEnvironment/upload/wm_1927.pdf .

498. Ibid.

499. Timothy Sandefur, *Cornerstone of Liberty: Property Rights in 21ˢᵗ –Century America* (Washington, DC: Cato Institute, 2006), 5-10.

500. Ibid, 90-106.

501. Ibid, 120-122.

502. Ibid.

503. Ibid, 123-124.

504. Ibid, 109-112.

505. Ibid, 79-90.

506. Ibid, 79-82.

507. Steven Malanga, "Illegal in More Ways than One: Identity theft in America goes hand and hand with illegal immigration.," City Journal's website, Spring 2008. From the City Journal's website on May 16, 2008, webpage URL is: http://www.city-journal.org/printable.php?id=2574 .

508. Greg Stohr, "Exxon Valdez Award Questioned at U.S. Supreme Court (Update3)," Bloomberg.com, February 27, 2008. From the Bloomberg.com website on May 8, 2008, webpage URL is: http://www.bloomberg.com/apps/news?pid=20670001&refer=news&sid=ajFkglZna8uo .

509. Jackie Crosby, "Lost laptop? Sue for millions!," StarTribune.com, February 13, 2008. From the StarTribue.com website on May 8, 2008, webpage URL is: http://www.startribune.com/templates/Print_This_Story?sid=15571092 .

510. James A. Dorn, "A Minimum Wage Hike Is the Wrong Direction for America," *Cato Institute,* January 30, 2007. From the Cato Institute's website on May 30, 2008, webpage URL is: http://www.cato.org/pub_display.php?pub_id=7221 .

511. Carl F. Horowitz, "Keeping the Poor Poor: The Dark Side of the Living Wage,"

Cato Institute, Policy Analysis No. 493, October 21, 2003. From the Cato Institute's website on May 30, 2008, webpage URL is: http://www.cato.org/pubs/pas/pa493.pdf

512. Ibid.

513. Jerry Taylor and Jagadeesh Gokhale, "Pay Bosses More!," *Cato Institute,* February 27, 2007. From the Cato Institute's website on May 30, 2008, webpage URL is: http://www.cato.org/pub_display.php?pub_id=8022 .

514. Timothy Sandefur, *Cornerstone of Liberty: Property Rights in 21st –Century America* (Washington, DC: Cato Institute, 2006), 83-85.

515. Jerry Taylor and Peter Van Doren, "Economic Amnesia: The Case against Oil Price Controls and Windfall Profit Taxes," *Cato Institute,* Policy Analysis No. 561, January 12, 2006. From the Cato Institute's website on May 30, 2008, webpage URL is: http://www.cato.org/pubs/pas/pa561.pdf .

516. "Challenging Price Controls on Homes: *Florida Home Builders Association v. City of Tallahassee,*" Pacific Legal Foundation's website. From Pacific Legal Foundation's website on May 20, 2008, webpage URL is: http://community.pacificlegal.org/NETCOMMUNITY/Page.aspx?pid=326&srcid=269 .

517. "Federal Court Refuses to Enforce Unfair Sales Act: Raj Bhandari Seeks to Vindicate Entrepreneurs Statewide," *Institute for Justice,* October 17, 2007. From the Institute for Justice's website on May 16, 2008, webpage URL is: http://www.ij.org/include/media_functions.asp?path=/economic_liberty/wi_gas/10_17_07pr.html&cmd=print_out .

518. "Contract Provisions on Liability Should Be Respected: *Lanier at McEver, L.P. v. Planners & Engineers Collaborative, Inc.,*" Pacific Legal Foundation's website. From Pacific Legal Foundation's website on May 8, 2008, webpage URL is: http://community.pacificlegal.org/NETCOMMUNITY/Page.aspx?pid=349&srcid=273 .

519. "Supporting the Integrity of Contract Provisions: *Circuit City Stores, Inc. v. Gentry,*" Pacific Legal Foundation's website. From Pacific Legal Foundation's website on May 8, 2008, webpage URL is: http://community.pacificlegal.org/NETCOMMUNITY/Page.aspx?pid=474&srcid=273 .

520. Alan Reynolds, "Dissecting the Bailout Plan," *Cato Institute,* December 10, 2007. From the Cato Institute's website on May 30, 2008, webpage URL is: http://www.cato.org/pub_display.php?pub_id=8834 .

521. Michael I. Krauss, "Restoring the Boundary: Tort Law and the Right to Contract," *Cato Institute,* Policy Analysis No. 347, June 3, 1999. From the Cato Institute's website on June 2, 2008, webpage URL is: http://www.cato.org/pubs/pas/pa347.pdf .

522. "New Mexico Ends Unconstitutional Censorship of Interior Designers," *Institute for Justice,* April 6, 2007. From the Institute for Justice's website on May 15, 2008, webpage URL is: http://www.ij.org/include/media_functions.asp?path=/economic_liberty/nm_interiordesign/4_6_07pr.html&cmd=print_out .

523. Ibid.

524. Ibid.

525. Daniel J. Mitchell, "Corporate Taxes: America is Falling Behind," *Cato Institute,* Tax and Budget Bulletin No. 48, July 2007. From the Cato Institute's website on June 2, 2008, webpage URL is: http://www.cato.org/pubs/tbb/tbb_0707_48.pdf .

526. Ibid.

527. William Beach, Rea S. Hederman, Jr., and Guinevere Nell, "Economic Effects of Increasing the Tax Rates on Capital Gains and Dividends," *The Heritage Foundation,* WebMemo No. 1891, April 15, 2008. From The Heritage Foundation website on June 2, 2008, webpage URL is: http://www.heritage.org/Research/Taxes/upload/wm_1891.pdf .

528. Please see, for example, the following references:
    (a) "Victory for Minneapolis Taxi Entrepreneurs," *Institute for Justice,* December 19, 2007. From the Institute for Justice's website on May 15, 2008, webpage URL is: http://www.ij.org/include/media_functions.asp?path=/economic_liberty/mn_taxi/12_19_07pr.html&cmd=print_out .
    (b) "Cambridge Entrepreneur Wins Fight With City Hall," *Institute for Justice,* June 4, 2007. From the Institute for Justice's website on May 15, 2008, webpage URL is: http://www.ij.org/include/media_functions.asp?path=/economic_liberty/ma_jitney/6_4_07pr.html&cmd=print_out .

529. Timothy Sandefur, *Cornerstone of Liberty: Property Rights in 21ˢᵗ –Century America* (Washington, DC: Cato Institute, 2006), 83-85.

530. John Berlau, "SOXing It to the Little Guy: How Sarbanes-Oxley Hurts Small Investors *and* Entrepreneurs," *Competitive Enterprise Institute,* CEI OnPoint No. 112, June 7, 2007. From the Competitive Enterprise Institute's website on May 19, 2008, webpage URL is: http://cei.org/pdf/5954.pdf .

531. Ibid.

532. Henry N. Butler and Larry E. Ribstein, *The Sarbanes-Oxley Debacle: What We've Learned; How to Fix It* (Washington, DC: AEI Press, 2006), 75-81.

533. "Seattle B&B Can Remain Open for Business: Lawsuit Challenging B&B Regulations Ends As City Dismisses Citation of Greenlake Guesthouse," *Institute for Justice,* February 27, 2007. From the Institute for Justice's website on May 15, 2008, webpage URL is: http://www.ij.org/include/media_functions.asp?path=/economic_liberty/seattlebb/2_27_07pr.html&cmd=print_out .

534. John Berlau, "SOXing It to the Little Guy: How Sarbanes-Oxley Hurts Small Investors *and* Entrepreneurs," *Competitive Enterprise Institute,* CEI OnPoint No. 112, June 7, 2007. From the Competitive Enterprise Institute's website on May 19, 2008, webpage URL is: http://cei.org/pdf/5954.pdf .

535. Houman B. Shadab, "The Challenge of Hedge Fund Regulation: As other nations expand access to hedge funds, should the U.S. adopt tighter regulation?," *Regulation,* Spring 2007, 36-41. From the Cato Institute website on May 16, 2008, webpage URL is: http://www.cato.org/pubs/regulation/regv30n1/v30n1-1.pdf .

536. Please see, for example, the following references:
    (a) David Kelley, "Capitalist Heroes," *Cato Institute,* October 11, 2007. From the Cato Institute's website on June 2, 2008, webpage URL is: http://www.cato.org/pub_display.php?pub_id=8740 .
    (b) Alexander Green, "Oil Company Profits: Just Who is Gouging Whom?," *The InvestmentU e-Letter,* Issue #653, March 23, 2007. From The InvestmentU website on June 2, 2008, webpage URL is: http://www.investmentu.com/IUEL/2007/20070323.html .

537. Jonathan Williams and Scott A. Hodge, "Oil Company Profits and Tax Collections: Does the U.S. Need a New Windfall Profits Tax?," *Tax Foundation,*

Fiscal Fact No. 41, November 9, 2005. From the Tax Foundation's website on June 2, 2008, webpage URL is: http://www.taxfoundation.org/news/printer/1168.html .

538. "Plaintiffs Lawyers Abuse "Unfair Competition" Law To Stifle Competition: *Doe v. Wal-Mart Stores, Inc,"* Pacific Legal Foundation's website. From Pacific Legal Foundation's website on June 3, 2008, webpage URL is: http://community.pacificlegal.org/NETCOMMUNITY/Page.aspx?pid=467&srcid=2 73 .

539. Ibid.

540. Please see, for example, the following references:
   (a) "Arizona Gardeners and Landscapers File Economic Liberty Lawsuit Against Structural Pest Control Commission: Agency Helps Big Business Weed Out Competition," *Institute for Justice*, September 28, 2005. From the Institute for Justice's website on June 3, 2008, webpage URL is: http://www.ij.org/include/media_functions.asp?path=/economic_liberty/ az_weeds/9_28_05pr.html&cmd=print_out .
   (b) "Victory for Vintners In Wine Wars!: Institute for Justice, Small Wineries and Consumers Toast U.S. Supreme Court Ruling," *Institute for Justice*, May 16, 2005. From the Institute for Justice's website on June 3, 2008, webpage URL is: http://www.ij.org/include/media_functions.asp?path=/economic_liberty/ ny_wine/5_16_05pr.html&cmd=print_out .

541. Richard Vedder and Wendell Cox, *The Wal-Mart Revolution: How Big-Box Stores Benefit Consumers, Workers, and the Economy* (Washington, DC: AEI Press, 2006).

542. "Vindicating Vioxx," *The Wall Street Journal,* May 31, 2008, A10. From The Wall Street Journal's website on June 1, 2008, webpage URL is: http://online.wsj.com/article_print/SB121218857343634215.html .

543. Greg Forster, "Monopoly vs. Markets: The Empirical Evidence on Private Schools and School Choice," *Milton and Rose D. Friedman Foundation,* School Choice Issues In Depth, October 2007.

544. Max Schulz, "California's Potemkin Environmentalism: A celebrated green economy produces pollution elsewhere, ongoing power shortages, and business-crippling costs," City Journal's website, Spring 2008. From the City Journal's website on May 16, 2008, webpage URL is: http://www.city-journal.org/printable.php?id=2564 .

545. Ibid.

546. Jack Spencer and Nick Loris, "Uranium Mining Is Important for Securing America's Energy Future," *The Heritage Foundation,* WebMemo No. 1866, March 25, 2008. From The Heritage Foundation website on May 19, 2008, webpage URL is: http://www.heritage.org/Research/EnergyandEnvironment/upload/wm_1866.pdf .

547. Please see, for example, the following references:
   (a) Paul Giannamore, "Local Mines Could Close: Murray fights EPA over refuse site and salamanders," *The Intelligencer, Wheeling News-Register,* May 3, 2008. From The Intelligencer, Wheeling News-Register's website on June 3, 2008, webpage URL is: http://theintelligencer.net/page/content.detail/id/509009.html? showlayout=0 .
   (b) Sarah Hurst, "Petition calls for Cook Inlet coal mining ban: Alaska DNR commissioner to decide if reclamation is possible in salmon-rich region; developer continuing with baseline studies," *Mining News,* Volume 12, No. 25, June 24, 2007.

From the Petroleum News' website on June 3, 2008, webpage URL is:
http://www.petroleumnews.com/pnarchpop/070624-22.html .

548. Max Schulz, "California's Potemkin Environmentalism: A celebrated green economy produces pollution elsewhere, ongoing power shortages, and business-crippling costs," City Journal's website, Spring 2008. From the City Journal's website on May 16, 2008, webpage URL is: http://www.city-journal.org/printable.php?id=2564 .

549. Ibid.

550. Ibid.

551. Ibid.

552. Robert Fink, "Not-in-my-backyard feelings stop needed oil refineries," *JSOnline: Milwaukee Journal Sentinel,* March 22, 2008. From JSOnline: Milwaukee Journal Sentinel's website on May 19, 2008, webpage URL is: http://www.jsonline.com/story/index.aspx?id=730865&format=print .

553. Nick Loris, "Omnibus Prohibits Oil Shale Development," *The Heritage Foundation,* WebMemo No. 1754, December 18, 2007. From The Heritage Foundation website on August 11, 2008, webpage URL is: http://www.heritage.org/Research/EnergyandEnvironment/upload/wm_1754.pdf .

554. Robert Fink, "Not-in-my-backyard feelings stop needed oil refineries," *JSOnline: Milwaukee Journal Sentinel,* March 22, 2008. From JSOnline: Milwaukee Journal Sentinel's website on May 19, 2008, webpage URL is: http://www.jsonline.com/story/index.aspx?id=730865&format=print .

555. Ben Lieberman, "The Good and Bad Approaches to Affordable Energy Policy," *The Heritage Foundation,* WebMemo No. 1927, May 19, 2008. From The Heritage Foundation website on May 19, 2008, webpage URL is: http://www.heritage.org/Research/EnergyandEnvironment/upload/wm_1927.pdf .

556. Max Schulz, "California's Potemkin Environmentalism: A celebrated green economy produces pollution elsewhere, ongoing power shortages, and business-crippling costs," City Journal's website, Spring 2008. From the City Journal's website on May 16, 2008, webpage URL is: http://www.city-journal.org/printable.php?id=2564 .

557. Ben Lieberman, "Beware of Cap and Trade Climate Bills," WebMemo No. 1723, *The Heritage Foundation*, December 6, 2007. From The Heritage Foundation website on August 9, 2008, webpage URL is: http://www.heritage.org/Research/Economy/upload/wm_1723.pdf .

558. "Carbon tax? City is first to try it: Boulder surcharge on coal aims to reduce emissions tied to global warming," MSNBC.com, November 10, 2006. From the MSNBC.com on May 27, 2008, website URL is: http://www.msnbc.msn.com/id/15651688/print/1/displaymode/1098/ .

559. Phil English, "The Cruelest Tax Increase of All," Human Events' website, March 12, 2008. From the Human Events' website on June 4, 2008, webpage URL is: http://www.humanevents.com/article.php?print=yes&id=25443 .

560. Jonathan Williams and Scott A. Hodge, "Oil Company Profits and Tax Collections: Does the U.S. Need a New Windfall Profits Tax?," *Tax Foundation*, Fiscal Fact No. 41, November 9, 2005. From the Tax Foundation's website on June 2, 2008, webpage URL is: http://www.taxfoundation.org/news/printer/1168.html .

561. Michael Tanner, "The Grass Is Not Always Greener: A Look at National Health Care Systems Around the World," *Cato Institute,* Policy Analysis No. 613, March 18, 2008. From the Cato Institute's website on June 6, 2008, webpage URL is: http://www.cato.org/pubs/pas/pa-613.pdf .

562. Michael F. Cannon and Michael D. Tanner, *Healthy Competition: What's Holding Back Health Care and How to Free It* (Washington, DC: Cato Institute, 2005), 1-14.

563. John S. O'Shea, "Ending the Physician Payment Crisis: Another Reason for Major Medicare Reform," *The Heritage Foundation,* WebMemo No. 1931, May 20, 2008. From The Heritage Foundation website on June 5, 2008, webpage URL is: http://www.heritage.org/Research/HealthCare/upload/wm_1931.pdf .

564. Connie Marshner, "Health Insurance Reform: What Families Should Know," *The Heritage Foundation,* WebMemo No. 1739, December 13, 2007. From The Heritage Foundation website on June 5, 2008, webpage URL is: http://www.heritage.org/Research/HealthCare/upload/wm_1739.pdf .

565. Ibid.

566. Ibid.

567. Ibid.

568. Michael F. Cannon and Michael D. Tanner, *Healthy Competition: What's Holding Back Health Care and How to Free It* (Washington, DC: Cato Institute, 2005).

569. Ibid, 1-14 and 111-138.

570. Ibid.

571. Ibid.

572. Ibid.

573. Ibid, 139-143.

574. Greg D'Angelo and Robert E. Moffit, "Congress Must Not Ignore the Medicare Trustees' Warning," *The Heritage Foundation,* WebMemo No. 1869, March 27, 2008. From The Heritage Foundation website on June 5, 2008, webpage URL is: http://www.heritage.org/research/healthcare/upload/wm_1869.pdf .

575. Ibid.

576. Michael F. Cannon and Michael D. Tanner, *Healthy Competition: What's Holding Back Health Care and How to Free It* (Washington, DC: Cato Institute, 2005), 35.

577. Michael Tanner, "The Grass Is Not Always Greener: A Look at National Health Care Systems Around the World," *Cato Institute,* Policy Analysis No. 613, March 18, 2008. From the Cato Institute's website on June 6, 2008, webpage URL is: http://www.cato.org/pubs/pas/pa-613.pdf .

578. "Socialized Medicine's Waiting Room," *The Limbaugh Letter*, November 2007, Vol. 16, No. 11, 12.

579. Ibid.

580. Ibid.